FREEDOM'S UNFINISHED REVOLUTION

FREEDOM'S UNFINISHED REVOLUTION

AN INQUIRY INTO
THE CIVIL WAR AND RECONSTRUCTION

THE AMERICAN SOCIAL HISTORY PROJECT

William Friedheim
with Ronald Jackson

Joshua Brown, Visual Editor
Bret Eynon and Stephen Brier, Supervising Editors

THE NEW PRESS · NEW YORK

The publisher is grateful for permission to reprint the following copyrighted material.
Every reasonable effort has been made to contact copyright holders.
Any errors will be corrected in future printings.

Excerpt from *Freedom Road* by Howard Fast. Copyright © 1944 by Howard Fast.

Excerpt from an interview with Bernice Johnson Reagon quoted in
The Eyes on the Prize Civil Rights Leader, Eyes on the Prize Production Team.

"Tar Baby" from *The Days When the Animals Talked* by William J. Faulkner. Copyright © 1977 by
William J. Faulkner. Reprinted by permission of Marie Brown Associates.

Excerpt from *Black Reconstruction in America* by W. E. B. DuBois is reprinted
by permission of David Graham DuBois.

LIBRARY OF CONGRESS CATALOGING-IN-PUBLICATION DATA

Friedheim, William.
    Freedom's unfinished revolution: the Civil War and Reconstruction / William Friedheim
with Ronald Jackson, authors.
        p. cm.
    "A primary source text and document reader from the authors of Who built America?"
    "The American social history project."
    Includes bibliographical references (p.) and index.
    Summary: Primary historical documents, artwork, and exercises present the Civil War
and Reconstruction.
    ISBN 1-56584-198-0
    1. United States—History—Civil War, 1861–1865—Sources.
    2. Reconstruction—Sources. [1. United States—History—Civil War, 1861–1865—Sources.
    2. Reconstruction—Sources.] I. Jackson, Ronald. II. Title.
E464.F74   1996
973.7—dc2095-4885   CIP
AC

PUBLISHED IN THE UNITED STATES BY THE NEW PRESS, NEW YORK
DISTRIBUTED BY W. W. NORTON & COMPANY, INC., NEW YORK

Established in 1990 as a major alternative to the large, commercial publishing houses,
The New Press is a full-scale nonprofit American book publisher outside of the university presses.
The Press is operated editorially in the public interest, rather than for private gain;
it is committed to publishing in innovative ways works of educational, cultural, and community value
that, despite their intellectual merits, might not normally be commercially viable.
The New Press's editorial offices are located at the City University of New York.

BOOK DESIGN BY CHARLES NIX AND HALL SMYTH
MAPS BY JOSHUA BROWN
PRODUCTION MANAGEMENT BY KIM WAYMER

PRINTED IN THE UNITED STATES OF AMERICA

98 99 9 8 7 6 5 4 3 2

CONTENTS

> DOCUMENT *1. Historian W. E. B. DuBois argues that slaves played a key role in their own emancipation.*

PART ONE: SLAVERY, SECTIONAL STRIFE, AND WAR

> DOCUMENTS *1. An interview with an ex-slave by the Federal Writers Project in the 1930s • 2. Nat Turner tells the story of his 1831 slave revolt • 3. An African-American folktale • 4. A militant call for freedom in 1829 by an African-American abolitionist • 5. Frederick Douglass: "If there is no struggle, there is no progress," 1857 • 6. A slavemaster reacts to Nat Turner's slave revolt, 1831.*

> DOCUMENTS *1. An ex-slave tells of the impact of the 1850 Fugitive Slave Act on free black communities • 2. Rescuing a fugitive slave from bounty hunters, 1859 • 3, 4, 5. The southern press applauds the beating of an abolitionist senator, 1856 • 6. A letter to John Brown in prison, 1859 • 7. A death row letter from a fugitive slave who raided Harpers Ferry with John Brown in 1859.*

PART TWO: THE CIVIL WAR

> DOCUMENTS *1. Abraham Lincoln: "My paramount aim is to save the Union," 1862 • 2. Harriet Tubman: Kill the Snake Before It Kills You, 1862 • 3. Frederick Douglass: "We strike at the effect and leave the cause unharmed," 1861 • 4. African Americans offer to recruit freedom fighters for the Union Army, 1861 • 5. "Contraband" slaves change how Union soldiers think about slavery, 1862 • 6. An escaped slave joins Union forces, 1862 • 7. A southern newspaper sees slavery as a military*

Foreword by Eric Foner

The Civil War era, the most pivotal period in American history, is also one of the least understood. This is especially true of Reconstruction, the period which followed the war, in which the nation sought to come to terms with the conflict's most important legacies—the consolidation of the Union and the destruction of slavery.

Freedom's Unfinished Revolution: An Inquiry Into The Civil War and Reconstruction presents a vivid and up-to-date account of the crucial years from 1861 to 1877. Drawing on the most recent historical scholarship, it reflects how our understanding of the period has changed during the past generation. Central to these changes is a new appreciation of the key role played by African Americans in bringing about emancipation, securing the Union's victory, and establishing the agenda for the nation's first postwar attempt to create a truly interracial democracy. As the book shows, the slaves who seized the opportunity presented by the war to escape from their plantations forced the issue of emancipation to the forefront of public debate in 1861 and 1862. The 200,000 black men who served in the Union Army and Navy during the war's final two years played a major role in the North's triumph. And the efforts of former slaves to breathe substantive meaning into the freedom they acquired—demanding personal autonomy, access to education, civil rights, the vote, and land—led to sweeping changes in inherited patterns of race relations. During Reconstruction, the nation's laws and constitution were rewritten to establish, for the first time, the principle of equal citizenship for all Americans, regardless of race. In the South, a breathtaking transformation of political life occurred, in which former slaveholders were ousted from power and former slaves and their allies, for a time, governed the region. Blacks did not achieve all they desired—especially on the economic front—but their demands did much to the nation's political agenda during Reconstruction.

Peopled by a remarkable cast of characters, from well-known figures such as Abraham Lincoln to obscure former slaves, *Freedom's Unfinished Revolution* details the immense changes the Civil War era brought to American life. It also makes clear that the issues central to those years remain unresolved questions in American society today—the role of the federal government in protecting the rights of individuals, the relationship between force and consent in eliciting allegiance to democracy, and the place of African Americans in our political and social life. No one who wishes to understand the origins of American society's deep divisions can afford to ignore the Civil War and its aftermath. *Freedom's Unfinished Revolution* is an excellent place to begin.

ERIC FONER
DeWitt Clinton Professor of History
Columbia University

Foreword by the Teachers Advisory Committee

This book grew out of the acknowledgment that the Civil War and Reconstruction are essential for students to understand, yet are difficult subjects to teach. The history of late-nineteenth-century and much of twentieth-century America is incomprehensible without an understanding of the Civil War and Reconstruction. The impact of that era is present today in newspapers and on television, in literature and the arts, in political debates and demographic patterns. Civil rights movements, racial conflicts, and changing ideas of national identity and citizenship are clearly tied to the 1860s and 1870s.

The roots of these developments, however, are complex. Issues, events, actors, and relationships in those crucial years are complicated and sometimes elusive. The materials available to teachers also present problems. Standard texts tend to reduce the Civil War to the decisions of politicians and generals. The war may emerge as merely a terrible tragedy, leaving students with no clear sense of the social, economic, political, and moral strands that led to war, the issues that divided the nation, or the role of ordinary people in these events.

While the Civil War is usually oversimplified, the Reconstruction era is often a daunting subject, with such a variety of players, events, issues, and arenas that teachers fear that students will be overwhelmed. Conversely, the rich evidence of African Americans in shaping the war and Reconstruction is missing from many textbooks. Students may mistakenly conclude that the role of African Americans in those years and the issues that they articulated are primarily history for African Americans and not history essential for understanding the nation as a whole.

This book arose out of the need and desire to create a textbook for high-school students that would make this pivotal moment of national war and national reconstruction come alive for them. The goal was to create a book that teachers would want to use, that addressed their concerns and reflected actual classroom experience. The book was also to be a text that students would want to use—a book that would provoke thought and encourage students to play an active role in making sense out of historical data.

Teachers took part in the book's earliest conceptual stage. William Friedheim is a historian and teacher. He brought to the writing of this book years of teaching experience and a commitment to student-based inquiry. Ronald Jackson is a writer and filmmaker, who has produced educational materials on social issues for a broad public. In addition to these writers, teachers actively engaged in discussions of the scope, focus, and purpose of the book. They pored over drafts, made suggestions, and debated points of presentation, in a truly collaborative venture. Advisory meetings became exciting colloquia on history and pedagogy.

Within these pages, teachers and students will find a rich panoply of documents, including diaries, letters, newspapers, records of historic meetings, field reports, songs, and congressional hearings. Voices and scenes emerge: freedpeople creating new lives in the Sea Islands; bread rioters in Richmond during the war; soldiers describing their experiences in battle; political leaders debating the future of the South; African-American ministers meeting with General Sherman during the war. Teachers and students will also find a striking collection of illustrations that not only illuminate the past but also raise questions about the power and use of visual imagery. Photographs of African-American soldiers and officeholders, for example, convey a deep sense of the human actors and urgency in this historical drama. Engravings depict details of work and family life. Pictures, which became important tools for reporting during the Civil War, provide students with valuable exercises in the power of images to enlighten and deceive. As they study political cartoons, students can explore the changing nature and perception of African-American life. Students can also analyze artists' depictions of historical events: the arraignment of John Brown, the raising of a Confederate flag in Savannah, Georgia, or African-American troops liberating slaves in the South.

The text has the historical information that students need in order to explore the many issues embedded in the war and Reconstruction. Teachers will also find classroom-proven teaching devices that help make the text accessible: prereading exercises; definitions and questions that help students review and expand their understanding of the text; maps; timelines; and a bibliography at the end of the book. Suggested activities for each chapter provide a possible starting point for further study. Activities such as role plays, research projects, debates, creative writing, and visual literacy exercises help build critical thinking skills. Many of these activities also involve collaborative learning and actively engage students in collectively discovering knowledge and making sense of history. Chapter activities and questions throughout the text also encourage students to make connections between the past and the present. Issues of civil rights, questions of freedom and equality, the power of racial tensions, the continuity of family, culture and community institutions, and the tactics of protest become clearer when viewed through the lens of the Civil War and Reconstruction.

Teachers will probably find that this book can be used in a variety of ways. *Freedom's Unfinished Revolution* can enhance courses in United States history and African-American history. Chapters are also valuable for social studies units on such topics as social change, war and revolution, the United States Constitution, civil rights, and culture and community development. Teachers can have students read the entire book, or they can focus on particular chapters or units that tie in with the themes of their course.

Historians debate and disagree about historical interpretations as they consider the underpinnings of contemporary society. This book invites students to do the same: to inquire, interpret, and debate—to take part in the continuing process of historical understanding.

TEACHERS ADVISORY COMMITTEE
Bruce Baskind, Victoria Missick, Patricia Oldham, Frank Poje, David Silberberg
April 1995

Preface

Freedom's Unfinished Revolution was created by the American Social History Project (ASHP), a group of historians, educators, and artists based at the City University of New York. Founded in 1981 by the late distinguished social historian Herbert G. Gutman and Stephen Brier, ASHP seeks to revitalize interest in history by reconceiving the ways the past is studied and presented. The project's texts, videos, and interactive multimedia materials are designed to help teachers and students explore the ways that "ordinary" Americans have shaped our nation.

Freedom's Unfinished Revolution is inspired by the historical synthesis presented in *Who Built America?* ASHP's two-volume, college-level text. Seeking to create a new book that would encourage high-school teachers and students to explore the Civil War and Reconstruction eras in some depth, we have written a dozen short narrative chapters to which we have added scores of additional primary source documents, illustrations, and teaching ideas that clarify and extend the basic historical narrative.

The pedagogical framework of *Freedom's Unfinished Revolution* reflects ASHP's years of work with high-school and college students and teachers. As part of its mission, ASHP organizes a range of faculty seminars that help teachers work together and explore ways to use social history to transform their classrooms. The discussions taking place in these programs in New York City and other urban high-school systems across the country have taught us how to develop pedagogy that puts students at the center of active, collaborative classrooms. We are pleased to acknowledge the lessons we have learned from faculty and student participants in these programs. We want especially to thank the five teachers who served as advisors to *Freedom's Unfinished Revolution*—Bruce Baskind, Victoria Missick, Patricia Oldham, Frank Poje, and David Silberberg—for reading endless drafts, making valuable and insightful suggestions, and helping us to better understand the ways this book could be a resource for teachers and students. The staff of ASHP's education programs—Linda Ellman, Eleanor Morley, and Elisabeth A. Dorsey—also provided comments and criticisms.

We want to acknowledge ASHP production assistant Mario Freison, who undertook the time-consuming process of gathering illustrations and permissions, and Ruth Misheloff, who thoroughly edited the text and located several critical images in the project's final stages. The scholarly work of Eric Foner has informed our understanding of Reconstruction in countless ways over the years, and we benefitted greatly from his reading of an earlier draft. We would also like to thank Susan Barber for sharing her original research on the Richmond bread riots.

ASHP is grateful to the Aaron Diamond Foundation, which provided the funding that allowed The New Press and ASHP to develop *Freedom's Unfinished Revolution*. Special thanks to Norm Fruchter, Vincent McGee, and Irene Diamond for their vision and their staunch commitment to educational innovation. And finally, we want to thank our New Press editor, Ellen Reeves, for shepherding the project and the designers Charles Nix and Hall Smyth, for creating an inviting and stimulating format the helps bring the Reconstruction era to life.

FREEDOM'S UNFINISHED REVOLUTION

GETTING THE NEWS. By the mid-nineteenth century, Americans experienced major changes in the way they received news. The invention of the telegraph permitted journalists to dispatch reports from distant locations to newspaper offices, vastly increasing the speed that news reached the public. In addition, by midcentury, new weekly illustrated newspapers provided extensive pictorial coverage of events in the form of wood engravings. City-dwellers purchased daily and weekly newspapers "hot off the presses" from shops or newsboys (as pictured here). But the United States was still a rural society, and most Americans received these newspapers through the mail or read selections reprinted in small local papers.

C. G. Bush, *Harper's Weekly*, May 18, 1867. American Social History Project.

INTRODUCTION
HISTORY IS US

Let us introduce you to a format common to this book. Every chapter (1) begins with a prereading exercise, (2) invites you to interpret documents, and (3) suggests classroom activities based on those documents.

This introduction does the same. Documents and activities follow page 6, and a prereading exercise begins immediately below.

BEFORE READING. *Free-write for five minutes about the word history. Write nonstop. Write whatever comes to your mind when you think about history. You can write about positive reactions to history, negative reactions, thoughts about what history means, views about its relevance or irrelevance. But whatever you do, keep on writing for the full five minutes.*

When finished, read aloud in pairs what you wrote.

Then, as a class, discuss:

- *What is history?*
- *Should we study history? Why, or why not?*
- *Who creates history?*
- *Is history relevant?*

Now read the introduction. After you complete the reading, continue the discussion of the questions above.

This is a book about slavery, war, and freedom. Just as important, it is a book about human drama and change.

Between 1860 and 1877, relationships between white and blacks, rich and poor, and North and South were turned inside out. By sharpening our focus on these seventeen years, we can compress changes that built up over half a century and exploded into a second American revolution. That revolution took place during the Civil War (1861–65) and its aftermath, known as Reconstruction (1865–77). What happened, and what didn't happen, during the second American revolution had profound consequences for the future of American democracy and race relations.

Before we try to make sense of that revolution, we need to define some terms and discuss some basic issues about history, including how it is taught.

What is history? The question seems simple enough, but historians and nonhistorians continue to argue, frequently and with great intensity, about the definition, substance, and value of history.

As professional historians and educators, we think history is both important and relevant. History can tell us a lot about the past, ourselves, and the world we live in. But it can enlighten only us if we—students and teachers—approach history as participants in its continuing development, as active interpreters of its meaning and content.

The authors of this text come to history with certain assumptions about what it is and how to study it:

1. History Is the Record of Change

The history of slavery, the Civil War, and Reconstruction is more than a mere compilation of dates and facts. We study this history to gain an understanding of a period that radically transformed the United States and who we are as Americans. But if we only memorize famous battles, elections, court cases, and political compromises, the history becomes flat, one-dimensional, boring, and irrelevant. We lose the drama of particular events, and, regrettably, cannot put them in a larger context. History becomes disconnected from the rest of the American experience. It has no cause and effect and little meaning. What makes the period interesting and pertinent to our own lives is how it changed American democracy, race relations, politics, and economic development. Some of these changes were positive, some were negative. Yet all of them affect Americans living on the edge of the twenty-first century.

2. History Is the Study of Human Relationships, Behavior, and Interaction

Change does not simply happen. It has causes that precede it and consequences that follow it. In the center of change are human actors: strong and weak, female and male, rich and poor, black, brown, yellow,

and white. Often they come from different places and backgrounds, bringing a range of emotions, motives, and interests to their actions. As they interrelate, adapt, resist, cooperate, and clash, they move and shake the world around them. There was immense human drama and significance, for example, in the encounters between slaves and masters. Those encounters are central to understanding the history of the South from slavery to freedom. As conditions changed from bondage to liberty, relationships between ex-slaves and ex-masters turned on their head. These are the elements of high drama. It is also fascinating and relevant history.

"OUR SPECIAL ARTIST." The pictorial press relied upon artists to cover the news. Once the Civil War started, some artists, such as *Harper's Weekly*'s Winslow Homer (shown here), drew images on location, either from personal observation or after interviewing eyewitnesses to events. Other artists, usually located at newspaper offices, sketched from photographs (which could not yet be reproduced for publication).

Winslow Homer, *Harper's Weekly*, June 14, 1862. American Social History Project.

3. History Shapes the Lives of Ordinary People, and Ordinary People in Turn Shape History

In most history textbooks, the lives of ordinary people are missing or, at best, exist on the outer margins of the history covered. Most U.S. history texts focus on political history and the actions and decisions of elites: presidents, senators, corporate leaders, and the rich and/or famous. Chapters are usually organized around presidential administrations with titles like "Lincoln and the Civil War," "Presidential Reconstruction," "Silent Calvin Coolidge and the Roaring Twenties," "The New Deal of Franklin Roosevelt," and "The Reagan Era."

Presidents and politics are crucial to an understanding of U.S. history, but so are ordinary Americans. It is true that decisions of war, peace, and everyday politics made by rich and powerful men have a huge impact on the lives of most Americans. In this sense, ordinary men and women are shaped by history often made by others. But at crucial junctures, ordinary people have changed the course of history. At times, history has been made at the grassroots, where masses of people have organized into farm, labor, civil rights, and other movements to defend and extend their rights. Just as often, ordinary people influence history by everyday responses to the conditions and possibilities of their lives.

As a case in point, this text will look at how slaves, both before and after emancipation, in both organized movements and day-to-day existence, helped change the course of nineteenth-century American history.

Rather than structure our text around presidents, we have centered it around the theme of freedom. We look at how both white and black nineteenth-century Americans, sometimes with very conflicting notions about liberty and equality, struggled to achieve freedom and give it meaning. We found that we could tell this story only if we looked at both political and social history, famous and ordinary Americans, and U.S. society from bottom up and top down. In other words, we don't focus on ordinary people to the exclusion of presidents, plantation owners, and corporate leaders. Nor do we focus on themes of social history—work, family, culture, religion, and community life—to the exclusion of political history. Rather, we try to examine how these different actors and themes overlap, conflict, and connect with one another.

THE ENGRAVER. The artist's sketch had to go through several steps before it reached the page of an illustrated newspaper. The sketch was first transferred to the surface of a block of wood. From there, an engraver cut out the design. For large pictures, the wood was divided into sections and distributed to a team of engravers, who worked on the separate parts. As depicted in this illustration from an 1852 magazine, engraving was an intensive job that required long hours hunkered over a magnifying glass. After the wood was cut (and, in the case of the larger pictures, rejoined), a metal impression was taken of the block, which was then fastened to printing presses.

Yankee Notions (September 1852). American Social History Project.

4. History Is Observed and Interpreted Through Many Eyes

How do we know what happened in the past? How, for example, can we discover what life was like on a slave plantation? Most of the descriptions of plantation life were written by slavemasters. They brought particular interests, motives, and perspectives to their descriptions of plantation life. That doesn't mean that we should disregard their diaries as historical evidence, but rather take into account that these documents present only one point of view.

If we look at plantation life through the eyes and experiences of a slave, we get a very different perspective. But since it was against southern law to teach slaves how to read and write, there are many fewer descriptions written from their point of view. There are, however, narratives written by ex-slaves. And there are also other pieces of evidence that tell us how slaves resisted and adapted, and how they looked at themselves, their families, fellow slaves, and plantation masters. Songs and folktales, for instance, passed down by word of mouth from generation to generation, provide many clues about the hopes, fears, values, culture, and survival tactics of African-American slaves.

As the historian sifts through the past, he or she looks for clues, pieces together various types of evidence, and evaluates testimony from different sources with different interests in what was happening. It makes a difference if the source is black or white, male or female, northern or southern, planter or slave, rich or poor white.

The history we study filters through many eyes, including those of our investigator, the historian. He or she may bring a particular outlook, motives, and values to the investigation of history. The historian makes very human decisions when determining what leads to pursue and what evidence to examine, select, ignore, and emphasize.

History also filters through popular culture. Movies, television, songs, books, plays, art, photographs, political cartoons, and even comic books portray history. And like the historian, the creators of these works have a point of view. Consider *Birth of a Nation* (1915) and *Gone with the Wind* (1939). These two movies, which reached record-breaking audiences, shaped—and, we

PHOTOGRAPHIC WAGON. Once the war began, many photographers went into the field. The lengthy process of taking and developing glass-plate negatives required them to devise traveling darkrooms like the one depicted in this photograph. Photographers could not set up their equipment during combat, but they were able to capture the detail of everyday life in the army and the terrible aftermath of battle.

Division of Photographic History, National Museum of American History, Smithsonian Institution.

would argue, grossly distorted—the views of tens of millions of twentieth-century Americans about the Civil War and Reconstruction.

In sum, history is contested terrain. The study of history in all of its forms—written, oral, film, scholarly, and popular—filters and interprets the past. As you hear, see, and read history, including this text, you should try to figure out its point of view and biases, and consider what evidence it draws upon to reach its conclusions.

Does this mean that all history is suspect? We think not. The fact that history reflects human bias does not make it invalid. But it does suggest that our response to history must be active, not passive. That means (1) looking at the study of history with a critical eye and (2) interpreting and expanding our knowledge of history rather than passively swallowing or memorizing a version predigested for us by an author or teacher. Ultimately, the critical test of our interpretation and knowledge of history is in the evidence.

Who We Are

We have just spent several paragraphs arguing that history filters through many eyes, including those of the historian. Hence, it is only fair that we tell you who we are and what agenda we bring to the study of history.

All of the authors and history editors of this book either are, or have been, associated with the American Social History Project (ASHP).

From its start in 1981 to the present, the work of ASHP has been driven by one overriding question: How can we present American history to the widest possible audience?

That question raises several more. Can we do this in ways that makes history accessible, understandable, and interesting? Can we do it in ways that include all Americans in history? And can we do it in ways that encourage audiences to interact with the history we produce, that is, to think about the past, debate it, interpret it, and make connections to their own lives?

We leave it to you—and others who read and view our multimedia (print, video, and computer) materials—to judge whether or not we have succeeded. Over the past fifteen years, we have:

- *created a widely read, two-volume college textbook,* Who Built America? Working People and the Nation's Economy, Politics, Culture and Society;
- *produced an award-winning series of videos used in more than 700 schools and colleges;*
- *developed a ground-breaking CD-ROM,* Who Built America? From the Centennial Celebration of 1876 to the Great War of 1914.

In 1989, with funding from major foundations, we began taking these materials into high-school classrooms, first in New York, and now across the country. In the process, we learned a lot from students and teachers, and even more about what kinds of materials high schools need. The result has been the development of a wealth of ASHP curriculum packages for secondary schools.

However, this is our first high-school text, which, based on our successful college text, we wrote in consultation with several high-school teachers. They tested some of the earlier drafts of this text in their classrooms and gave us lots of smart advice about what would work and what would not. The end product is this book.

5. History Is the Art of Investigation

Like a good detective, a historian must ask the relevant questions, interpret evidence, make inquiries, explore connections, and verify facts. As the detective/historian accumulates more knowledge, he or she develops a better understanding of the events under investigation.

In this text, we invite you to become a historian/detective. In particular, we encourage you to do three things:

1. Put our text under the detective's magnifying glass. Question it when you think it is wrong. Expand, clarify, modify, or develop our interpretation when you think it is right.

2. Examine evidence from original sources. Look at diaries, speeches, petitions, songs, folktales, illustrations, and newspaper editorials. Listen to the voices of ordinary people as you read documents about slave resistance, debates about war aims, and firsthand accounts of poor whites and blacks voting and directing the affairs of southern governments after the Civil War.

3. Look for new evidence. Ask what evidence we have missed and what additional information we need to find out.

This text encourages you to examine historical evidence. For your study and analysis, it presents source documents both written and visual. Printed historical sources range from diaries, speeches, government documents, letters, editorials, and debates, to songs, folktales, and even excerpts from novels. The breadth of visual sources—lithographs, illustrations, cartoons, caricatures, and photographs—is just as diverse. We are asking you to examine these documents as primary—meaning firsthand—historical evidence. Draw on them to make judgments and interpretations about slavery, the Civil War, and Reconstruction.

As you inspect each document, evaluate its source and what point of view it represents.

Consider what audience the document seeks to reach, and how its form (e.g., a speech, a debate, a letter, an illustration, an excerpt from a novel) shapes its message. How does language or imagery in the account affect the reader or viewer? How does the document connect to other events, people, places, things, or themes? What can we learn from it as we assemble our picture of history?

At the end of each chapter, there are suggested activities. In keeping with our general approach, the activities seek to promote historical debate and investigation. They focus on questions about point of view, historical interaction and connections, and change. Most of the exercises emphasize learning through writing and collaboration. We believe that writing encourages thinking and that collaboration in small groups creates a supportive environment in which people can raise questions, test ideas, give and receive feedback, analyze historical evidence, assess cause and effect, debate historical interpretations, and reach their own conclusions about the history they study. But our end-of-chapter suggestions offer a range of classroom applications that are by no means limited to writing and group activities. We encourage students and teachers to use these exercises, modify and improve them, or substitute others that may be considered more appropriate or creative.

Our intent was to create text and activities that make history provocative, dramatic, and very connected to our own lives. We present history not as a finished work but one in progress. Join us as we investigate, interpret, debate, and expand our understanding of freedom's unfinished revolution.

Should Documents Be Recorded in Dialect?

A lot of the voices that you will read in this text are those of slaves both before and after emancipation. Very often their statements were recorded on paper in dialect by whites. A question arises, however: When historians quote these sources, should they do so in dialect or not? Some historians do, claiming that presenting the voice in dialect makes it more genuine.

In this text, however, we use these documents but remove the dialect. We do this for two reasons: First, the documents are easier to read and understand without the dialect, and second, those who recorded the dialect may not have done so accurately.

For example, in 1865, a Virginia plantation mistress recorded the comments below made by one of her recently emancipated slaves. She believed in inequality and considered the ex-slave her inferior, and thus may have presented his speech patterns in a way to portray him as ignorant. Hence, in chapter 8, we use the document but remove the dialect. We did not, however, revise the grammar.

THE DOCUMENT
as it appears in chapter 8:

Seems like we do all the work and [only] get a part. There ain't going to be no more master and mistress, Miss Emma. All is equal. I done hear it from the courthouse steps. All the land belongs to the Yankees now, and they're going to divide it out among the colored people. Besides, the kitchen of the big house is my share. I helped build it.

— CYRUS, *a freedman, to his former mistress, Emma Mordecai, after the fall of Richmond, April 1865*

THE DOCUMENT
as originally recorded by Emma Mordecai:

Seems lak we'uns do all the wuck and gits a part. Der ain't goin' ter be no more Master and Mistress, Miss Emma. All is equal, I done hear it from de cotehouse steps.... All de land belongs to de Yankees now, and dey gwine to divide it out 'mong de colored people. Besides, de kitchen ob de big house is my share. I help built hit.

— CYRUS, *a freedman, to his former mistress, Emma Mordecai, after the fall of Richmond, April 1865*

What do you think: Should the documents be presented in dialect, or not?

W. E. B. DuBois: Did Slaves Play a Key Role in Their Own Liberation?

For more than one hundred years, historians have debated who freed the slaves. In 1935, W. E. B. DuBois, in his classic work Black Reconstruction in America, *challenged what was then a prevailing view among historians of the Civil War era — that African Americans played a minor role in their own freedom. His argument appears below. (The argument continues today. See the debate under the heading "Who Freed the Slaves?" in chapter 3.)*

DOCUMENT ONE

[In 1928, a U.S. historian wrote that] "American negroes are the only people in the history of the world, so far as I know, that ever became free without any effort of their own…."

One but has to read the debates in Congress and state papers from Abraham Lincoln down to know that the decisive action which ended the Civil War was the emancipation and the arming of the black slave; that as Lincoln said: "Without the military help of the black freedmen, the war against the South could not have been won." The freedmen, far from being the inert [passive] recipients of freedom at the hands of philanthropists [charity-givers], furnished 200,000 soldiers in the Civil War who took part in nearly 2000 battles and skirmishes, and in addition perhaps 300,000 others as effective laborers and helpers. In proportion to population, more Negroes than whites fought in the Civil War. These people, withdrawn from the support of the Confederacy, with the threat of the withdrawal of millions more, made the opposition of the slaveholder useless, unless they themselves freed and armed their own slaves. This is exactly what they started to do; they were only restrained by realizing that such action removed the very cause for which they began fighting. Yet one would search current histories [in 1935, when DuBois wrote this statement] almost in vain to find a clear statement or even faint recognition of these perfectly well-authenticated facts.

— W. E. B. DUBOIS

Examining the document

•*What is the response of DuBois to the argument that African Americans played no role in their own freedom?* •*What evidence does DuBois offer to support his answer?* •*DuBois claims that by withdrawing "from the support of the Confederacy," slaves made "the opposition of the slaveholder useless." How could slaves withdraw their support? How could such withdrawal weaken the war effort of the Confederacy?* •*What, according to DuBois, restrained slaveholders from freeing and/or arming their slaves to fight in the war against the North?*

Suggested Activities

DISCUSSION

Do you think DuBois right? Did African Americans play a central role in their own emancipation? Is the evidence he presents convincing? If you were a detective/historian, what else would you want to find out in order to determine whether or not African Americans played a central role in their own liberation? As a group, make a list of questions and issues to investigate. As you read the text and documents in this book, try to answer the questions on your list. You might also want to explore other sources if the text does not provide enough information.

VISUAL LITERACY

Do pictures present an accurate view of reality? Study the illustration titled "Our Special Artist" on page 2. Does the special artist present a faithful view of what happened? Is his portrait of events colored by his own point of view? Do still, movie, and television pictures of contemporary events reflect the point of view of those who produce them? Can we use these pictures as historical evidence of what happened?

Compare pictorial coverage during the period of the Civil War and the present.

APPLETON'S STEREOSCOPIC EMPORIUM ON LOWER BROADWAY, NEW YORK CITY.
Photographs could not be published directly in newspapers but, like artist's sketches, had to be "translated" into wood engravings. Nevertheless, Americans could view photographs of the war in exhibitions and purchase copies in commercial shops. As shown in this picture, the most popular form of photography was the stereograph, composed of two images of the same scene that, when viewed through a special device, conveyed a three-dimensional effect.
Division of Photographic History, National Museum of American History, Smithsonian Institution.

FROM DAWN TO DUSK. Men, women, and children pick cotton under the watchful eye of an overseer.

Prints and Photographs Division, Library of Congress.

PART ONE

SLAVERY, SECTIONAL STRIFE, AND WAR

TIMELINE

EVENTS LEADING TO THE CIVIL WAR

1619	The first African slaves are brought to North America.
1777–1820	Northern states, starting with Vermont, abolish slavery.
1787	The Founding Fathers write a "three-fifths compromise" into the Constitution, counting each slave as three-fifths of a free person for purposes of determining a state's representation in Congress.
1793	Eli Whitney perfects the cotton gin, making the cultivation of cotton with slave labor profitable.
1800–65	Thousands of slaves escape north using the Underground Railroad.
1807	Slave trade from Africa to the United States ends.
1820	The Missouri Compromise: Missouri enters the Union as a slave state, Maine as a free state. Slavery is prohibited in the west above a line extending from Missouri's southern border to the Rocky Mountains.
1829	David Walker, a free black, publishes his *Appeal*, urging slave resistance.
1831	William Lloyd Garrison publishes the first issue of the abolitionist newspaper the *Liberator*.
1831	Nat Turner's slave revolt.
1832	South Carolina asserts its right to declare U.S. laws null and void in the state, talks of secession, but retreats when President Andrew Jackson threatens force.
1832	The American Antislavery Society (AAS) is founded.
1836	Southern congressmen gain passage of the "Gag Rule," directing Congress to ignore all antislavery petitions.
1845	The former Mexican territory of Texas is annexed by the United States as a slave state.
1846–48	War with Mexico. The United States annexes half of Mexico.

"RATION DAY." A weekly newspaper report on the operations of a plantation shows a master distributing provisions. The engraving suggests that this planter provided his slaves with a varied and nutritious diet, which was not typically the case. The picture fails to show the gardens and other methods slaves used to supplement often meager or boring fare.

Harper's Weekly. American Social History Project.

1846–49	Bitter debate in Congress over the Wilmot Proviso, which would have prohibited slavery in newly annexed territories. The proviso is defeated.
1850	Compromise of 1850: California enters the union as a free state, but a new Fugitive Slave Law makes it easier to hunt escaped slaves in the North.
1852	Harriet Beecher Stowe's novel, *Uncle Tom's Cabin,* exposes the horrors of slavery and becomes a best-seller.
1854	The Kansas-Nebraska Act sets aside the Missouri Compromise line; the territories of Kansas and Nebraska can choose whether to be slave or free states.
1854	The Republican party is founded. It opposes the extension of slavery to the western territories.
1856	"Bloody Kansas": War breaks out between pro- and antislavery forces in Kansas.
1856	Senator Charles Sumner, an abolitionist, is beaten unconscious in the chamber of the U.S. Senate by a proslavery congressman.
1857	The Dred Scott decision: The Supreme Court rules that the new western territories have no right to prohibit slavery. Chief Justice Roger Taney declares that no black person in the United States has "any rights which the white man is bound to respect."
1859	John Brown leads a raid on the federal arsenal at Harpers Ferry, [West] Virginia, to seize weapons for an antislavery guerrilla war. He is captured and hanged.
1860	Lincoln is elected president on a Republican party platform opposed to the expansion of slavery. In response, most southern states secede by early 1861.

INTRODUCTION

The growth of the United States from the end of the Revolution (1783) to the beginning of the Civil War (1861) was breathtaking. In just over seventy-five years, a small, mainly agricultural nation on the Atlantic Ocean grew into a powerful, diverse economy, stretching across the continent to the Pacific. From the original thirteen states, the nation multiplied to thirty-three. By 1860, Americans manufactured, mined, and harvested a wealth of goods—textiles, shoes, iron, coal, lumber, grains, beef, sugar, tobacco, cotton, and other riches— which moved across continents and oceans to American and world markets, symbolizing U.S. economic progress and abundance.

It was an era marked by prosperity and conflict. Those who produced the wealth did not equally share its benefits. Tensions between classes, between races, between nationalities, and between men and women, as well as between geographical sections, divided increasing numbers of Americans. But one issue much more than any other split the nation: slavery.

MARKET—1. The place or region where goods are bought and sold (as in the foreign market for cotton or the Dallas market for computers). 2. The demand for a product (as in the market for beef). 3. A particular group of buyers (as in the teenage market for sneakers).

In what ways did the United States change between the American Revolution and the Civil War?

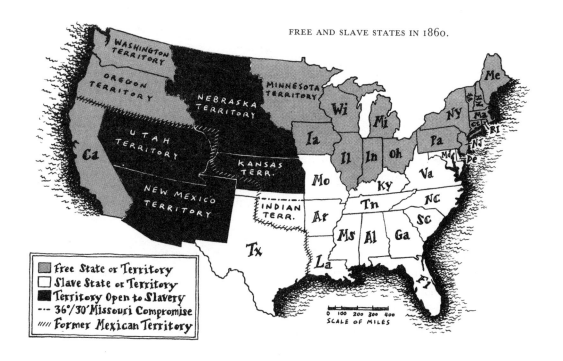

FREE AND SLAVE STATES IN 1860.

Free State or Territory
Slave State or Territory
Territory Open to Slavery
--- 36°/30′ Missouri Compromise
//// Former Mexican Territory

Initially, most white Americans living north of slavery expressed little concern about the "peculiar institution" of slavery, or were openly hostile toward African Americans. But between 1820 and 1860, the extent and speed of westward expansion raised unsettling questions about slavery and race in general for all Americans. Would the new western territories come into the Union as free or slave states? What would happen to the balance of power between free and slave states in the U.S. Senate? Who would control the land in the West: slaveholding planters, capitalist entrepreneurs, or pioneer farmers and workers? The future of the West, and of the whole nation, depended on the answers to these political and economic questions.

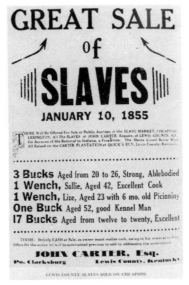

GREAT SALE of SLAVES

JANUARY 10, 1855

THERE Will Be Offered For Sale at Public Auction at the SLAVE MARKET, CHEAPSIDE, LEXINGTON, All The SLAVES of JOHN CARTER, Esquire, of LEWIS COUNTY, KY, On Account of His Removal to Indiana, a Free State. The Slaves Listed Below Were All Raised on the CARTER PLANTATION at QUICK'S RUN, Lewis County, Kentucky.

3 Bucks Aged from 20 to 26, Strong, Ablebodied
1 Wench, Sallie, Aged 42, Excellent Cook
1 Wench, Lize, Aged 23 with 6 mo. old Picininny
One Buck Aged 52, good Kennel Man
17 Bucks Aged from twelve to twenty, Excellent

TERMS: Strictly CASH at Sale, as owner must realize cash, owing to his removal to Indiana. Offers for the entire lot will be entertained previous to sale by addressing the undersigned.

JOHN CARTER, Esq.
P.o. Clarksburg   Lewis County, Kentucky

LEWIS COUNTY SLAVES SOLD ON CHEAPSIDE

PEOPLE FOR SALE, 1855.
The twenty-three slaves to be sold belonged to a Kentucky planter named John Carter. He decided to "liquidate his assets" before moving to the free state of Indiana.

John Winston Coleman, *Slavery Times in Kentucky* (1940).

Why did slavery become such an important issue during this period?

But it was not only westward expansion and development that pushed slavery to center stage in American life. Slavery became a key moral and emotional issue after 1830 because of the growing resistance of slaves themselves and the militancy of black and white abolitionists. Americans reacted with fierce passion to Nat Turner's slave revolt in 1831; to abolitionist rallies and literature; to the successes of the underground railroad in transporting slaves to freedom; to confrontations between escaped slaves and the bounty hunters who pursued them into free states in the North and West; to Harriet Beecher Stowe's brutal descriptions of slavery in her 1852 best-selling novel, *Uncle Tom's Cabin,* to John Brown's attempt in 1859 to arm slaves by raiding a federal arsenal at Harpers Ferry, [West] Virginia.

For forty years, political leaders in the nation's two major parties, the Whigs and Democrats, tried first to avoid the slavery issue, then to reach a compromise. From 1820 to 1860, Congress engineered a series of political settlements—the 1820 Missouri Compromise, the Compromise of 1850, the 1854 Kansas-Nebraska Act—aimed at maintaining a rough balance of political power in the U.S. Senate between slave and free states.

"PECULIAR INSTITUTION"—slavery, particularly as it became unique or peculiar to the South after 1800. By the mid–nineteenth century, the South became one of the few regions in the entire Western Hemisphere where slavery still existed.

CAPITALIST—one who hires wage labor to produce goods and/or services for profit

ENTREPRENEUR—an investor or businessperson

MILITANCY—aggressive action and attitudes in behalf of a cause

ABOLITIONISTS—those who wanted to outlaw slavery and free all slaves

After the Sale. Slavery, and particularly slave auctions, left a lasting impression on many foreign visitors to the South. One of them was a British artist, Eyre Crowe, who witnessed a Richmond auction in 1853 and later painted this scene showing slaves preparing to be transported to new owners in the deep South.

Eyre Crowe, *After the Sale: Slaves Going South from Richmond*, c. 1861, oil on canvas, 27 ⅛ x 36 ⅛ inches (1957.27). Chicago Historical Society.

But by 1860, the raw emotions dividing the sides left little room for compromise. In the presidential election of that year, a new party—the Republican party— and a new candidate, Abraham Lincoln, took a position that made a political settlement of the slavery issue nearly impossible. Lincoln won the presidency on a platform that called for prohibition of the expansion of slavery into the new western territories, but allowed slavery to continue in the old South. The slaveholding class that ruled the South would not permit even this compromise. By early 1861, the South seceded from the Union rather than accept limits to slavery's westward expansion. Within a year, Americans would be fighting other Americans in the bloodiest war in U.S. history.

UNDERGROUND RAILROAD—a network of free blacks and sympathetic whites who helped slaves escape north

BOUNTY HUNTERS—those who pursued and captured runaway slaves for a reward

WHIGS—a major political party, 1832–60. Advocated strong federal government to promote commerce and economic expansion.

DEMOCRATS—a major political party, 1800 to the present. Before the Civil War, called for less federal power and more state and local power.

SECEDE—to withdraw

DOCUMENT ONE

…I remember Mammy told me about one master who almost starved his slaves. Mighty stingy, I reckon he was.

Some of them slaves was so poorly thin they ribs would kind of rustle against each other like corn stalks a-drying in the hot winds. But they gets even one hog killing time, and it was funny, too, Mammy said.

They was seven hogs, fat and ready for fall hog-killing time. Just the day before Old Master told off they was to be killed, something happened to all them porkers. One of the field boys found them and come-a-telling the master: "The hogs is all died, now they won't be any meats for the winter."

When the master gets to where the hogs is a-laying, they's a lot of Negroes standing around looking sorrow-eyed at the wasted meat. The master asks: "What's the illness with 'em?"

"Malitis," they tells him, and they acts like they don't want to touch the hogs. Master says to dress them anyway for they ain't no more meat in this place.

He says to keep all the meat for the slave families, but that he's afraid to eat it hisself account of the hogs got malitis.

"Don't you know what is malitis?" Mammy would ask the children when she was telling of the seven fat hogs and seventy lean slaves. And she would laugh, remembering how they fooled Old Master so's to get all them good meats.

"One of the strongest Negroes got up early in the morning," Mammy would explain, "long 'fore the rising horn called the slaves from their cabins. He skitted to the hog pen with a heavy mallet in hand. When he tapped Mister Hog 'tween the eyes with a mallet, 'malitis' set in mighty quick, but it was a uncommon 'disease,' even with hungry Negroes around all the time."

—JOSIE JORDAN *in an interview
with the Federal Writers Project in the 1930s.
Included in B.A. Botkin, ed.,*
A Folk History of Slavery, *1945*

CHAPTER ONE

THE RESISTANCE TO SLAVERY GROWS

Thinking About Historical Evidence
"Malitis"

BEFORE READING. *What follows is an account of an incident on a slave plantation passed down from one generation of African Americans to the next.*

Read the account as a piece of historical evidence. Then, in small groups, discuss these questions:

What does the account tell us about daily life on the plantation? About the relationship between slave and master? How do we judge the accuracy of this or any other account?

What else do we need to know to get a fuller picture of daily life on a slave plantation? Make a list of questions. How can we find the answers? What other specific kinds of historical evidence (material things, spoken and written words) would we want to gather to get an accurate picture of daily life on the plantation?

After you have read chapter 1, reconsider Document One and the questions about evidence.

ESCAPE. This icon, or symbol, appeared on notices about fugitive slaves in the classified section of the Mobile, Alabama, *Commercial Register* in the 1830s.

Commercial Register, June 16, 1832, Prints and Photographs Division, Library of Congress.

In 1860, on the eve of the Civil War, slightly under four million African-American slaves lived and labored in the South. Most worked in agriculture, creating immense wealth for world markets by cultivating and harvesting cotton, tobacco, sugar, and rice. Planters in the South and merchants in the North and in Europe became fabulously rich buying and selling goods produced by enslaved African labor in America.

European settlers brought the first African slaves to North America in 1619. Over the next 250 years, the South developed an agricultural economy, a way of life, and a system of political and social relationships based on the exploitation of African labor. The system of slavery influenced almost every aspect of southern behavior and interaction among blacks, among whites, and between the two races.

Early in the seventeenth century, slavery spread to the North. But it was never as central to the economy and development of the North, nor as rooted and widespread as it was in the South. After the American Revolution (1775–83), the North developed a more diversified market economy based on free labor. Massachusetts abolished slavery in 1780, and over the next several decades other northern states did the same.

In the first half of the nineteenth century, the question of slavery increasingly divided North and South. By the 1830s, resistance to the system by slaves in the South and abolitionists in the North was changing the course of nineteenth-century American history.

MARKET ECONOMY—A system of production and distribution based on the free exchange (buying and selling) of goods, services, and labor.

Resistance: 1831

The year 1831 marked a major turning point in opposition to slavery.

In Boston, Massachusetts, on New Year's Day, William Lloyd Garrison published the first issue of the *Liberator,* a newspaper that became the nation's most famous abolitionist journal. The *Liberator* had an immediate and dramatic impact. Slaveholders denounced its publication; abolitionists rallied to its support. No longer could the

What made the year 1831 a turning point in the resistance to slavery?

planter class in the South afford to take slavery's continued existence for granted. From this point on, the institution came under constant, intense public attack. With a new urgency, slaveholders united to defend their "peculiar institution."

"AM I NOT A WOMAN AND A SISTER?" An engraving from abolitionist George Bourne's 1837 pamphlet, *Slavery Illustrated in Its Effects upon Women.*

George Bourne, *Slavery Illustrated in Its Effects upon Women* (1837). Prints and Photographs Division, Library of Congress.

In August 1831, the bloodiest slave revolt in U.S. history threw slaveholders and other white southerners into a state of utter panic. Nat Turner, a Virginia-born slave preacher who claimed that he had had a vision from God to revolt [see Document Two], led fellow slaves in a daring but ultimately unsuccessful bid for freedom. Sixty whites and more than one hundred African Americans died in the insurrection and its eventual suppression by authorities in Southampton County, Virginia. Apprehended and executed with thirteen others, Turner in death became a figure larger than life. His deed captured the imagination of slaveholders and slaves alike, stirring fears in one and exciting hopes in the other.

First the *Liberator*, then Turner's revolt—in just eight months, slavery had been rocked by major assaults from within and without.

INSURRECTION—A revolt against authority.

Resistance: The Slaves

Nat Turner was only the latest of martyred slaves who had revolted or conspired against their masters. Across generations and regions, word of mouth told of uprisings and plots led by Gabriel Prosser in 1800, Denmark Vesey in 1822, and now Turner. The plantation grapevine spread news of insurrections by escaped slaves and their Indian allies during the Seminole wars (1812, 1835). Each of these acts of armed defiance failed. Yet their legend provoked alarm among masters and inspired continued resistance among slaves.

That resistance took many forms, much of it woven into the fabric of everyday life.

In the face of daily, seemingly unending oppression, slaves found ways to undercut the authority of their masters and make their own lives less unbearable.

What made all of this possible was a system of social, religious, and family support that enabled slaves to transfer survival strategies, moral values, and cultural traditions from seniors to adults to children. Elders sang songs and told folktales, full of both obvious and hidden meanings,

Joseph Cinque. In July 1839, captive West Africans rebelled and took over the Spanish slave ship *Amistad.* They ordered the crew to sail to Africa but, instead, the *Amistad* was taken on a meandering course until it was waylaid by a U.S. Navy ship. The Africans were charged with the murder of the captain and jailed in New Haven, Connecticut. Abolitionists came to their support, and former president John Quincy Adams represented them in court. After a long legal battle, the Supreme Court freed the "mutineers" in 1841. The following year they returned to Africa. "Our hands are now clean for we have striven to regain the precious heritage we received from our fathers," wrote Joseph Cinque, the leader of the rebellion. His portrait was painted by Nathaniel Jocelyn in 1839.

Nathaniel Jocelyn, *Joseph Cinque,* 1839, oil on canvas, 30 1/4 x 25 1/2 inches. The New Haven Colony Historical Society.

that not only entertained but educated family and kin of all ages. At church services full of emotion and meaning, often held under cover of darkness in isolated woods and out of earshot of the plantation master, slaves absorbed lessons from biblical dramas. Preachers narrated Old Testament tales of good triumphing over evil, of the weak outwitting the strong, and of the oppressed escaping their tormentors—David and Goliath, Samson and Delilah, Jonah and the whale, and the parting of the Red Sea as Israelites fled slavery in Egypt.

In what ways did African Americans resist slavery?

Nourished by extended family networks and a form of Christianity heavily influenced by African religion, a distinct African-American culture developed. This culture gave slaves strength and a sense of self and group identity that helped them to endure, which also included acts of everyday resistance.

Sometimes this defiance took the form of a daily tug-of-war between slave and master over the pace and intensity of work in the fields. The planter and his overseers had the force of the whip and the rule of government authority and law. But slaves could sabotage work by breaking tools, injuring work animals, inflicting self-injury, faking illness, going slowly, or, in the case of women, claiming pregnancy. Many slaves pretended not to understand the simplest instructions. In a few instances, rebellion escalated into barn-burnings or the poisoning of a master.

How did religion and family help slaves to endure and resist slavery?

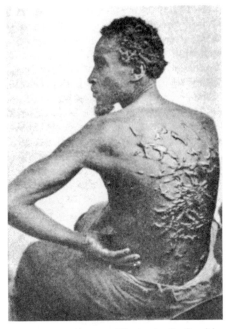

A MAP OF SERVITUDE. The back of a Louisiana slave named Gordon, photographed in 1863 after he escaped to Union forces.

Prints and Photographs Division, Library of Congress.

"FIVE GENERATIONS ON J. J. SMITH'S PLANTATION, BEAUFORT, SOUTH CAROLINA."
An African-American family photographed in 1862.

Timothy H. O'Sullivan, 1862. Prints and Photographs Division, Library of Congress.

Plantation Burial. Funerals were sad occasions in the slave quarters, but they also provided African Americans with an opportunity to confirm their community identity. They were often held at night so that friends and families from neighboring farms could attend.

John Antrobus, *Plantation Burial*, 1860, oil on canvas, 53 x 81 ½ inches (1960.46). The Historic New Orleans Collection.

Some slaves hid in the woods for a few days in order to gain bargaining power against a master or overseer. A field hand might sneak away to evade a whipping or the oppressive labor of the planting or harvesting season. Once the daily work routine eased, for example, after a harvest, the escaped slave would return. He or she might face the whip, but there was also the chance the master might lighten the work load because slave labor was essential to producing the enormous amounts of cotton, tobacco, and rice that planters sold in world markets. Better that the planter reduce the brutal pace of labor than have large numbers of his hands absent for days at a time during the planting or harvesting season.

Thousands of slaves, however, resisted by trying to run away, usually to the North or Canada, thereby escaping slavery altogether. Surrounded by southern whites and their organized military patrols, however, the majority of runaways were caught, whipped, and in some instances sold away from their families to discourage other slaves from plotting to escape. Yet a remarkable "underground railroad" managed to transfer thousands to freedom.

The Underground Railroad was a network of many hundreds of free blacks and white sympathizers who concealed, guided, housed, clothed, and sheltered runaway slaves in their flight north. The best known of these northern "conductors" was Harriet Tubman. An escaped slave, Tubman returned to the South nineteen times, repeatedly risking recapture and summary execution. She personally led three hundred slaves to freedom.

Resistance by African Americans to slavery took many forms, some open and militant, others more indirect. Compare the forms revealed in the following documents.

Nat Turner's Confessions: "The Serpent Was Loosened"

Before he was hanged, Nat Turner, leader of the most famous slave revolt in U.S. history, told his story to an interviewer. In this excerpt, Turner relates that a voice from God directed him in the summer of 1831 to strike against his Virginia master and other whites.

DOCUMENT TWO

And the spirit appeared to me again, and said, as the Savior had been baptized, so should we also; and when white people would not let us be baptized by the church, we went down into the water together in the sight of many who reviled [insulted] us, and were baptized by the Spirit. After this I rejoiced greatly and gave thanks to God. And on the 12th of May, 1828, I heard a loud noise in the heavens and the Spirit instantly appeared to me and said that the Serpent was loosened, and Christ had laid down the yoke he had borne for the sins of men, and that I should take it on, and fight against the Serpent, for the time was fast approaching when the first should be last and the last should be first.

QUESTION: Do you not find yourself mistaken now?
ANSWER: Was not Christ crucified?

And by signs in the heaven that it would make known to me when I should commence the great work, and until the first sign appeared I should conceal it from the knowledge of men; and on the appearance of the sign (the eclipse of the sun, last February), I should arise and prepare myself to slay my enemies with their own weapons. And immediately on the sign appearing..., I communicated the great work for me to do to four in whom I had the greatest confidence (Henry, Hark, Nelson and Sam)....

Since the commencement of 1830, I had been living with Mr. Joseph Travis, who was to me a kind master and placed the greatest confidence in me; in fact I had no cause to complain of his treatment to me. On Saturday evening, the 20th of August, it was agreed between Henry, Hark, and myself to prepare a dinner the next day for the men we expected, and then to concert a plan, as we had not determined on any....

...It was quickly determined that we should commence at home (Mr. Travis) on that night, and until we had armed and equipped ourselves and gathered sufficient force, neither age nor sex was to be spared—which was generally adhered to....

I took my station in the rear, and, as it was my object to carry terror and devastation wherever we went, I placed fifteen or twenty of the best armed and most to be relied on in front, who generally approached the houses as fast as their horses could run. This was for two purposes—to prevent their escape and to strike terror to the inhabitants. [Turner then proceeds to describe the "terror and devastation" caused by the insurrection.]

—*From* THE CONFESSIONS OF NAT TURNER,
edited by T. R. Gray, who interviewed Turner
in prison in November 1831

Brer Rabbit: "Tar Baby"

Folktales played an important role in the everyday struggle of slaves to endure and resist the inhumanity and oppression of plantation life. Slave families drew on this oral tradition to entertain and educate their young. Through folktales, slaves passed on wisdom, moral values, and survival strategies from one generation to the next. The tales included stories of trickery, and even treachery, which were in part a commentary on plantation life and a means of expressing hostility toward the master in a disguised form.

This oral tradition borrowed heavily from African culture. For example, tricksters in animal form were prominent in both African and African-American folklore. Brer Rabbit, a legendary trickster in the African-American folk tradition, takes center stage in the "Tar Baby" story that follows.

DOCUMENT THREE

Brer Wolf studied and studied to find a way to catch Brer Rabbit. He scratched his head, and he pulled his chin whiskers until by and by he said, "I know what I'll do. I'll make me a tar baby, and I'll catch that good-for-nothing rabbit."†

And so Brer Wolf worked and worked until he had made a pretty little girl out of tar. He dressed the tar baby in a calico apron and carried her up to the well, where he stood her up and fastened her to a post in the ground so that nobody could move her. Then Brer Wolf hid in the bushes and waited for Brer Rabbit to come for some water. But three days passed before Brer Rabbit visited the well again. On the fourth day, he came with a bucket in his hand.

When he saw the little girl, he stopped and looked at her. Then he said, "Hello. What's your name? What are you doing here, little girl?"

The little girl said nothing.

This made Brer Rabbit angry, and he shouted at her, "You no-mannered little snip, you! How come you don't speak to your elders?"

The little girl said nothing.

"I know what to do with little children like you. I'll slap your face and teach you some manners if you don't speak to me," said Brer Rabbit.

Still the little girl said nothing.

And then Brer Rabbit lost his head and said, "Speak to me, I say. I'm going to slap you." With that, Brer Rabbit slapped the tar baby in the face, and his right had stuck.

"A-ha, you hold my hand, do you? Turn me loose, I say. Turn me loose. If you don't, I'm going to slap you with my left hand. And if I hit you with my left hand, I'll knock the daylights out of you."

But the little girl said nothing. So Brer Rabbit drew back his left hand and slapped the little girl in her face, bim, and his left hand stuck.

"Oh, I see. You're going to hold both my hands, are you? You better turn me loose. If you don't I'm going to kick you. And if I kick you, it's going to be like thunder and lightning!" With that, Brer Rabbit drew back his right foot and kicked the little girl in the shins with all his might, blap! Then his right foot stuck.

"Well, sir, isn't this something? You better turn my foot loose. If you don't I've got another foot left, and I'm going to kick you with it, and you'll think a cyclone hit you." Then Brer Rabbit gave that little girl a powerful kick in the shins with his left foot, blip! With that his left foot stuck, and there he hung off the ground, between the heavens and the earth. He was in an awful fix. But he still thought he could get loose.

So he said to the little girl, "You've got my feet and my hands all stuck up, but I've got one more weapon and that's my head. If you don't turn me loose, I'm going to butt you! And if I butt you, I'll knock your brains out." Finally, then, Brer Rabbit struck the little girl a powerful knock on the forehead with his head, and it stuck, and there he hung. Smart old Brer Rabbit, he couldn't move. He was held fast by the little tar baby.

Now, Brer Wolf was hiding under the bushes, watching all that was going on. And as soon as he was certain that Brer Rabbit was caught good by his little tar baby, he walked over to Brer Rabbit and said, "A-ha, you're the one who wouldn't dig a well. And you're the one who's going to catch his drinking water from the dew off the grass. A-ha, I caught the fellow who's been stealing my water. And he isn't anybody but you, Brer Rabbit. I'm going to fix you good."

"No, sir, Brer Wolf, I haven't been bothering your water. I was just going over to Brer Bear's house, and I stopped by here long enough to speak to this little no-manners girl," said Brer Rabbit.

"Yes, you're the one," said Brer Wolf. "You're the very one who's been stealing my drinking water all this time. And I'm going to kill you."

"Please, sir, Brer Wolf, don't kill me," begged Brer Rabbit. "I haven't done anything wrong."

"Yes, I'm going to kill you, but I don't know how I'm going to do it yet," growled Brer Wolf. "Oh, I know what I'll do. I'll throw you in the fire and burn you up."

"All right, Brer Wolf," said Brer Rabbit. "Throw me in the fire. That's a good way to die. That's the way my grandmother died, and she said it's a quick way to go. You can do anything with me, anything you want, but please sir, don't throw me in the briar patch."

"No, I'm not going to throw you in the fire, and I'm not going to throw you in the briar patch. I'm going to throw you down the well and drown you," said Brer Wolf.

"All right, Brer Wolf, throw me down the well," said Brer Rabbit. "That's an easy way to die, but I'm surely going to smell up your drinking water, sir."

"No, I'm not going to drown you," said Brer Wolf. "Drowning is too good for you." Then Brer Wolf thought and thought and scratched his head and pulled his chin whiskers. Finally he said, "I know what I'm going to do with you. I'll throw you in the briar patch."

"Oh, no, Brer Wolf," cried Brer Rabbit. "Please, sir don't throw me in the briar patch. Those briars will tear up my hide, pull out my hair, and scratch out my eyes. That'll be an awful way to die, Brer Wolf. Please, sir, don't do that to me."

"That's exactly what I'll do with you," said Brer Wolf all happy-like. Then he caught Brer Rabbit by his hind legs, whirled him around and around over his head, and threw him way over into the middle of the briar patch.

After a minute or two Brer Rabbit stood up on his hind legs and laughed at Brer Wolf and said to him, "thank you, Brer Wolf, thank you. This is the place where I was born. My grandmother and grandfather and all my family were born right here in the briar patch."

And that's the end of the story.

† *Tar was often spread on fences by masters to catch slaves who, out of hunger or mischief, would sneak into fields and orchards to steal food. Tar stuck on the hands would betray the "guilty" slave.*

Source: WILLIAM J. FAULKNER, The Days When the Animals Talked. *Copyright 1977 by William J. Faulkner.*

Examining the documents

•*Why is Nat Turner convinced that his rebellion is just and right?* •*What factors determined the timing of his rebellion?* •*What does the "Tar Baby" story show us about survival and the everyday relationship between master and slave on the plantation?* •*What is the significance of the briar patch and of the animals (wolf, rabbit) chosen as characters in this story?*

Resistance: Abolitionists and Anti-Abolitionists

Escaped slaves like Harriet Tubman and Frederick Douglass became powerful leaders of the antislavery cause; so did African Americans born into freedom.

By 1790, there were 59,000 free African Americans in the United States: 27,000 in the North and 32,000 in the South. Forty years later, the total increased to 319,000.

As their numbers increased, African-American institutions and organizations began to flourish in the North: churches, newspapers, political organizations, mutual aid societies, schools, boarding houses, small business, and, quite significantly, antislavery societies.

Militant antislavery movements in free black northern communities generally pre-dated and spurred organized efforts by white abolitionists. Newspapers edited by white and black abolitionists found an eager, active, and large following among African Americans in the North.

MUTUAL AID SOCIETY—an organization whose members, as needed, provide aid and assistance to one another

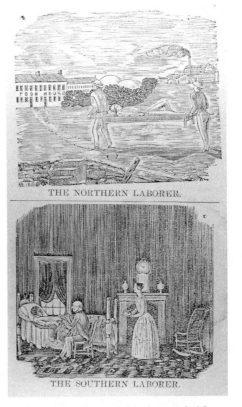

THE NEGRO AS HE WAS.

THE NORTHERN LABORER.

THE NEGRO AS HE IS.

THE SOUTHERN LABORER.

THE BENEFITS OF SLAVERY. Two pages from a proslavery pamphlet published around 1860 present the contrasting fates of unfree and free labor: while fortunate slaves are civilized and, in old age, cared for by benevolent masters, the northern wage worker faces exhaustion and poverty.

From the private collections of Larry E. Tise, Harrisburg, Pennsylvania.

THE WHIPPING OF AMOS DRESSER. A theology student traveling through Nashville, Tennessee, in 1835 was one of the many abolitionist victims of proslavery repression. Dresser was discovered to be carrying antislavery literature in his luggage. He was abducted during the night, brought to a public square, and whipped before a cheering crowd.

Amos Dresser, *The Narrative of Amos Dresser…* (1836). American Antiquarian Society.

"FREE NEGROES IN THE NORTH." Apologists for slavery often constructed a grotesque picture of free blacks in the North. According to this etching published during the Civil War, without the supervision of benevolent masters, northern African Americans descended into violence and degradation.

V. Blada (A.J. Volck), *Sketches from the Civil War in North America, 1861, '62, '63* (1863).
Print Collection, Miriam and Ira Wallach Division of Art, Prints, and Photographs, The New York Public Library,
Astor, Lenox, and Tilden Foundations.

Five years before William Lloyd Garrison published the first issue of the *Liberator,* free blacks in the Massachusetts General Colored Association were organizing antislavery activities. One member, David Walker, published a call to action in 1829 directed to the slaves themselves. His seventy-six-page pamphlet, known as *Walker's Appeal,* urged slaves to "Arise, arise! Strike for your lives and liberties. Now is the day and the hour."

Walker's Appeal caused a sensation among both slaveholders and abolitionists.

Why did Walker's Appeal cause such a sensation?

Its uncompromising, angry tone brought a new militancy to the entire antislavery movement. The governors of Georgia and North Carolina and city officials in Richmond, Savannah, and New Orleans denounced Walker. But free blacks, slaves, and even a white printer in Milleridge, Georgia, smuggled copies of *Walker's Appeal* into the South.

A reward of $1,000 was offered in the South for David Walker's corpse; $10,000 if he were captured and returned alive. Bounties were also put on the heads of other abolitionists. Georgia offered a $5,000 reward for the trial and conviction "under the laws of this state" of William Lloyd Garrison, publisher of the *Liberator.* With each act of resistance by slaves and abolitionists, and with each counter-action by southern slaveholders, divisions within the nation widened.

BOUNTY—a reward or payment

"FAMILY AMALGAMATION AMONG THE MAN-STEALERS." An illustration from an 1834 antislavery pamphlet depicts an unlikely domestic scene in a plantation household, with slave children joining their owners at the dinner table. Some antislavery advocates viewed the potential for intimacy between whites and blacks as one of the demoralizing effects of the "peculiar institution."

George Bourne, *Pictures of Slavery in the United States* (1834). Prints and Photographs Division, Library of Congress.

Walker's Appeal: "We Must and Shall Be Free"

David Walker was born a free man in the slave South in 1785. Sometime after his thirtieth birthday, he moved north to Boston's free black community, where he became active in the antislavery movement. Below is an excerpt from Walker's 1829 Appeal.

DOCUMENT FOUR

Never make an attempt to gain our freedom or *natural* right from under our cruel oppressors and murderers until you see our way clear—when that hour arrives and you move, be not afraid or dismayed....

...we are men as well as they. God has been pleased to give us two eyes, two hands, two feet, and some sense in our heads as well as they. They have no more right to hold us in slavery than we have to hold them....

...Let no man of us budge one step, and let slave-holders come to beat us from our country. America is more our country than it is the whites—we have enriched it with our *blood and tears*. The greatest riches in all of America have arisen from our blood and tears: and they will drive us from our property and homes, which we have earned with our *blood*....

Our sufferings will come to an end, in spite of all the Americans this side of eternity. Then we want all the learning and talents among ourselves, and perhaps more to govern ourselves. — "Every dog must have its day," the American's is coming to an end.

...I speak Americans for your good. We must and shall be free, I say, in spite of you. You may do your best to keep us in wretchedness and misery, to enrich you and your children, but God will deliver us from under you. And woe, woe, will be to you if we have to obtain our freedom by fighting. Throw away your fears and prejudices then, and enlighten us and treat us like men, and we will like you more than we now hate you.... Treat us like men, and there is no danger but that we live in peace and happiness together....

—*Excerpt from* WALKER'S APPEAL, *September 28, 1829*

Examining the document

• *Walker argues that slaves have the right to be free. According to Walker, where do they get that right?*

• *Why does Walker believe that "America is more our [the slaves'] country than it is the whites"?*

• *Does Walker feel that he is part of America?*

Conflict accelerated with the founding of the American Antislavery Society (AAS) in 1832. Over the next three years, the AAS campaign to blanket both free and slave states with abolitionist literature provoked a furious response in the South. In July 1835, a crowd in Charleston, South Carolina, broke into a post office, seized stacks of AAS literature, and publicly set them afire. South Carolina officials approved this riotous behavior. The postmaster general of the United States, ignoring the unlawful destruction of mail, refused to intervene.

What kind of reaction was there in the South to abolitionist literature? How did this reaction intensify sectional conflict?

But the AAS persisted. It swamped Congress with antislavery petitions signed by millions of Americans. In response, southern congressmen in 1836 persuaded their colleagues to pass a "Gag Rule" that trampled the constitutional right to petition the government. The rule ordered Congress to ignore "all petitions, memorials, resolutions, propositions, or papers relating in any way or to any extent whatever to the subject of slavery."

What contradictory attitudes existed toward race and slavery in the North? How were these attitudes reflected in northern attitudes toward western expansion?

The antislavery movement continued to agitate, but it met contradictory reactions in the North. Many white northerners despised slavery *and* black people alike, seeing both as threats to the livelihood of white workingmen. The small but growing black population of the free states lived on the margins of society, generally confined to menial and low-paying occupations that did not compete with white labor. In many midwestern states, free blacks were by law denied residence.

All the same, most white northerners, even the most racist, hotly opposed the extension of slavery from the South to the West. Northern farmers wanted western lands held free for settlement as single-family homesteads. Many urban Americans shared the farmers' dream of working and owning land in the West. These would-be frontier farmers feared that southern planters would grab most of the western lands for large plantations worked by slave labor. The self-interest of these northerners fostered both antiblack and antislavery attitudes.

Parts of the abolitionist movement reflected the same contradictory views. Some white antislavery reformers opposed racial oppression hundreds of miles away in the slave South, but turned a blind eye to discrimination and exploitation of free blacks on their own doorstep. A number of white abolitionists were haughty and disdainful toward African Americans in the movement.

The abolitionist movement had its imperfections; nevertheless, it made an enormous contribution to the history of freedom in the United States by mobilizing millions of citizens to confront slavery as a moral disgrace of the nation's character. At the same time, westward expansion compelled all Americans to face slavery as an issue vital to the nation's political and economic future. Eventually, the political, economic, and moral issues would converge, and the nation would be torn apart by war.

Frederick Douglass: "If There Is No Struggle, There Is No Progress"

Growing sectional strife after 1850 increased the tensions within the abolitionist movement between its more moderate and militant wings. In the following speech, ex-slave Frederick Douglass makes the case for a more militant approach to abolition.

DOCUMENT FIVE

Let me give you a word of the philosophy of reforms. The whole history of the progress of human liberty shows that all concessions yet made to her august claims have been born of earnest struggle....If there is no struggle, there is no progress. Those who profess to favor freedom and yet deprecate agitation are men who want crops without plowing the ground. They want rain without thunder and lightning. They want the ocean without the roar of its mighty waters. The struggle may be a moral one or it may be a physical one, or it may be both moral and physical, but it must be a struggle. Power concedes nothing without a demand. It never has and it never will.

— FREDERICK DOUGLASS
in a speech in Rochester, N.Y., 1857

Examining the document

• *What is Douglass's main message?*
• *Would Turner and Walker (Documents Two and Four) agree with that message? Why or why not?*

A Planter's Reaction to Nat Turner's Revolt: "A Horrible, Heart-Rending Tale"

DOCUMENT SIX

I have a horrible, heart-rending tale to relate....

...[A] band of insurgent slaves (some of them believed to be runaway slaves from neighboring swamps), had turned out on Sunday night last, and murdered several whole families, amounting to 40 or 50 individuals.

The insurrection was represented as one of a most alarming character.... Unfortunately, a large number of the...male population was absent at camp [religious] meeting some miles off...and the panic with which they [the slaves] struck at the moment prevented the assembling of a force sufficient to check [them]....

As soon as this intelligence [information] was received, our authorities met, and decided to make an immediate application to Col. House, commanding at Fortress Monroe, who at 6 o'clock this morning embarked on the steam boat *Hampton*, with three companies and pieces of artillery for Suffolk. These troops were re-inforced by detachments from the U.S. ships *Warren* and *Natchez*, the whole amounting to nearly 300 men.

...[T]he few slaves who have rushed headlong into the arena, will be shot down like crows or captured and made examples of. The militia are collecting in all the neighboring counties, and the utmost vigilance prevails....

—*A Virginia planter's report in the* NILES WEEKLY REGISTER, August 27, 1831

For research: in-depth investigation

What happened when Nat Turner led slaves in revolt? Why did he undertake the rebellion? What were the effects? How important was this event historically?

There are conflicting interpretations of Turner's revolt. Document Six excerpts a southern white planter's report on the revolt. Turner himself gives another account in Document Two, but Turner's words were transcribed and edited by T. R. Gray, a white southerner. In our time, William Styron based his novel *The Confessions of Nat Turner* (1967) mainly on Gray's version of what Turner said, yet was challenged by critics for viewing Turner, a black slave, from a white southerner's perspective. In some history books used today, the rebellion gets little or no attention while claiming a lot of attention in others, but with a variety of interpretations and emphases.

Suggested Activities

FOR RESEARCH (CONTINUED)
Investigate the treatment of Nat Turner's rebellion in the following types of sources:

- a northern newspaper from the time
- a Virginia newspaper from the time
- an abolitionist newspaper from the time (for example, the *Liberator*)
- several high-school U.S. history texts
- several standard college U.S. history texts
- several African-American history texts

Divide the investigation of these sources among members of the class. Consider other sources (like Gray's version of the *Confessions*, Styron's novel, essays by Styron's critics, or more detailed historical studies of the rebellion).

As you read each source, notice the author's *assumptions*, that is, those ideas and beliefs the writer takes as naturally, self-evidently true, and try to infer the author's *agenda*—what he or she wants readers to think, feel, or do.

When your research is complete, compare findings. What similarities and differences in interpretation did you and others find among the sources? How do you explain them? How do the interpretations in the sources compare with the discussion of Turner's rebellion in *this* text?

What personal conclusions do you draw about Turner's revolt and its importance in U.S. history? On what do you base your conclusions?

REACTING TO VISUAL EVIDENCE
Take one minute to study the announcement of "People for Sale, 1855," on page 14. Free-write your reactions for five minutes. Share what you write with classmates.

VIDEO OPTION: *Doing as They Can*
Document One is the basis for the "malitis" story in *Doing as They Can,* an American Social History Project video that can be used to supplement this chapter. If you see the video, consider these questions.

Write for five minutes then share what you wrote with another student before the class as a whole discusses the video.

- What does the title *Doing as They Can* mean?
- Is the "malitis" story a good example of "Doing as They Can"?
- In the video and reading, what other examples of "Doing as They Can" can you cite?

FREE-WRITING AND DISCUSSION
Read Document Six on page 34. Write a brief summary. Then free-write for five minutes on each of the following:

- You are a Virginia slavemaster. You have just read the report of Nat Turner's rebellion in the *Niles Weekly Register*. What are you thinking?
- You are a Virginia slave who has just overheard the slavemaster read the article aloud to his overseer. What are you thinking?

Pair up with a classmate and read your summary and writing. Drawing on what you learned from the text, the documents, and your free-writing, discuss why Turner's revolt was such a turning point in (1) the planter's growing defensiveness and defiance about slavery, and (2) the increasing resistance by slaves and the abolitionist movement.

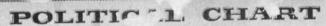

"POLITICAL CHART OF THE UNITED STATES." An 1856 Republican map delineates the geographic contours of slavery. A portrait of Republican presidential candidate John C. Frémont is displayed at the top of the document.

CHAPTER TWO

WESTWARD EXPANSION, SECTIONAL STRIFE, AND CIVIL WAR

BEFORE READING. Study *"The Political Chart of the United States,"* the 1856 Republican party map on page 36. Identify as many of the following before you read the chapter. As you read, complete any identifications that you cannot do initially.

1. The slave states in 1856.
2. The free states in 1856.
3. All the states and territories that were once part of Mexico.
4. The two states admitted by the Missouri Compromise of 1820.
5. The Missouri Compromise line.
6. The free state admitted to the Union by the Compromise of 1850.
7. The Kansas-Nebraska territory.
8. The slave state Dred Scott was taken from and the free state and territory he was taken to.

Westward Expansion and National Division

Whatever their differences before the Civil War, most northern and southern whites agreed that rapid westward expansion and settlement were essential to the future well-being of the nation. Between 1820 and 1860, that expansion brought them into conflict with the Native Americans and Mexicans who occupied much of what was to become the American West. In turn, the success and speed with which the U.S. conquered Indians, absorbed Mexican territory, and pushed westward to the Pacific Ocean, raised questions that would provoke tensions among those very Americans who favored expansion. Who would control the new western territories?

Who would reap the benefits of expansion? Northern capitalist developers and investors? pioneers cultivating small family farms? or a tiny but immensely powerful southern elite who envisioned a west of big plantations worked by slave labor?

Northern investors, merchants, manufacturers, promoters, and speculators envisioned rich, seemingly unlimited possibilities for economic development in the West. Their heads danced with images of railroads, mines, lumber camps, and commercial farms spreading across the continent—from the Mississippi River to the Pacific Ocean.

FAMILY, OR SUBSISTENCE, FARMS—farms that raise crops and livestock for family use rather than for sale. In 1800, American agriculture was dominated by subsistence farms. By 1900, there were relatively few of them.

But for many more Americans, particularly white northerners, the West became the place where they could fulfill the "American Dream" of individual progress and freedom. Most ordinary working Americans never made it west, but that did not stop them from dreaming of a family homestead that would guarantee their future independence and self-sufficiency.

In the era just before and after the Civil War, large numbers of Americans believed that with cheap land, hard work, a little luck, and a lot of cooperation from Mother Nature, a pioneer family could produce almost everything it needed to survive. That meant food, clothing, shelter, and everyday household items such as soap and candles and even quilts and curtains. A family with a flourishing homestead could declare independence from the bankers, manufacturers, and merchants who controlled the economic destiny of so many other Americans. Next to the plans of enterprising northern businessmen for railroads, mines, mills, big farms, and economic development, the pioneer family farm seemed modest in its ambitions.

But the struggling frontier farmer and capitalist businessman thinking about profits in the West had something very important in common: they both had a stake in keeping slave labor out of the West. If southern-style plantations were to dominate the new West, then there would be no place for economic developers, subsistence farmers, or anybody else, for that matter. By the 1850s, northerners with very different economic agendas for expansion were uniting for free labor and against slave labor in the West.

Southern planters, on the other hand, came to see control of the West as essential to the survival of slavery. As overworked tobacco, cotton, rice, and sugar lands in Virginia, South Carolina, and other old-South states became infertile from overuse, the West, particularly the Southwest, became increasingly attractive. The fertile soil of Mississippi and Texas promised rich-

COMMERCIAL FARMS—farms that produce specialized crops, such as cotton, beef, or wheat, for national and world markets. Today, virtually all U.S. agriculture consists of commercial farms.

HOMESTEAD—a small tract of land, often one sold by the government to families or individuals at very low prices on the condition that they settle and farm it

ACTIONS SPEAK LOUDER THAN WORDS.
"The Land of Liberty" is the title of this cartoon published in an 1847 edition of *Punch*, the British satirical weekly.

Punch, 1847. American Social History Project.

er yields and higher profits. Even planters in the upper South, where there were too many slaves and not enough fertile land, wanted to see the slave labor system spread to the Southwest so that they could sell their excess slaves at a profit to planters there.

Planters also saw the West as a "safety valve" for the growing discontent of southern whites who did not own slaves. The plantations monopolized the best land and resources, pushing poorer whites to the margins of society. To maintain its political and economic power, the slaveholding class needed the support of poor whites. The West offered new opportunities, particularly land, for poorer whites living on the edges of the slave economy. By opening the West to southern settlement, the planter class could defuse the unhappiness of lower-class whites in the South.

The rapid continental expansion of a diversified northern market economy based on free labor made the thrust westward even more urgent for southern planters. Slavery had flourished in the North in the seventeenth and eighteenth centuries, particularly in the Middle Atlantic states. But in the nineteenth century, as antislavery sentiment grew, northern states abolished the system.

To prevent free states in the North from using the federal government against the interests of slaveholders, planters needed to retain equal representation in the U.S. Senate. As the nation grew westward, that meant admitting one new slave state into the Union for every free state.

For the system of slavery, it was expand or die. The "peculiar institution" could not survive politically without new slave states. Nor could it survive economically without new, more fertile lands for both slaveholding and non-slaveholding southern whites. "There is not a slaveholder in this House or out of it," one Georgia politician told Congress in the 1850s, who doesn't know "perfectly well that whenever slavery is confined within certain limits, its future existence is doomed."

Why was the westward expansion of slavery essential to its survival in the United States?

REPRESENTATION IN THE U.S. SENATE—each state has two senators, regardless of population. If there were more free states than slave, the balance of power in the U.S. Senate between North and South would be broken.

Extending Westward Into Mexico

Both northern and southern expansionists focused their territorial ambitions on a vast expanse of land originally settled and still claimed by Native Americans, but officially governed by Mexico. In 1835, the nation of Mexico extended well beyond its present borders with the United States. Its flag flew over a vast territory stretching from Texas to California populated by (1) Native Americans, (2) Spanish-speaking farmers, ranchers, and herders (many of them of mixed European and Indian blood), and (3) increasing numbers of U.S. immigrants. In 1835, U.S. settlers in Texas (then a Mexican province) rebelled, declaring an independent republic a year later. Ten years later, in 1845, Congress approved the annexation of Texas into the Union as a slave state. Soon after, the new territory of Oregon came into the Union as a free state, maintaining the balance of power in the U.S. Senate between North and South.

Expansionists north and south now cast their eyes on a still bigger Mexican prize— the huge territory that today includes the states of California, Arizona, Nevada, New Mexico, and Utah. Expansionist fever swept the nation from the Gulf of Mexico to the Canadian border. After a number of border skirmishes, the United States declared war against Mexico on May 13, 1846. A vocal antiwar movement could not stem the westward tide across the continent. U.S. forces quickly overwhelmed the Mexican Army. By 1848, the United States had annexed half of Mexico—1.2 million square miles of land.

How did the massive extension of U.S. territory at Mexico's expense undercut thirty years of compromises? What were the compromises? How were they undercut?

The massive extension of U.S. territory at Mexico's expense undercut thirty years of compromises that had kept the scales of power balanced between free and slave states in the U.S. Senate. The Missouri Compromise in 1820 had set a precedent. First, it admitted one slave state (Missouri) and one free state (Maine) into the Union. Second, it drew a line west from Missouri's southern border to divide free and slave territories. But as both abolitionists and slaveholders surged into the lands newly seized from Mexico, the Missouri precedent unraveled.

The Conflict Sharpens

Almost immediately there was conflict over the spoils of the war with Mexico. In 1846, congressman David Wilmot of Pennsylvania proposed that slavery be prohibited in all the territories recently seized from Mexico. With overwhelming support from northern Congressmen, the Wilmot Proviso won approval in the U.S. House of Representatives. But the Senate ignored, then blocked its passage, and the proviso never became law. The debate over the Wilmot Proviso opened old wounds between North and South.

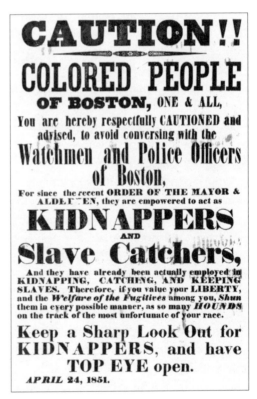

THE FUGITIVE SLAVE LAW. A notice posted by Boston abolitionist Theodore Parker in 1851.
Boston Public Library.

UNVEILED. After passage of the Fugitive Slave Law, escaped slave women living in the North sometimes wore veils when they appeared in public to avoid identification by slave catchers.

William Still, *The Underground Rail Road* (1872). American Social History Project.

Those wounds were further aggravated when California, one of the territories taken from Mexico, applied in 1849 for admission into the Union as a free state. California's application threatened the even balance between free and slave states in the U.S. Senate.

But with the Compromise of 1850, North and South avoided—or more accurately, delayed—a struggle that threatened to rip the Union apart. Congress agreed to admit California as a free state, to prohibit the slave trade in Washington, D.C., where it once had flourished, yet permitted slavery in the new territories of New Mexico and Utah.

In addition, as part of the 1850 compromise, slave owners got a new Fugitive Slave Law. It denied a jury trial to anyone accused of escaping slavery, gave marshals tremendous leeway to pursue slaves into free states, and empowered the federal government to prosecute northern whites who shielded runaways. The Underground Railroad was put in jeopardy. Moreover,

PROVISO—a clause in a document that imposes a restriction or condition

FREEDOM OR DEATH. Soon after passage of the Fugitive Slave Law, Margaret Garner fled from her
Kentucky master with her four children. Slave catchers followed her to Ohio. Faced with capture,
Garner killed two of her children rather than have them return to slavery. The surviving children were taken
from her and, on the return trip to Kentucky, Garner drowned herself in the Ohio River.
Her story inspired an acclaimed nineteenth-century painting by Thomas S. Noble
(on which this engraving is based) and Toni Morrison's Pulitzer Prize-winning novel, *Beloved*.

Harper's Weekly, May 18, 1867. American Social History Project

bounty hunters sometimes wrongfully seized free blacks born in the North as escaped slaves. These frequent dramas between hunters and hunted shocked many and prodded the moral conscience of many northern citizens.

How did the Fugitive Slave Law undermine these sectional compromises?

In response, black Americans and their white allies used force to protect fugitive slaves, sometimes attacking and even killing their pursuers. It was against this background that *Uncle Tom's Cabin*, Harriet Beecher Stowe's 1852 novel about slavery and slave hunters, appeared as a serial in an abolitionist newspaper. When eventually published as a book, it sold 300,000 copies, electrifying northern readers.

"A BOLD STROKE FOR FREEDOM." On Christmas Eve, 1855, slave catchers caught up
with a group of teenaged slaves who had escaped by wagon from Loudon County, Virginia.
But the posse was driven off when Ann Wood, leader of the group, brandished weapons
and dared the pursuers to fire. The fugitives continued on to Philadelphia.

William Still, *The Underground Rail Road* (1872). American Social History Project.

"POLICE CONVEYING SIMS TO THE VESSEL." Thomas Sims escaped slavery in Georgia,
but in April 1851 he was arrested in Boston and, under the Fugitive Slave Law,
returned to his owner. The city's abolitionist movement agitated for his release and large
crowds surrounded the courthouse in which Sims was incarcerated. But these efforts,
which included plans to forcibly free the prisoner, did not succeed. This illustration from
a Boston illustrated weekly shows how Sims was conducted by three hundred armed police
and marshals to a navy ship that carried him back to slavery. Upon his return south,
Sims was sold to a new master in Mississippi. He escaped in 1863.

Gleason's Pictorial Drawing Room Companion, May 10, 1851. American Social History Project.

Harriet Brent Jacobs: "Reign of Terror"

"Reign of terror." Those words were used by Harriet Brent Jacobs, an escaped slave, to describe the impact of the Fugitive Slave Law on African Americans in the North.

Scenes of bounty hunters with bloodhounds in search of escaped slaves became common in the North. With the law on their side, slave catchers sometimes wrongly captured free African Americans, claiming that they were escaped slaves.

In this excerpt, Harriet Jacobs describes the fear and anguish created by the Fugitive Slave Law in New York City's black community.

DOCUMENT ONE

[A]n event occurred of disastrous import to the colored people [of New York City]. The slave Hamlin [James Hamlet], the first fugitive that came under the new law, was given up by the bloodhounds of the north to the bloodhounds of the south. It was the beginning of a reign of terror to the colored population. The great city rushed on in its whirl of excitement.... But while fashionables were listening to the thrilling voice of Jenny Lind in Metropolitan Hall, the thrilling voices of poor hunted colored people went up, in an agony of supplication, to the Lord, from the Zion's church. Many families who had lived in the city for twenty years, fled from it now. Many a poor washer woman, who by her hard labor, had made herself a comfortable home, was obliged to sacrifice her furniture, bid a hurried farewell to friends, and seek her fortune among strangers in Canada. Many a wife discovered a secret she had never known before—that her husband was a fugitive and must leave her to insure his own safety. Worse still, many a husband discovered that his wife had fled from slavery years ago, and as "the child follows the condition of its mother," the children of his love were liable to be seized and carried to slavery. Everywhere in those humble homes, there was consternation and anguish. But what cared the legislators of the "dominant race" for the blood they were crushing out of trampled hearts?

...I was suspect to...[being a fugitive]; and so were hundreds of intelligent and industrious people around us. I seldom ventured into the streets....I went as much as possible through the back streets and by-ways. What a disgrace to a city calling itself free, that inhabitants, guiltless of offense, and seeking to perform their duties conscientiously, should be condemned to live in such incessant fear, and have nowhere to turn for protection! This state of things, of course, gave rise to many impromptu vigilance committees. Every colored person and every friend of their persecuted race, kept their eyes wide open.

— HARRIET BRENT JACOBS,
Incidents in the Life of a Slave Girl, *1861*

Harriet Tubman: Rescuing a Fugitive Slave

Militant black and white abolitionists organized opposition to the Fugitive Slave Law. In 1859, Harriet Tubman (an ex-slave and leader of the Underground Railroad) played a central role in rescuing a fugitive slave named Charles Nalle in Troy, N.Y. Defying police and a judge, Tubman and others snatched Nalle from his captors and delivered him to safety. Nalle's lawyer, Martin Townsend, tells how this happened.

DOCUMENT TWO

When Nalle was brought from Commissioner Beach's office into the street, Harriet Tubman who had been standing with the excited crowd, rushed...to Nalle, and running one of her arms around his manacled arm, held onto him without ever loosening her hold through the more than half-hour's struggle...to the dock, where Nalle's liberation was accomplished. In the melee, she was repeatedly beaten over the head with policemen's clubs, but she never for a moment released her hold....

True, she had strong and earnest helpers in her struggle, some of whom had white faces as well as human hearts....But she exposed herself to the fury of sympathizers with slavery, without fear, and suffered their blows without flinching....

—*Reported in* SARAH BRADFORD, Harriet, the Moses of Her People, *1884*

Examining the documents

•*In the North, how did the Fugitive Slave Law change the lives of African Americans?*
•*What evidence do you have of such changes in these documents?*

The Compromise of 1850 thus sowed the seeds of deeper divisions over slavery. The Kansas-Nebraska Act of 1854 further widened the split. The act was viewed by its sponsor, Senator Stephen Douglas of Illinois, as an impetus for economic development of the western Great Plains. To gain passage, however, Douglas needed the support of southern senators.

Douglas gained southern backing by agreeing to scrap the provision of the 1820 Missouri Compromise that prohibited slavery north of the Missouri Compromise line. The Kansas-Nebraska territories were in fact above the line. Under the act, the future of the territories as either "free" or "slave" would be decided in a vote by residents.

Bloody Kansas

Once the Kansas-Nebraska Act became law in 1854, all hell broke loose. Organized groups of both slaveholders and abolitionists migrated to Kansas. An undeclared guerrilla war erupted in what came to be called "Bloody Kansas." With each act of intimidation, arson, and murder by both sides, emotions grew uglier and differences were settled by force.

In the end, the antislavery forces prevailed. The northern settlers in Kansas who called themselves abolitionists opposed

GUERRILLA WAR—a war fought by small bands of men using hit-and-run tactics and the element of surprise

BLEEDING KANSAS. A daguerreotype (an early form of photograph) taken in Topeka, Kansas Territory, during the summer of 1856, shows a free-state artillery battery.
Kansas State Historical Society.

slavery on moral grounds and pushed to outlaw it everywhere in the United States. But a majority in Kansas avoided the label "abolitionist," and instead opposed slavery on the basis of narrower self-interest—which often was laced with racism. Consider this resolution adopted by Free Soilers in Pittsburg, Kansas:

> If the Douglas [Kansas-] Nebraska bill should ever go into peaceful operation, which we doubt, it would forever Africanize the heart of the North American continent and divide the free states of the Atlantic from the free states of the Pacific by colonies of African bondsmen and thereby exclude the free white race of the North from [Kansas and Nebraska]....

Majority antislavery sentiment in Kansas wanted the western territories kept free for white settlement only.

In May 1856, against the backdrop of "Bloody Kansas," abolitionist Senator Charles Sumner of Massachusetts gave a fiery speech denouncing proslavery activists in the territory of Kansas and their supporters in the U.S. Congress. The next day, while Sumner sat defenseless at his Senate desk, Congressman Preston Brooks of South Carolina beat him unconscious with a cane.

"Bloody Kansas" may have been the point beyond which further compromise was impossible. By 1854, the old two–party structure of Whigs and Democrats was virtually destroyed. Both parties were hopelessly divided by slavery into northern and southern wings. The Whig party would dissolve; the Democratic party would barely survive the 1850s, only to grow again and prosper after the Civil War.

By 1854, the Republican party was founded, which mobilized northerners around the themes of "free soil, free labor, free men." In 1856, Republicans united opposition to the extension of slavery in the West and ran John C. Frémont for president. Frémont lost nationwide, but captured eleven of the sixteen free states.

Why did "all hell break loose" with the passage of the Kansas-Nebraska Act?

Unlike the Whig and Democratic parties, Republicans neither retreated from the issue of slavery, nor to compromise it away. They identified slavery as *the* issue dividing the nation. In 1855, Congressman Abraham Lincoln, who later became the first Republican president, asked, "Can we as a nation continue together *permanently—forever*—half slave and half free?" As the Republican party grew, southern slave-holders panicked, and sectional and political tensions increased.

Why were southern slaveholders so concerned about the rise of the Republican party?

FREE SOILERS—those who called for outlawing slavery in the western territories

BONDSMEN—slaves

"Let Us Have a Caning or Cowhiding Every Day"

In several of his speeches just days before Congressman Preston Brooks assaulted him, Senator Charles Sumner of Massachusetts roused the anger of southern slaveholders and their supporters. Sumner characterized proslavery forces in Kansas as "murderous robbers," "assassins," and "thugs" guilty of "incredible atrocities." The southern press responded with unflattering and sometimes inflammatory commentary about the senator. The tirades against Sumner continued, and even escalated, after Brooks's assault on the Massachusetts senator. The southern press was almost unanimous in applauding Brooks's deed. Excerpted here are endorsements by three Virginia newspapers.

DOCUMENT THREE

A glorious deed! A most glorious deed!! Mr. Brooks, of South Carolina, administered to Senator Sumner, a notorious abolitionist from Massachusetts, an effectual and classic caning. We are rejoiced. The only regret we feel is that Mr. Brooks did not employ a slave whip instead of a stick. We trust the ball may be kept in motion. Seward [another abolitionist senator] should catch it next.

—*The* RICHMOND WHIG, *1856*

DOCUMENT FOUR

We entirely concur with the *Richmond Whig*, that if thrashing is the only remedy by which the abolitionists can be controlled, that it will be well to give Senator William H. Seward a double dose at least every other day until it operates freely on his political bowels.

—*The* PETERSBURG INTELLIGENCER, *May 1856*

DOCUMENT FIVE

Good!—good!!—very good!!! The abolitionists have been suffered to run too long without collars. They must be lashed into submission. Sumner, in particular, ought to have nine-and-thirty [lashes] every morning....Senator Wilson...[is] also dying for a beating. Will not somebody take him in hand....If need be, let us have a caning or cowhiding every day.

—*The* RICHMOND EXAMINER, *May 1856*

Examining the documents

•*Why do you think the three Virginia newspapers (Documents Three, Four, and Five) cheered the beating of Sumner and then called for more violence against other abolitionist senators?* •*What do these editorials tell us about relations between North and South in 1856?* •*At this point, could the Civil War have been avoided? If so, how? If not, why not?*

From Dred Scott to John Brown

The divide between North and South grew more pronounced in 1857 with the Supreme Court's decision in the Dred Scott case. Dominated by southerners and their sympathizers, the Court rejected the claim to freedom of a Missouri slave named Dred Scott, whose master had taken him to Illinois and the Wisconsin territory, both of which prohibited slavery. Speaking for the Court, Chief Justice Roger Taney dismissed Scott's argument. Slaves were property, Taney said. He and the majority of justices then ruled unconstitutional all laws that restricted the free movement of property. Since Scott was property, the Court's ruling meant that no territory could interfere with the right of his slave-master to own slaves. But Taney went further: He maintained that Scott had no right to bring suit because no black person in the United States could become a citizen and enjoy "any rights which the white man was bound to respect."

The decision had staggering implications. If the Supreme Court chose to take its opinion in the Dred Scott case to its logical extreme, it could legalize slavery in every state and territory in the Union. The northern public was mortified. Proslavery forces in the South became even bolder in their demands. The Dred Scott decision had brought the nation to the brink of war.

For John Brown, a militant white abolitionist, the Dred Scott decision reaffirmed the moral necessity of taking direct action against slavery. In October 1859, Brown led a small band of black and white antislavery fighters in a bold assault on the federal arsenal at Harpers Ferry, [West] Virginia. Their goal was to capture a large store of weapons, liberate slaves, and then retreat to the hills. From there, they hoped to launch more raids on slave plantations and to wage a guerrilla war against local slaveholders.

Their plan quickly collapsed, however. Caught, tried, and hung, Brown and his men in life and death excited fierce passions in both the South and the North. Most slaveholders saw Brown as the devil in human form; most black and white abolitionists regarded Brown's raiders as righteous and moral crusaders.

How did "Bloody Kansas," the Dred Scott decision, and John Brown's Harpers Ferry raid bring the nation to the brink of war? What were the "staggering implications" of the Dred Scott case?

"THE ARRAIGNMENT." A *Harper's Weekly* artist sketched John Brown and his coconspirators as they were charged with treason and murder in a Charleston, Virginia, courtroom.

Porte Crayon (David Hunter Strother), "The Arraignment," *Harper's Weekly,* November 12, 1859. American Social History Project.

"Your Martyr Grave Will Be a Sacred Altar"

To southern planters, Brown symbolized everything that was evil. But many abolitionists and African Americans considered Brown and his raiders heroes. As the following documents reflect, the raid struck a sharp moral and emotional chord in the African-American community.

DOCUMENT SIX

Dear Friend: Although the hands of Slavery throw a barrier between you and me, and it may not be my privilege to see you in the prison house, Virginia has no bolts or bars through which I dread to send you my sympathy. In the name of the young girl sold from the warm clasp of a mother's arms to the clutches of a libertine or profligate [a completely immoral and shameless person], — in the name of the slave mother, her heart rocked to and fro by the agony of her mournful separations — I thank you that you have been brave enough to reach out your hands to the crushed and blighted of my race. You have rocked the bloody Bastille [a famous prison stormed and liberated during the French Revolution in 1789]; and I hope from your sad fate great good may arise to the cause of freedom. Already from your prison has come a shout of triumph against the giant sin of our country....

We may earnestly hope that your fate will not be a vain lesson, that it will intensify our hatred of Slavery and love of Freedom, and that your martyr grave will be a sacred altar upon which men will record their vows of undying hatred to that system which tramples on man and bids defiance to God. I have written to your dear wife, and sent her a few dollars, and I pledge myself to you that I will continue to assist her....

—Letter to John Brown, in prison, from a free black woman,
FRANCES ELLEN WATKINS,
Kendallville, Indiana, November 25, 1859

"I Could Not Die for a Better Cause"

Among the Harpers Ferry raiders captured and sentenced to death was John Copeland, a fugitive slave. A reporter from the Baltimore Sun *quoted Copeland as he walked to the gallows on December 16, 1859: "If I am dying for freedom, I could not die for a better cause—I had rather die than be a slave." Six days earlier, he wrote this letter to his brother.*

DOCUMENT SEVEN

Dear Brother:...It was a sense of the wrongs that we have suffered that prompted the noble but unfortunate John Brown and his associates to attempt to give freedom to a small number, at least, of those who are now held by cruel and unjust laws, and by no less cruel and unjust men. To this freedom they were entitled by every known principle of justice and humanity, and for the enjoyment of it God created them. And now, dear brother, could I die in a more noble cause? Could I, brother, die in a manner and for a cause which could induce true and honest men more to honor me, and the angels more readily to receive me to their happy home of everlasting joy above...? And were it not that I know that the hearts of those to whom I am attached by the nearest and most enduring ties of blood relationship—yea by the closest and strongest ties that god has instituted—will be filled with sorrow, I would almost as [soon] die now as at any time, for I feel that I am now prepared to meet my maker....

—JOHN A. COPELAND,
sentenced to death for participating in the
Harpers Ferry Raid, in a letter to his brother,
December 10, 1859

Examining the documents

•*Why did Brown excite such passions among both defende and opponents?*

Lincoln's Election and Southern Secession

Abraham Lincoln, the Republican leader and soon-to-be presidential candidate, still thinking that conflict between North and South could be avoided, made a point of publicly condemning John Brown's raid. But the white, slaveholding elite in the South saw little difference between Lincoln and Brown.

Elected president in November 1860, Lincoln was ready to make concessions to the slaveholding South. But he drew the line at the extension of slavery, a position that he had taken consistently throughout the 1850s and which he had explained in a famous speech in Peoria, Illinois, in 1856:

WILLIAM WALKER'S "FILIBUSTERS" RELAX
AFTER THE BATTLE OF GRANADA.

Slaveholders went to great extremes to expand slavery, turning to Mexico, western territories and even Central America. Supported by fifty-eight mercenaries, the Tennessee-born William Walker "invaded" Nicaragua in May 1855. Within six months he succeeded in exploiting civil unrest in the country and declared himself president. Walker's government, which opened the country to slavery, was recognized by the United States in 1856. But a year later, he was overthrown by forces financed by his former sponsor, railroad entrepreneur Cornelius Vanderbilt.

J. W. Orr, *Frank Leslie's Illustrated Newspaper*, May 3, 1856.
American Social History Project.

The whole nation is interested that the best use shall be made of these [new western] territories. *We want them for homes for free white people. This they cannot be, to any considerable extent, if slavery shall be planted within them.* Slave states are the places for poor white people to remove from, not to remove to. New free states are the places for poor people to go to, and better their condition. For this use the nation needs these territories. [Emphasis added.]

It was a position that welcomed free whites to the West and excluded African Americans, whether slave or free. What mattered to the planters, though, was not Lincoln's support of white privilege but his uncompromising position against the expansion of slavery.

What was Lincoln's position on the West? Whom did he want to settle there? Whom did he want to exclude? When Lincoln was elected president, why did southern states secede?

By early 1861, Lincoln's unvarying stand on excluding slavery from the new western territories triggered the secession of southern states from the Union. Most planters understood that without expansion, slavery could not survive.

The United States had reached a turning point in its history. The future of its democratic institutions, economic development, and territorial expansion would hang in the balance until the issue of slavery was resolved.

Suggested Activities

POINT OF VIEW

In the drama leading up to the Civil War, there were many different people with many different points of view. A master and a slave might see the same event differently. So might a northerner and a southerner.

To explore these conflicting viewpoints, organize into small groups and divide up the roles and the writing topics below.

1. Editorial writer for the *Richmond Whig* (see Document Three). Write an editorial in response to the raid led by John Brown on Harpers Ferry.

2. Harriet Brent Jacobs (see Document One). Write a letter to the abolitionist newspaper the *North Star*, edited by ex-slave Frederick Douglass. Your letter is a response to the editorial comments on the beating of Sumner in the three Virginia newspapers included in Documents Three, Four, and Five.

3. A southern planter who has had problems with runaway slaves. Write a letter to the editor of the *Petersburg Intelligencer* (see Document Four) responding to the account of Harriet Tubman's role in the rescue of Charles Nalle (see Document Two).

4. John Brown. Write an answer to the letter you received from Frances Ellen Watkins (Document Six).

5. A free black living in the North. Write a letter to Abraham Lincoln responding to his speech in Peoria, Illinois (quoted on page 53).

First, discuss the point of view of your assigned character. Then, in your group, do the writing. After reading and discussing the writing within your group, present a group summary to the rest of the class. Finally, as a whole class, discuss whether or not conflict between these views could have been resolved without a Civil War. In other words, by the 1850s, was war between North and South inevitable?

POSITION PAPER

Is violence justifiable? If so, under what circumstances? These questions were especially relevant in the 1850s. The three Virginia newspapers in Documents Three, Four, and Five give a rousing cheer for the violence committed against Senator Sumner. Supporters of John Brown defended his use of force at Harpers Ferry.

The Civil War became an ultimate act of violence. But can a society survive repeated acts of violence and war?

Was violence justified in the events leading up to the Civil War? If so, when and why? If not, why not? In writing, explain your position on these questions. Then read and discuss your position papers in small groups.

SORTING AND INTERPRETING THE CAUSES OF THE CIVIL WAR

Historians often disagree as they interpret events. Their interpretations, however, need to pass the challenge of evidence and logic. You will join the debate about the events leading up to the Civil War. As you develop your position, you need to put it to the test of evidence and reason.

Study the timeline preceding the introduction to section one. Choose the *three* events you think *most* important in causing the Civil War. Then select the *two* you consider *least* important.

With a small group of classmates, try to reach a consensus on the three most and the two least important causes. Develop arguments for your own choices, listen to the reasoning of other students, and, when necessary, make concessions to more persuasive arguments.

Groups will report their choices, and the discussion leading to them, for whole-class debate on the causes of the Civil War.

CREATIVE WRITING

Choose any illustration or image reproduced in the chapter that you find interesting. Write a one-page story about it. Share and read aloud stories with a classmate. Explain why you chose the image you wrote about.

VISUAL LITERACY/CREATING A DIARY

Take the role of one of the characters in the picture "Unveiled" on page 41. Write a diary about what is happening from that person's point of view. Share and discuss diary entries with classmate.

VIDEO OPTION: *Doing as They Can*

To prepare for this exercise, review the last ten minutes of *Doing as They Can*, one of the videos produced by the ASHP that can be used with this text. This final section of the video is based on Harriet Brent Jacobs's account of the terrifying consequences of the Fugitive Slave Law. After watching the video, reread chapter two's analysis of the Fugitive Slave Law. Also review Harriet Jacobs's account in Document One and the description of Harriet Tubman's rescue of a fugitive slave in Document Two.

In the voice of Harriet Jacobs, write a letter to the *New York Times*. The purpose of your letter is to convince the largely white readership of the *Times* to oppose the Fugitive Slave Law. Draw on the personal experience of fugitive slaves to add drama and impact to your letter.

Some of the *Times*'s readers in the 1850s clearly opposed slavery, but many did not feel very concerned about it. Have this audience in mind as you make your case against the Fugitive Slave Law.

Read and discuss letters with others in the class.

"THE FIRST FLAG OF INDEPENDENCE RAISED IN THE SOUTH, BY THE CITIZENS OF SAVANNAH, GA., NOVEMBER 8, 1860." According to this lithograph, the earliest symbol of secession was the "Don't Tread on Me" snake—an image familiar to many Americans, having appeared on numerous flags

PART TWO

THE CIVIL WAR

TIMELINE

1860   Lincoln is elected president in November.

1861   The seven lower southern states secede from the Union by February.

P. G. T. Beauregard orders Confederate troops on April 12 to fire on the Union garrison at Fort Sumter, South Carolina. The Civil War begins.

In late May, Union General Benjamin Butler employs escaped slaves at Fortress Monroe, Virginia, and declares them to be contraband (confiscated property) of war.

Four more states, in the upper South, join the Confederacy by June, bringing the total number of seceded states to eleven.

The Confederate Army wins a major victory in Virginia at Bull Run in July.

The U.S. Congress passes the First Confiscation Act in August, declaring that owners will lose rights to slaves used in the Confederate war effort.

1862   Union military morale sinks to a low point in early summer with a series of retreats and defeats in Virginia.

The U.S. Congress passes the Second Confiscation Act in July, declaring that owners participating in the Confederate rebellion against the Union will lose rights to their slaves, even if their slaves are not used in the war effort.

The U.S. War Department in August authorizes the recruitment of African-American soldiers on the Union-occupied Sea Islands off the coast of South Carolina.

1863   President Lincoln issues an Emancipation Proclamation on New Year's Day, declaring all slaves free in Confederate-held territory. He announces a new Union policy to recruit and enlist African Americans into the U.S. military. By war's end, almost 200,000 African-American troops serve.

Slave resistance in the South grows as more and more African Americans slow down production on southern plantations and flee to Union lines.

The U.S. Congress passes a Draft Law in March that allows draftees to hire substitutes.

Confederate women, protesting high prices for scarce food, riot in Richmond, Virginia. Over the next year, food protests spread to several other southern towns and cities.

African-American soldiers rebuff a Confederate attack at Milliken's Bend, Louisiana, in June.

In July, the tide of the war turns in the Union's favor with major victories at Gettysburg (Pennsylvania), Vicksburg (Mississippi), and Port Hudson (Louisiana).

Protests against the March Draft Law turn into a week-long riot in New York City in July. Troops, rushed back from the front at Gettysburg, help put down the protest.

In July, Union soldiers, led by waves of African-American soldiers, storm Fort Wagner, South Carolina, only to be driven back in some of the fiercest fighting of the war.

African-American soldiers in the Third South Carolina Volunteers, protesting unequal pay in the Union military, put down their rifles in November. The U.S. Army puts down the protest and executes its leader, Sergeant William Walker.

1864   In March, the U.S. Congress makes the pay of black soldiers equal to whites, retroactive to January 1.

Confederate troops under the command of General Nathan Bedford Forrest, who would found the Ku Klux Klan after the war, massacre surrendering black Union soldiers in April at Fort Pillow, Tennessee.

The famed "Virginia" army, under Confederate General Robert E. Lee, suffers a series of defeats after midyear. Battlefield deaths and an increasing rate of desertion sharply reduce the numbers and effectiveness of Lee's troops.

The Union reelects Lincoln president in November.

The army of Union general William Tecumseh Sherman cuts a path of "scorched earth" in the late fall and early winter across Georgia and the Carolinas, uprooting large populations. More than 40,000 refugee slaves follow, slowing down Sherman's advance.

1865   General Sherman and Secretary of War Edwin Stanton meet with twenty black ministers in Savannah on January 12 to discuss the fate of slaves whose lives have been uprooted by Sherman's army.

Sherman, in response to advice from the ministers, in January issues Special Field Order Number 15, which sets aside land on the islands and coast of South Carolina, Georgia, and northern Florida for settlement exclusively by ex-slaves.

The U.S. Congress in late January sends the Thirteenth Amendment—abolishing slavery in its entirety—to the states for ratification.

The U.S. Congress in March establishes a Bureau of Refugees, Freedmen, and Abandoned Lands (the Freedmen's Bureau) to oversee the transition from slavery to freedom and, where possible, to distribute land to ex-slaves for settlement.

The war ends with the surrender of the Confederate Army at Appomattox Court House, Virginia, on April 9.

Vice President Andrew Johnson becomes president when Lincoln is assassinated on April 14.

The Thirteenth Amendment passes the states by December and becomes the law of the land.

INTRODUCTION

As he campaigned for president in November 1860, Abraham Lincoln promised not to abolish slavery in the South. But he drew a sharp line against extending the South's "peculiar institution" to the new western territories and states. But even Lincoln's moderate position alarmed southern planters, who believed slavery needed to expand in order to survive. They feared that the election of a president so intent on imposing limits on slavery would send a clear signal of encouragement to African-American slaves to defy their masters.

With Lincoln's election in November 1860, many slave owners became convinced that the only way to protect their right to own slaves was to separate or secede from the United States and establish their own proslavery country. By February 1861, the lower South states most dependent on slave labor (South Carolina, Mississippi, Florida, Alabama, Georgia, Texas, and Louisiana) seceded from the United States and formed an independent nation, which they called the Confederate States of America, or the Confederacy. Over the next three months, four more states—Virginia, Tennessee, North Carolina, and Arkansas—joined the Confederacy.

IMPORTANT CIVIL WAR SITES

The secession of the first states and the formation of the Confederacy sent the economy of the North into a tailspin. Stock market prices plummeted, banks closed, stores went out of business, and workers lost their jobs. Seeking to avoid war with the South, many northerners tried to find a peaceful way to bring the southern states back into the Union. Some northerners proposed new laws that would make slavery legal and permanent in the South, while others opposed compromise of any kind.

Pulled in different directions, President Lincoln at first sought to avoid war or the use of military force. Yet he needed to show his antislavery supporters that he was prepared to stand firm in defense of the Union and against the extension of slavery into the western territories.

In the spring of 1861, just two months after the Confederacy was formed, Lincoln found an opportunity to show his resolve against the seceding states, yet stop short of initiating hostile military action. He sent reinforcements and a supply ship to Fort Sumter, which guarded the important harbor in Charleston, South Carolina. Union soldiers at the fort had run low on medical supplies and food. Since the president didn't want to be accused of starting a war with the South, he announced that the ship was on a peaceful mission, and that his troops would take no action against the Confederacy unless southern troops interfered. The Union supply ship set sail for Fort Sumter on April 8.

Jefferson Davis, president of the new Confederate States of America, now faced a problem. If he blocked the Union supply ship, he and the Confederacy would have to take responsibility for starting a war. On the other hand, if Davis allowed the Union ship to reach Fort Sumter, he would be permitting a foreign country, the United States, to supply and maintain a fort on Confederate territory. Davis and his advisers decided to take military action, demanding the immediate surrender of the troops in the fort. The commanding officer at Fort Sumter refused to yield, and on April 12 Confederate troops attacked; two days later Fort Sumter surrendered. The Civil War had begun.

Was Lincoln willing to start a war to bring the seceding states back into the Union? What was his purpose in resupplying Fort Sumter?

Neither Abraham Lincoln nor Jefferson Davis could have possibly foreseen that the strategic military and political game they played at Fort Sumter would soon escalate into a brutal, total war that would last four years and consume the lives of over 600,000 white and black Americans.

The Civil War radically changed the United States, marking the triumph of the system of free labor throughout the country and hastening the development of American industrial capitalism. Even more dramatic, the Union's victory radically transformed the society of the South, destroying the system of slave labor that for two hundred and fifty years shaped the region's political, economic, social, and cultural life. In the process, African Americans took part on center stage, becoming integral players in both the war and the period of Reconstruction to follow.

How did the Civil War radically transform the United States?

CHAPTER THREE
WAR AIMS: UNION OR FREEDOM

BEFORE READING. *Once the shooting war began, President Abraham Lincoln insisted that the U.S. government was fighting to preserve the Union. He did not want to risk losing the support of four slave states fighting on the Union side: Delaware, Kentucky, Missouri, and Maryland. Consequently, Lincoln went to great lengths to assure loyal slaveholders in these states that the key northern war aim was "union," and not "freedom" (the abolition of slavery).*

But radicals in his own party, abolitionists, and almost everyone in the African-American community in the North wanted to turn the war for union into a crusade for freedom. The issue was not secession or union, they argued, but slavery or freedom.

The three documents that follow reflect the northern debate over war aims, presenting the positions of President Abraham Lincoln and two leading abolitionists, Harriet Tubman and Frederick Douglass, both of whom had escaped from slavery many years earlier.

Which war aim would you support: "union" or "freedom"? After reading the documents below, write a paragraph stating and explaining your stand.

When you have completed the chapter and discussed the controversy over war aims with classmates, reread what you wrote. Would you still take the same position?

"FREED NEGROES CELEBRATING PRESIDENT LINCOLN'S DECREE OF EMANCIPATION."
An engraving in the French pictorial weekly *Le monde illustré* presents a somewhat fanciful depiction of African-Americans' response to the Emancipation Proclamation.

Jacob, *Le monde illustré*, March 21, 1863 (ICHi-22095). Chicago Historical Society.

DOCUMENT ONE

My paramount aim in this struggle is to save the Union, and is not either to save or destroy slavery. If I could save the Union without freeing any slaves, I would do it, and if I could save it by freeing all the slaves I would do it; and if I could save it by freeing some and leaving others alone I would also do that.

— ABRAHAM LINCOLN *in an open letter to Horace Greeley, editor of the* New York Tribune, *published August 25, 1862*

Harriet Tubman: Kill the Snake Before It Kills You

DOCUMENT TWO

God won't let Master Lincoln beat the South until he does the right thing. Master Lincoln, he's a great man, and I'm a poor Negro but this Negro can tell Master Lincoln how to save money and young men. He can do it by setting the Negroes free. Suppose there was an awful big snake down there on the floor. He bites you. Folks all scared, because you may die. You send for doctor to cut the bite; but the snake is rolled up there, and while doctor is doing it, he bites you again. The doctor cuts out that bite; but while he's doing it, the snake springs up and bites you again, and so he keeps doing it, till you kill him. That's what Master Lincoln ought to know.

— HARRIET TUBMAN, *quoted in a letter by Lydia Maria Child, January 21, 1862*

Frederick Douglass: "We Strike at the Effect and Leave the Cause Unharmed"

DOCUMENT THREE

... [T]here is but one effectual way to suppress and put down the desolating war which the slaveholders ... are now waging.... Fire must be met with water, darkness with light, and war for the destruction of liberty must be met with war for the destruction of slavery. ... [Fighting only to save the Union,] we strike at the effect, and leave the cause unharmed. Fire will not burn it out of us—water cannot wash it out of us, that this war with the slaveholders can never be brought to a desirable termination until slavery, the guilty cause of all of our national troubles, has been totally and forever abolished.

—*Excerpts from three editorials by* FREDERICK DOUGLASS *in the* Douglass Monthly, *May, July, and August 1861*

Examining the Documents

•*What determines President Lincoln's stand on slavery?* •*Harriet Tubman uses the image of a snake to make a point about how President Lincoln should wage the war. What is her point?* •*Frederick Douglass criticizes the Union's war policy by arguing that "we strike at the effect and leave the cause unharmed." What does he mean? What is the cause and what is the effect?*

The Debate Over War Aims

In the late winter and early spring of 1861, when eleven southern states seceded from the Union, they formed the Confederate States of America with a clear purpose: to defend slavery and preserve a way of life. The military goal of the Confederate Army was defensive, not offensive. There was no need for the South to invade or defeat the North. The task of its army, plain and simple, was to safeguard Confederate territory and uphold its "peculiar institution."

What difference did it make whether the North's war aim was union or freedom?

How did the aims of the North and South differ after the secession of the southern states?

The North, on the other hand, had a bigger job. To maintain the Union, its army had to invade the South, defeat the Confederate Army, overthrow the Confederate government, and force eleven southern states back into the Union. Its diplomats had to isolate the Confederacy from international support. And its navy had to stop ships from entering southern ports with military goods and food.

How did these differences influence each section's military and diplomatic strategy?

President Lincoln and his advisers believed that they could defeat the South without abolishing slavery. Convinced that the North's victory would be quick and easy, they did not even bother to mobilize thousands of African Americans in the North who were ready and eager to fight for the liberation of their people. Lincoln hesitated to make such a move, fearing it might antagonize the four slaveholding states that remained loyal to the Union. For both political and military reasons, Lincoln made union rather than freedom his central war aim.

The March of the Seventh Regiment Down Broadway.
Newspaper artist Thomas Nast sketched the tumultuous send-off of New York's National Guard regiment on April 19, 1861. Eight years later, Nast completed this oil painting of the scene.

Thomas Nast, *The March of the Seventh Regiment Down Broadway,* 1869, oil on canvas, 5 feet 6 inches x 8 feet. The Seventh Regiment Fund, Inc.

CAUGHT IN THE MIDDLE. An illustration in a May 1862 issue of *Harper's Weekly* depicts one way that the institution of slavery contributed to the Confederacy's war effort. According to the caption, the northern newspaper artist observed this "struggle between two Negroes and a rebel captain" through a telescope. The captain "insisted upon their loading a cannon within range of [Union] Sharpshooters.... [He] succeeded in forcing the Negroes to expose themselves, and they were shot, one after the other."

Mead, *Harper's Weekly*, May 10, 1862. American Social History Project.

But northern abolitionists and Radical Republicans—an influential congressional minority in Lincoln's own party—saw things differently. They scoffed at the idea that Lincoln could preserve the Union without destroying slavery. Slavery, they contended, was precisely the issue that divided the Union into two nations— one free, the other slave. Southern states had seceded to defend their "peculiar institution"; the North could only bring them back by totally demolishing slavery. According to this line of argument, the North needed to transform a war to preserve the Union into one for freedom.

Why did the Lincoln administration hesitate to mobilize African Americans to fight the Confederacy? What were the consequences of this hesitancy?

When describing slavery and calling for its destruction, the rhetoric of Radical Republicans and abolitionists blazed with moral fire, using words such as "sinful," "evil," and "depraved." Eventually, the Radical Republicans won the day by combining their righteous passion with very practical arguments about the military benefits of freedom as a war aim.

They emphasized that the slave gave the South a critical advantage: slaves did the work of feeding and clothing the Confederate Army, thus freeing white southerners for military duty. Consequently, if freedom became the North's war aim, the military advantage would shift from the Confederacy to the Union. Slaves would become a military asset for the North if they were granted freedom, since they would now have every incentive to sabotage southern production and/or run away to the Union side.

How did slavery give the South an initial advantage in fighting the war?

Lincoln and his generals eventually saw the military wisdom of the Radical Republicans' argument for freedom as a war aim. Two factors accounted for their shift: (1) slaves forced the issue, particularly in Virginia, by escaping in increasing numbers to northern lines; and (2) the North suffered staggering military defeats in the first two years of the war.

RHETORIC—the persuasive use of language

DOCUMENT FOUR

Washington, April 23rd, 1861

Hon. Simon Cameron,
Secretary of War

Sir: I desire to inform you that I know of some three hundred reliable colored free citizens of this City, who desire to enter the service in defense of this City.

I have been three times across the Rocky Mountains in the service of the Country with [General John] Frémont and others.

I can be found in the Senate Chambers, as I have been employed about the premises for some years.

Yours respectfully,
Jacob Dodson (Coloured)

Battle Creek [Michigan]
October 30th, 1861

Hon. Simon Cameron,
Secretary of War

Dear Sir: ...I wish to solicit the privilege of raising from five to ten thousand free men to report in sixty days to take any position that may be assigned (sharpshooters preferred). We would like white persons for superior officers.

If this proposition is not accepted we will, if armed and equipped by the government, fight as guerrillas....

A part of us are half breed Indians and legal voters of the state of Michigan. We are all anxious to fight for the maintenance and preservation of the principles promulgated [announced] by President Lincoln and we are sure of success if allowed the opportunity. In the name of God answer immediately.

Yours fraternally,
G. P. Miller, M.D.

Cleveland, Ohio
15th November, 1861

Hon. Simon Cameron,
Secretary of War

Sir: ...[W]e would humbly and respectfully state that we are colored men (legal voters); all voted for the present administration.

The question now is will you allow us the poor privilege of fighting, and, if need be, dying, to support those in office who are our own choice? We believe that a regiment of colored men can be raised in this State, who, we are sure would make as patriotic and good soldiers as any other.

What we ask of you is that you give us the proper authority to raise such a regiment, and it can and shall be done.

We could give you a thousand names, as either signers or references, if you required....

W. T. Boyd
J. T. Alston

P.S. We await your reply.

—*Samples of letters written to Secretary of War Simon Cameron offering to enlist African-American soldiers for the Union Army, 1861*

Examining the document

•*If you were Secretary of War Cameron, what evidence could you use to convince your commander-in-chief, President Lincoln, to allow the recruitment of African Americans into the Union Army in 1862? What objections might President Lincoln raise to your argument?*

The Contraband Policy: A First Step Toward Emancipation

In the spring of 1861, a Confederate commander in the Virginia Tidewater issued an order putting all male slaves in the region to work for his army. Slave labor erected the Confederate military batteries at Sewall's Point, putting Union troops under General Benjamin Butler at a serious tactical disadvantage. But slaves building these batteries, seeing an opportunity for freedom, fled during the night of May 23, 1861, to Butler's outpost at Fortress Monroe, Virginia.

Butler understood the importance of these slaves "as a means of offense in the enemy's hands." But his commander-in-chief, President Lincoln, was hesitant to free slaves because it might offend loyal slaveholders in pro-Union states. Butler, however, argued "that as a military question it would seem to be a measure of necessity to deprive [the Confederacy] of their [slaves'] services." In fact, the escaped slaves also provided Butler with crucial information about Confederate positions and military

Why did General Benjamin Butler declare slaves "contrabands" of war? What was the significance of his contraband policy?

"CONTRABANDS" COMING INTO THE UNION LINES. A sketch by *Frank Leslie's Illustrated Newspaper* "special artist" Edwin Forbes shows a group of African Americans entering the Union camp at Hanover Town, Virginia.

Edwin Forbes, May 29, 1864. Prints and Photographs Division, Library of Congress.

strength. Eventually, with Lincoln's approval, Butler declared the escaped slaves "contrabands" of war—riches the slave-owners lost their rights to when the Confederacy rebelled.

A contraband slave was in effect an emancipated slave. The "contraband" policy was a first timid but important step toward full-scale emancipation. Lincoln maintained that this was not a policy of abolition but merely a tactic of war. Yet it opened the door, if ever so slightly, toward freedom.

TIDEWATER—the fertile low coastal lands of Virginia

BATTERY—an emplacement for artillery

CONTRABAND—seized property

A Northern Disaster at Bull Run Leads to the First Confiscation Act

Defeats on the battlefield also moved Lincoln's government away from union and toward freedom as the North's primary war aim. From the out-set, the Confederacy had three clear military advantages: (1) they could draw on slave labor; (2) they were fighting a defensive war on familiar territory; and (3) they drew on the best generals trained at West Point, most of whom were southerners.

What moved the Lincoln administration to change its war aim from union to freedom?

"CONTRABANDS" IN CUMBERLAND LANDING, VIRGINIA. A photograph taken in May 1862.
James F. Gibson, May 14, 1862. United States Military History Institute.

The first major battle of the Civil War took place on July 21, 1861, at Bull Run in northern Virginia, as a Union force of 30,000 attacked a Confederate army of 22,000 men. Treating the approaching battle like a summer picnic, many northern civilians traveled from Washington, D.C., to Bull Run to see the battle. But Bull Run turned into a major defeat for the North, in which 600 died, and the picnicking northerners ended up running for their lives. Horrified by the Union defeat, many Unionists began to realize, perhaps for the first time, that the war was going to be long and hard.

The Battle of Bull Run convinced many in Congress that it was time to try to deny the South its slave labor force—one of the Confederacy's most important advantages in the war. Passing the first of two confiscation acts in August 1861, Congress proclaimed that any slave owner whose slaves were used by the Confederate Army would lose all rights to those slaves.

CONFISCATION—seizure of property or wealth

"THE STAMPEDE FROM BULL RUN—FROM A SKETCH BY OUR SPECIAL ARTIST."
Northern illustrated newspapers dispatched "special artists" to cover the war. These artists' sketches, engraved on wood blocks and published in *Harper's Weekly, Frank Leslie's Illustrated Newspaper,* and other weekly periodicals, were the North's major source of war pictures. A few short-lived southern illustrated papers appeared, but it was the *Illustrated London News* that most actively portrayed the Confederate point of view. Its "special artist" Frank Vizetelly sketched this rout of Union forces on July 21, 1861.
Frank Vizetelly, *Illustrated London News,* August 17, 1861. American Social History Project.

A Union
General on
Contrabands:
"They Will
Submit to Any
Difficulty,
Perform Any
Duty, Incur
Any Danger."

*In the testimony that
follows, a general tells
Congress how contraband
slaves served his army
and had a dramatic
impact on the way Union
soldiers thought about
slavery and freedom.*

DOCUMENT FIVE

In September and October last, and perhaps as late as November [1861], in two or three instances, orders came from the headquarters of the army of the Potomac, directing that such and such persons—naming them—claiming to have slaves in one of my camps…should be permitted to search the camp, and reclaim their slaves. I addressed a communication…stating that such steps would likely lead to disorder and mischief in the camps; because in several instances the sympathies of the men [Union soldiers] had been excited by seeing slaves, reclaimed under such circumstances, very harshly treated….

The most valuable and reliable information of the enemy's movements in our vicinity that we have been able to get derived [originated] from Negroes who came into our lines….

…They will submit to any privation [lack of basic comforts], perform any duty, incur any danger. I know an instance in which four of them recently carried a boat from the Rappahannock River [Virginia], passing through the enemy's pickets successfully, to the Potomac and crossed over to my camp and reported themselves there. They gave us information of the enemy's force which was communicated to headquarters; a service upon which it would be difficult to fix a price. These services rendered by these men are known to the soldiers, and contribute, I presume, largely to the sympathy they feel for them….

…There was one case in the 5th regiment where a man named Cox claimed some slaves. He was very badly treated by the soldiers. He came there with an order from the division headquarters for two or three slaves. He pointed out who they were and undertook to take them away; but the soldiers pounced upon him and beat him severely….He went away without his slaves.

With our people there was a feeling of indignation against it, from the lowest to the highest; it was a universal feeling.

—*Testimony of* GENERAL DANIEL E. SICKLES
*before the Joint Committee on the Conduct of the War,
37th [U.S.] Congress, Third Session, 1862*

A Runaway Slave: "Freedom Will Reign Despite Earth and Hell"

The following document tells a moving but complex story. On one level, the document is a simple tale: John Boston runs away from his master and seeks the protection of a Union regiment from Brooklyn, New York.

But there are complications. First of all, Boston is the slave of a Maryland planter, and Maryland is a slave state fighting on the side of the Union. Second, Boston's flight to freedom means that he must leave his wife (the document that follows is a letter to her). Third, the Brooklyn regiment is defying Union policy by giving Boston sanctuary. His master after all is a loyal Unionist in a border state that has sided with the North.

It's not clear whether Boston's wife is free or slave, or whether she ever got the letter. What is clear is that Maryland authorities seized the letter either before or after she got it. These officials then demanded that the Union Army return Boston to his owner. It is not known what happened to him. But the courage of John Boston — and that of thousands of others who fled to Union lines to escape slavery — became

---

DOCUMENT SIX

My Dear Wife:

It is with great joy that I take this time to let you know where I am. I am now in the safety of the 14th Regiment of Brooklyn. This day I can address you thank God as a free man. I had a little trouble in getting away, but as the Lord led the children of Israel to the land of Canaan so he led me to a land where freedom will reign despite earth and hell. Dear you must make yourself content that I am free from the slaver's lash. And as you have chosen the wise plan of serving the Lord I hope you will pray much and I will try by the help of God to serve him with all my heart. I am with a very nice man and have all that heart can wish. But my dear I can't express my great desire that I have to see you. I trust the time will come when we shall meet again. And if we don't meet on earth we will meet in heaven where Jesus reigns.

—JOHN BOSTON *to his wife, January 12, 1862*

A Southern Newspaper Boasts That Slavery Gives the Confederacy a Military Advantage

Practical military considerations moved the Lincoln administration and a number of conservative generals to see the importance of emancipation.

As the Confederate newspaper editorial in Document Seven makes clear, slave labor was a vital military asset for the South. In order to deny the Confederacy this asset, General Benjamin Butler argues in Document Eight for a policy that would allow the Union Army to use the labor of escaped slaves. Impressed by the logic of Butler's position, Lincoln allowed him to declare runaway slaves "contraband" property, in effect liberating them from their masters.

DOCUMENT SEVEN

The total white population of the eleven States now comprising the Confederacy is 6,000,000, and therefore to fill up the ranks of the proposed army (600,000) about ten per cent of the entire white population will be required. In any other country but our own such a draft could not be met, but the Southern States can furnish that number of men, and still not leave the material interests of the country in a suffering condition. Those who are incapacitated for bearing arms can oversee the plantation, and the Negroes can go on undisturbed in their usual labors. In the North, the case is different; the men who join the army of subjugation [oppression] are the laborers, the producers and the factory operatives. Nearly every man from that section, especially those from the rural districts, leaves some branch of industry to suffer during his absence. The institution of slavery in the South alone enables her to place in the field a force much larger in proportion to her white population in the North....The institution is a tower of strength to the South, particularly at the present crisis, and our enemies will be likely to find that the "moral cancer" about which their orators are so fond of prating, is really one of the most effective weapons employed against the union by the South.

—*Editorial in a Confederate newspaper,*
the MONTGOMERY ADVERTISER,
Alabama, November 6, 1861

General Benjamin Butler On Slavery
"As A Military Question"

DOCUMENT EIGHT

Sir: Since I wrote my last dispatch the question in regard to slave property is becoming one of very serious magnitude. The inhabitants of Virginia are using their Negroes in the batteries, and are preparing to send the women and children South. The escapes [of slaves] from them are very numerous and a squad [of escaped slaves] has come in this morning to my pickets bringing their women and children....Twelve of these Negroes I am informed have escaped from the erection of batteries on Sewall's Point which this morning fired upon my expedition as it passed by out of range. As a means of offense therefore in the enemy's hands these Negroes when able bodied are of...importance. Without them the batteries could not have been erected at least for many weeks. As a military question it would seem to be a measure of necessity to deprive their masters of their services. How can this be done? As a political question and as a question of humanity can I receive the services of a father and mother and not take the children? Of the humanitarian aspect I have no doubt. Of the political one I have no right to judge. I therefore submit all of this to your better judgement....

—*Letter from* GENERAL BENJAMIN BUTLER
to General-in-Chief Winfield Scott, May 27, 1861

*Examining
the documents*

*•In Document Five, what evidence is there that General Sickles's soldiers feel sympathy toward the slaves? Why do you think they feel this way?
•Describe Boston's emotions in Document Six. Does he have any misgivings about escaping? Explain. •According to the Confederate newspaper in Document Seven, why is slavery "one of the most effective weapons employed against the union by the South"? Do you think General Butler (Document Eight) would agree?*

The Call for Freedom Grows Louder

By the summer of 1862, northern military opinion took a sharp turn against slavery. As contraband labor built fortifications and performed essential noncombat tasks for the Union Army, the attitudes of many white Yankee soldiers toward slavery changed. For one thing, as Union soldiers fighting in the South saw the horrors of slavery for themselves firsthand, many became convinced that the enslavement of African Americans was morally wrong. Moreover, slaves in the South actively supported Union soldiers, guiding them through unfamiliar territory and providing information on the location of Confederate positions.

But the main factor turning northern public opinion against slavery and toward freedom was a succession of defeats suffered by the Union Army. The quick and easy victories once predicted never materialized. Northern papers reported grim news of extended battles, exhausted armies, and immense casualties. Union forces did win a few hard-earned victories during 1862, including a naval battle that secured the key port of New Orleans and a bloody struggle at Shiloh, Tennessee, where Confederate troops retreated after both sides had sustained monstrous losses (4,000 dead, another 16,000 wounded).

GAINES MILLS, JUNE 1862. Newspaper artist Alfred Waud hastily sketched the Confederate capture of Union cannon during the Battles of the Seven Days in Virginia. Suffering 4,000 casualties, Union forces retreated, losing an additional 2,800 soldiers as prisoners of war. The Confederate victory was sustained at the cost of 9,000 southern casualties.

Alfred R. Waud, June 27, 1862. Prints and Photographs Division, Library of Congress.

But then, in summer 1862, the North suffered a series of alarming defeats in Virginia's Shenandoah Valley at the hands of Confederate troops under the command of General "Stonewall" Jackson.

Morale in the North sank to rock bottom that June and July when Union general George B. McClellan ordered his troops to retreat during a crucial battle near Richmond, Virginia. General McClellan, known for his timid approach to military strategy, had proslavery views. His retreat at Richmond paved the way for an invasion of the North by the Confederate Army in Virginia led by General Robert E. Lee.

How did Butler's contraband policy and the two confiscation acts change the balance of military power between North and South?

Partly in response to developments on the battlefield, Congress in July 1862 passed a second Confiscation Act, this one more far-reaching than the first. It declared that slaves belonging to any slave owner who supported the Confederacy would be "forever free." The Congress also passed the Militia Act, allowing previously excluded African Americans into all branches of the military. These new laws encouraged even more slaves to escape, and by summer's end, the number of black men and women employed by the Union Army increased. First slowly, then dramatically, the balance of military power on the front lines changed between North and South.

The Bright Side. Harper's Weekly "special artist" Winslow Homer's 1865 painting, based on his wartime sketches, depicts black teamsters relaxing in a Union campsite. Unlike most images of African-American laborers, this unusual painting shows these men as distinct individuals (not as stereotypes). While the teamsters are shown resting, the supply wagons and mules in the background remind the viewer of the crucial role African Americans played in supplying ammunition and food to northern forces, and suggest that their relaxation is well earned.

Winslow Homer, *The Bright Side,*1865, oil on canvas, 13 ¼ x 17 ½ inches. The Fine Arts Museums of San Francisco, Gift of Mr. and Mrs. John D. Rockefeller 3rd (1979.7.56).

DOCUMENT NINE

I love my country...I have risked my life in its battles and am willing to do so again and again. I am deeply anxious to do my whole duty. But ...I cannot conscientiously force my boys to become the slavehounds of Kentuckians and I am determined that I will not....I will not make myself and my regiment a machine to enforce the slave laws of Kentucky and return slaves....If I go down in disgrace, it will be with a clear conscience; if I am right my friends must not let me go down....

—*Excerpts from a letter by* COLONEL SMITH D. ATKINS
to a friend, November 2, 1862

A Northern Soldier and Slaveholder Protests That Union Infantry "Hold the Negroes of My Neighbors and Myself"

DOCUMENT TEN

Mr. President: I deem it my privilege as a Citizen to make the following Complaint to you. While I have been absent from my home serving our Country in the field to the utmost of my humble ability, I have not only suffered large pecuniary [financial] loss from rebel depredations [plundering], but worse still, federal officers, particularly those of the 18th Michigan Infantry volunteers who have taken within their lines and hold the Negroes of my neighbors and myself. The regiment has now not less than twenty-five Negroes in Camp at Lexington Ky who belong to loyal union men...[including] one of mine....

When I became a soldier I sacrificed a large and lucrative practice as an attorney...and placed my property in this state at the mercy of our enemies—who have revenged themselves largely upon me—and now my utter ruin is to be completed by our own officers to promote a fanatical partisan [abolitionist] theory—which...does me and many loyal men of my state bold wrong for the supposed benefit to another race. Mr. President is this right and will you sanction it?...

—A letter to President Abraham Lincoln from slaveholder MARCELLUS MUNDY, *commander of a Kentucky regiment in the Union Army, November 27, 1862*

Examining the documents

• The writers of the letters in Documents Nine and Ten are both loyal Union soldiers. Why and how, then, do they differ?

The Emancipation Proclamation

There was a natural progression from General Butler's "contraband" policy to the two confiscation acts passed by Congress and finally to the Emancipation Proclamation. Three factors prompted Lincoln to move toward a policy of emancipation. Two we have already examined: the role of African Americans and the gloomy military situation. A third was the need to isolate the Confederacy from its main source of international support, Great Britain.

The Confederacy saw Britain, the major buyer of southern cotton, as an important potential source of economic aid. The South found supporters among the British business classes, but working people throughout England had a long-standing hatred of slavery and the rich planters, and they would not fully back the Union until Lincoln took a strong stand against slavery. Britain's support of the Confederacy would not alone have persuaded Lincoln to act on the issue of emancipation. But in the summer of 1862, with northern armies faltering on the battlefield and African Americans pushing for liberation, Lincoln announced his intention to issue a proclamation granting freedom to some slaves.

On January 1, 1863, the Emancipation Proclamation took effect. It freed more than three and a half million slaves in Confederate areas still fighting against the North but excluded almost half a million slaves in the four slaveholding states loyal to the Union and tens of thousands more in Union-controlled portions of Tennessee, Louisiana, and Virginia. The proclamation justified the elimination of slavery on military rather than moral grounds.

Why did Lincoln issue the Emancipation Proclamation? Whom did it free?

Despite these limitations, the Emancipation Proclamation set off wild celebrations among white and black abolitionists in the North and rejoicing prayer among slaves in the South. There was even jubilation among the slaves in loyal slaveholding states who had not been freed by the proclamation.

African Americans, slave and free alike, understood that the aims of the war had been dramatically changed and that the Union was on a new course. Freedom was in the air.

An 1862 cartoon from the northern satirical weekly *Vanity Fair* depicts the Confederacy's president, Jefferson Davis, trying to gain diplomatic recognition from a skeptical Great Britain. "I hardly think it will wash, Mr. Davis," Britannia comments in the cartoon's caption. "We hear so much about your colors running."

Howard, *Vanity Fair*, July 12, 1862. American Social History Project.

Who Freed the Slaves?

Did Lincoln free the slaves? Did the slaves free themselves? The answer to both questions is yes. But historians disagree on who played the key role in emancipation.

In 1994, two award–winning historians, James M. McPherson and Ira Berlin, debated the issue in the pages of a new academic journal, *Reconstruction*.

McPherson, a professor at Princeton University, readily conceded that slaves actively participated in their own emancipation. But Lincoln's role, McPherson argues, was even more central to the cause of freedom. In McPherson's words, Lincoln freed the slaves by:

- "Pronouncing slavery a moral evil that must come to an end and then winning the Presidency in 1860"
- "Provoking the South to secede"
- "Refusing to compromise on the issue of slavery's expansion, or Fort Sumter"
- "Knitting together a Unionist coalition [in] the first year of the war and committing to emancipation in the second"
- "Refusing to compromise this policy once he had adopted it"
- "Prosecuting the war to unconditional victory as commander-in-chief of the army of liberation."

McPherson supports his argument by pointing out that Lincoln was consistent and vocal in his attacks condemning slavery as immoral. Between 1854 and 1860, when he won the Republican nomination

"WRITING THE EMANCIPATION PROCLAMATION." From *Sketches from the Civil War in North America*, a collection of etchings by German immigrant artist (and dentist) Adalbert Johann Volck. A Baltimore pro-South Democrat, Volck depicted a drunken Lincoln (a liquor bottle sits on a side table) surrounded by symbols of Satanism and paintings honoring John Brown and slave rebellions, his foot planted on the Constitution.

V. Blada (A. J. Volck), *Sketches from the Civil War in North America, 1861, '62, '63* (1863). American Social History Project.

for president, Lincoln gave 175 speeches attacking slavery, calling it a "monstrous injustice." In these, McPherson suggests, Lincoln did more than make a moral case against slavery: he used his political genius to build a campaign against it. As a politician, he never moved too far ahead of his constituents. In 1860, he ran for president on a platform that made his election possible. He opposed the expansion of slavery, but at that point did not call for its abolition. Step by small step, he moved northern public opinion against slavery and turned a war for union into one for emancipation. The North could not have won the war and abolished slavery, McPherson maintains, if Lincoln in the first year of war had not kept a fragile Union coalition together—a coalition that included four slave states. "Lincoln's greatest skills as a political leader," McPherson concludes, "were his sensitivity to public opinion and his sense of timing." According to this line of argument, Lincoln announced his plans for an Emancipation Proclamation only at the point at which he could move a majority of northerners to support such a dramatic change in war aims.

Professor Ira Berlin of the University of Maryland strongly disagrees with McPherson. "Lincoln's Proclamation," he writes, "as its critics have noted, freed not a single slave." It applied only to slaves in Confederate-held territories. It did not free any slaves in territories liberated by Union armies or in the four slave states— Delaware, Kentucky, Maryland, and Missouri—fighting on the Union side.

"Indeed," comments Berlin, "the Proclamation's flat prose, ridiculed as having the moral grandeur of a bill of lading [a cargo list], suggests that the true authorship of African-American freedom lies elsewhere." Berlin insists that "the strongest advocates of emancipation were the slaves themselves."

> ...[A]s opportunities arose, slaves risked all for freedom. By abandoning their owners, coming uninvited into Union lines, and offering their assistance as laborers, pioneers, guides and spies, slaves forced federal soldiers at the lowest level to recognize their importance to the Union's success. The understanding travelled quickly up the chain of command. In time, it became evident to even the most obtuse [dull-witted] federal commanders that every slave who crossed into Union lines was a double gain: one subtracted from the Confederacy and added to the Union. The slaves' resolute determination to secure their liberty converted many white Americans to the view that the security of the Union depended on the destruction of slavery. Eventually, this belief tipped the balance in favor of freedom, even among those who had little interest in the question of slavery and no love of black people.

What evidence do McPherson and Berlin use to support their arguments? Who do you think is right? Who played the central role in turning a war for Union into one for freedom—Lincoln, or the slaves themselves? Who freed the slaves? Do the answers to these questions make any difference in how we interpret the Civil War?

The McPherson-Berlin debate: "Who Freed the Slaves?" Reconstruction, vol. 2, no. 3 (1994), pp. 35–44. McPherson, a professor of history at Princeton University, has written several highly praised books on the Civil War and Reconstruction. Berlin, a professor and former director of the Freedmen and Southern Society Project at the University of Maryland, is a leading interpreter of American slavery and coeditor of a four-volume documentary history of slavery, freedom, and the Civil War.

POSITION PAPER

It's June 1862. The war on the military front is not going well for the Union, and morale in the North is low. President Lincoln concedes the need to do something dramatic. Up to this point of the war, he has been extremely careful not to do anything that might lose the support of loyal slaveholders in the Union states of Delaware, Kentucky, Maryland, and Missouri. But he is now seriously exploring the possibility of issuing an Emancipation Proclamation.

Before he makes a decision, Lincoln wants to study the issue. He asks you, a trusted aide, to draw up a position paper to (1) consider the pros and cons of issuing an Emancipation Proclamation, and (2) make a recommendation about what he should do.

Write this position paper for President Lincoln outlining the arguments for and against emancipation, and then make a recommendation. Draw on and quote any relevant documents. Make sure that documents you use are dated before June 1862.

ROLE PLAY

Frederick Douglass is granted an audience with President Abraham Lincoln in late 1861. Douglass argues that the president should make his *main* war aim destroying slavery rather than preserving the Union. Lincoln takes the position he states in Document One.

Divide into two groups. Group 1: Choose someone to play Douglass and brainstorm arguments to present to Lincoln. (See Document Three.) Group 2: Choose someone to play Lincoln and prepare him or her to argue positions expressed in Document One.

Douglass and Lincoln will then debate. After a few minutes, others can join in by asking questions or making additional arguments.

After the debate, analyze why Douglass and Lincoln argued for different war aims.

ROLE PLAY

It's November 1862. What should government policy toward runaway slaves be in Kentucky, a slave state fighting on the Union side? As in the role play above, divide into two groups. Group 1: Prepare someone to play Smith D. Atkins (Document Nine). Group 2: Choose someone to take the role of Marcellus Mundy (Document Ten). Follow the same steps (preparation, debate, discussion) as in the role play above.

FOR DISCUSSION

What do you think prompted Lincoln to shift his views on emancipation? Was Lincoln's "paramount aim in this struggle," even *after* the Emancipation Proclamation, "to save the Union"? Or was it to "strike down slavery"? Discuss, citing evidence for your position.

VISUAL PORTRAYALS OF AFRICAN AMERICANS

Study all the illustrations and photographs in this chapter that include African Americans. Do any present African Americans as stereotypes? as racial caricatures? Which do you think most faithfully portray African Americans during the war? Discuss.

"INDUSTRY OF LADIES IN CLOTHING THE SOLDIERS, AND ZEAL IN URGING THEIR BEAUX TO GO TO WAR."
Southern white women's role in the Confederate cause, as interpreted in *The South: A Tour of Its Battle-fields and Ruined Cities*, published a year after the end of the war.

CHAPTER FOUR

THE HOME FRONTS

The War Diaries of Mary Boykin Chesnut

DOCUMENT ONE

APRIL 13, 1861. People talk before them as if they were chairs and tables and they make no sign. Are they stolidly stupid, or wiser than we are, silent and strong, biding their time?

JUNE 22, 1861. Yesterday some of the Negro men on the plantation were found with pistols. I have never seen aught [anything] about any Negro to show that they knew we had a war on hand, in which they had an interest.

NOVEMBER 11, 1861. [A friend] was in a state of abject fright because the Negroes show such exultation at the enemy's making good their entrance at Port Royal [on the South Carolina Sea Islands].

OCTOBER, 1863. I taught him [the family butler] to read… but he won't look at me now. He looks over my head. He scents freedom in the air. He was always very ambitious. I do not think that he ever troubled with books much, but then my father always said that Dick, standing in front of his sideboard, had heard all the subjects on earth or heaven discussed, and by the best heads in the world.

—*From the diary of* MARY BOYKIN CHESNUT

---

*BEFORE READING.
The following items
are from the diary of
Mary Boykin Chesnut,
an upper-class white
woman living on a
southern plantation
during the Civil War.*

Assignment

*In writing, answer the
following questions:
1. In the April 13 entry,
what does Chesnut mean
when she says, "People
talk before them as if
they were chairs and
tables and they make no
sign"? To whom does the
word "people" refer? the
words "them" and
"they"? Why do you think
"they make no sign"?
2. In the same entry,
how would you answer
her question "Are they
stolidly stupid, or wiser than we are, silent and strong, biding their time"?
3. In the June 22 entry, what does Chesnut mean by the phrase "in which they had
an interest"? 4. From the evidence in all four entries, why do you think tensions
increased as Union armies penetrated more deeply into the South?*

Women filling cartridges at the united states arsenal at Watertown, Massachusetts.
Winslow Homer, *Harper's Weekly,* July 20, 1861. American Social History Project.

The conflict between the Union and the Confederacy rapidly turned into a total war that transformed economic, political, and human relationships in the North and the South. With dramatic and at times even revolutionary results, the Civil War changed the ways men and women of different races and classes worked and interacted, as well as how they thought about and related to government.

In the North, a once small federal government, which played a minimal role in the economy, grew into a mammoth bureaucracy that became the biggest employer in the United States. As such, it mobilized the U.S. economy behind the Union war effort. The power of government was everywhere, organizing factories, farms, railroads, cities, and wage laborers to feed, clothe, and arm the Union forces.

The Lincoln administration established close ties with business, helping rising corporations with loans and tax breaks and granting valuable government orders for goods. With the help of government credit and land grants, railroads extended their lines and made huge profits by transporting military goods and men. A system of steep tariffs on imported manufactured goods gave American firms protection from foreign competition and encouraged the growth of U.S. industrial production.

> *How and why did the role of the U.S. government change during the war? How did these changes affect the lives of ordinary Americans?*

While government intervention benefitted industry, it did not necessarily help working Americans. Federal and state governments prohibited strikes and undercut the efforts of workers to organize labor unions. In turn, when the federal government borrowed

TARIFFS—taxes on foreign goods

heavily and began to print money to finance the war effort, inflation resulted. Inflation, meaning overvaluation of money, credit, and goods, made life particularly difficult for working people trying to make ends meet.

As the partnership between government and industry grew, it had to confront a big dilemma: how to increase war production when the labor force was shrinking. The Union Army recruited and drafted hundreds of thousands of working men. To replace them, and at the same time actually increase industrial output, business and government used a three-pronged strategy: (1) they further mechanized industry; (2) they encouraged more women to enter the work force; and (3) they drew on new sources of immigrant labor.

How were the Union government and Northern business able to increase war production at a time when military recruitment was shrinking the workforce?

Mechanical reapers, mowers, and women's labor transformed northern farms. Many women went to work in factories, arsenals, armories, food-processing plants, retail stores, offices, schools, and hospitals. Tens of thousands of "sewing women" worked under government contract for minimal wages in their homes making military uniforms. "We are unable to sustain life for the prices offered by contractors who fatten on their contracts by grinding immense profits out of the labor of operatives," wrote a group of Cincinnati seamstresses to President Lincoln in 1864. Yet even though most women's work paid pitifully low wages, it also opened up opportunities during and after the war in occupations once closed to female labor.

Industrialists set up organizations that actively recruited immigrants, particularly from Ireland and Germany. By 1863, for example, workers of Irish and German descent dominated significant sectors of the New York City labor force. Many Irish, German, and American-born workers in the city, prodded by antiwar Democrats, expressed great resentment toward the Republican national government, convinced that its no-strike, minimum wage, and inflationary policies were antilabor.

In March 1863, the government added fuel to the fire by passing a draft law that allowed the rich to escape service by hiring substitutes. Together with rising prices and declining wages, the new draft law fueled bitterness in many working-class wards,

What prompted the 1863 draft riots in New York City? How did the character of the riots change from beginning to end?

particularly in heavily Irish neighborhoods. In July, New York streets exploded in protest. But what started as a focused, militant antidraft demonstration soon escalated into an out-of-control riot. The crowd quickly turned its wrath against New York's small African-American community, ransacking and burning residences in black neighborhoods, and lynching a dozen African Americans. Only when Union troops were rushed back from the front at Gettysburg was order restored and the riot suppressed.

OPERATIVE—a skilled worker

ANTIWAR DEMOCRATS—members of the Democratic party who opposed the war, claiming that Lincoln's centralization of government power was unconstitutional and that his draft policy was unfair to the working classes

Who Served in the Union Army?

The Tammany Hall political club raised funds to pay substitutes for many New York City workers. In fact, only seven percent of those whose names were drawn in draft lotteries throughout the North actually served in the Union Army.

The preferred way to enlist troops, particularly in light of the intense resistance to the draft, was by offering bounties—cash grants—to volunteers. Federal and local governments, raising money by contributions and taxes, paid a half-billion dollars in bounties. Some volunteers received bounties of $1,000, more than three times the annual wage for an average worker. A few even became bounty jumpers: They would sign up in one town, receive their bounty, and promptly desert. Then they would go to another town and, under an assumed name, repeat the process.

Civil War historian James McPherson noted that "the half-billion dollars paid in bounties by the North represented something of a transfer of wealth from rich to poor—another version of the theme of 'rich man's war/poor man's fight.'"

The New York Draft Riots: lynching of a black man on Clarkson Street.

Illustrated London News, August 8, 1863. American Social History Project.

The social fabric of the Confederacy was also ripped apart by the war. By 1863, as the military situation in the South grew grimmer, social tensions between races and classes took on a particularly sharp edge.

As we discussed in chapter 2, there was a rising tide of slave resistance in the Confederacy from the beginning of the war to the end. Slaves increasingly escaped to Union lines and sabotaged production on the South's plantations. In her diary, Mary Chesnut (Document One) provides dramatic testimony of Confederate concern about growing slave defiance.

Inequities in the Confederacy's draft and impressment laws resulted in a complaining chorus of "rich man's war/poor man's fight" that echoed across the entire South. As in the North, the rich could hire substitutes; in addition, any white man owning twenty or more slaves was entitled to an exemption from service, which he could apply to himself, a son, or an overseer. Resentment grew against large slaveholders who had led the South into war, yet received special privileges protecting them from many of the conflict's hardships and dangers. Southern impressment laws allowing the military to commandeer food from farmers at below- market prices added to the discontent. By 1864, more and more poor white farmers—the very backbone of the Confederacy and its army—began to talk actively of peace. At war's end, the number of Confederate soldiers deserting actually exceeded those remaining in uniform.

Similar patterns developed in the North. As war industries grew, so did government bureaucracy, as well as the number of women who now had to run farms or worked producing war goods. Miserable wages and galloping inflation, coupled with the departure of husbands, brothers, fathers, and sons for the front, pushed many women and the households they managed to the brink of starvation.

But as women entered the wage-labor force and assumed even more responsibility for running their households, they became more militant. In April 1863, as the Confederate government diverted farm products from local markets for military purposes, the price of now scarce food skyrocketed. In Richmond, Virginia, the capital of the Confederacy, women rioted for bread. Food riots and protests, led by women, spread that spring to other southern cities.

Why did women riot in southern cities in 1863? How had the war changed their lives?

In the short run, the Confederate government suppressed these demonstrations. In the longer run, however, social relations were thrown into turmoil by the war and the impending defeat of the South. Once slaves began sabotaging the Confederate war effort, abandoning their masters, and defecting to Union lines, race relations in the South were turned on their head.

In the South, why did white, small farmers begin to waver in their support for the Confederacy?

Next, we will examine more closely the two 1863 riots that erupted out of the social and economic tensions generated by the war—the New York City draft riot and the Richmond, Virginia, bread riot.

IMPRESSMENT—recruitment by force of persons into the military

COMMANDEER—to seize.

A Brooklyn Mob Attacks African-American Workers: "Why Will You Not Put Away This Great Wickedness?"

Fears that emancipated slaves would move north to take jobs from Irish labor echoed repeatedly in Democratic party literature before and during the war. Spurred by such fears, an Irish mob set fire to a factory in Brooklyn in August 1862 with twenty-five African Americans inside, mainly women and children. Responding quickly, police were able to extinguish the blaze with minimal injury to people and property. An African-American newspaper responded with the following editorial. As you read it, consider whether or not the event it condemns forecasted the draft riots a year later.

DOCUMENT TWO

Irishmen! the day will come when you will find out that you are making a sad mistake in asserting to crush our liberties. Learn! O learn, that the protection of the feeblest of your fellow beings, is the only guarantee you have of the protection for your own liberty in this or any other land. We call upon the world to bear witness to the dreadful effects which the system of slavery has had upon the Irish people. In their own country they are kind and hospitable to our poor and constantly abused race; but here, so dreadfully corrupted do some of them become that they are prepared for the vilest deed of diabolism [devilishness] which it is possible for the brain of man to conceive, as is witnessed in their attempt to roast alive a number of people who never did them the least harm. Americans! we charge you before high Heaven and the whole civilized world with being the authors of this great wickedness. It was you who first taught them to hate us.... Why, our countrymen, will you not put away this great wickedness among you?

—*An editorial in the* ANGLO-AFRICAN, *August 9, 1862*

Examining the document

•*Why does the* Anglo-African *charge Americans, not Irishmen, with responsibility for the "great wickedness" of the fire?*
•*In the statement "the protection of the feeblest of your fellow beings, is the only guarantee you have of the protection for your own liberty in this or any other land," whom does "your" and "you" refer to?*
•*Who are "the feeblest of your fellow beings"?* •*What does the whole statement mean?*

Draft Riots of 1863

For five days in the summer of 1863, the streets of New York City erupted in fury. On Monday, July 13, thousands of working-men—artisans, industrial workers, and day laborers—closed factories and shops to protest the imposition of a federal military draft. After a morning rally in the newly completed Central Park, the crowd moved to the location of the draft lottery office downtown. By early afternoon, the building was in flames. Some demonstrators in the crowd then marched back up Fifth Avenue to 43rd Street. There, after routing terrified African-American children, they looted and torched the Colored Orphan Asylum.

What officials deemed a "riot" did not begin as one. The activities of Monday morning were part of a militant, focused protest. But arson, looting, drunkenness, destruction of property, and even murder characterized events from late Monday to early Friday. By Tuesday, a significant number of the original protesters dropped out; others joined in. Participation cut across generational, religious, and ethnic (but not racial) lines. As the week wore on, however, the crowd on the streets generally became younger, more Irish, and more Catholic.

What triggered the events of July 13–17, 1863? Who were the people who took to the streets early on the 13th? What was their mood? What did they target? How did the nature, behavior, and targets of the crowds change during the week of the riots?

IMPOSITION—the act of making something compulsory

DRAFT RIOTERS—NO. 1. Illustrated and written descriptions of a riot sometimes tell us more about the point of view of the newspaper editor, artist, or author than about the event itself. In this engraving from *Harper's Weekly*, rioters are shown looting a Second Avenue drugstore. The *Weekly*, which supported the Republican party and often espoused nativist (anti-immigrant) sentiments, caricatured the rioters in a way that emphasized their Irish ethnicity and brutality.

Harper's Weekly, August 1, 1863. American Social History Project.

Different participants had different motives, ranging from legitimate economic and political grievances to outright racism and criminal activity. The victims of the crowd's violent actions quickly moved beyond the draft, targeting the rich, the Republican party, abolitionists, political authorities, Protestants and, finally and most viciously, black New Yorkers. Mobs lynched several African-American men, leaving their dead bodies hanging from lamp-posts. By Friday, July 17, the death toll—white and black—had risen to more than one hundred.

The cause of all this death and destruction was triggered six days earlier when officials began drawing names for the North's first draft lottery. For those whose number came up in the draft lottery, there was a way out, particularly if they had access to money. The Conscription (or Draft) Act of March 1863 provided that a draftee could hire an "acceptable substitute," or pay the government $300 to find one. There was nothing new about hiring substitutes. It had been standard policy in the U.S. Army from the time of the Revolution to the Civil War. For most workingmen, though, the $300 fee was a small fortune, representing as much as a year's wages. The fee seemed to prove again that the Civil War was a "rich man's war/poor man's fight." "The Song of Conscripts," mocking the Conscription Act, sums up sentiment:

> We're coming, Father Abraham, three hundred
> thousand more
> We leave our homes and firesides with bleeding hearts
> and sore
> Since poverty has been our crime, we bow to thy decree;
> We are poor and have no wealth to purchase liberty.

In New York's predominantly Irish, working-class wards, sentiment ran strongly against the draft law, which seemed but one more example of heavy-handed Republican rule. Tammany Hall, the Democratic party machine that controlled much of New York City's government, had a strong and loyal following in these Catholic and Irish neighborhoods. Tammany circulated political leaflets in predominantly Irish and Democratic party precincts suggesting that the draft law was antiworker, anti-Irish, prorich and problack (African Americans were exempt from the draft because the U.S. Constitution did not recognize them as citizens). Fernando Wood, the former

MACHINE—a political organization

Democratic New York City mayor, argued in 1861 that "this war...is a war of abolitionists against Southern men and their rights....They are willing to spend Irish and German blood to secure a victory, and when they have secured it, they will bring the black laborer up into the North to steal the work and bread of the honest Irish and Germans."

Racial tension had divided Irish and African-American communities for more than a decade. Victimized by discrimination in the labor market, Irish and African Americans often competed for the same jobs.

Why was there opposition to the draft law? Why did sentiments against the law run so strongly in the largely Irish wards? How did the Republican and Democratic parties differ on the draft?

DRAFT RIOTERS—NO. 2. While *Frank Leslie's Illustrated Newspaper* also used Irish caricatures in its coverage of the Draft Riot, its portrayal of rioters varied. This engraving shows an orderly and uncaricatured "group of rioters marching down Avenue A." *Leslie's* readers included many Irish Catholic New Yorkers.

Frank Leslie's Illustrated Newspaper, August 1, 1863.
American Social History Project.

"BUYING A SUBSTITUTE IN THE NORTH DURING THE WAR."
Baltimore artist A. J. Volck depicted the Union Army as composed of immigrant
and native-born deviants and criminals. He was moved less by the inequities
of the northern draft law than by his sympathy for the South.

V. Blada (A. J. Volck), *Sketches from the Civil War in North America, 1861, '62, '63* (1863). Print Collection, Miriam and Ira Wallach Division
of Art, Prints, and Photographs, The New York Public Library, Astor, Lenox, and Tilden Foundations.

On the waterfront, the virtually all-Irish Longshoremen's Association sought to keep the workforce lily white. But when employers brought in black workers as strikebreakers—first in 1855 and again in early 1863—racial hostility escalated.

What role did race play in the July 1863 riots? Why was racial antagonism between some Irish and African Americans so intense?

Racism was widespread throughout New York and by no means confined to the poorer Irish wards. Yet a stereotype emerged that implied that racism was uniquely Irish. Many written and illustrated media accounts of the day depicted the Irish as unpatriotic, drunken louts bent exclusively on racial violence. Contrary to the stereotype, the New York Irish Catholic community did not hold a unified position on the war and the draft. Archbishop John Hughes supported conscription, condemned the riots, and traveled to Rome to visit the pope on President Lincoln's behalf to plead the Union's cause.

What evidence is there in the text that not all Irish opposed the war and the draft?

The 69th Regiment of the Union Army—
New York City's famed Irish Regiment—
went into battle against Confederate rebels
flying both the stars and stripes and the
green flag of Ireland. In July 1863, summoned back to Manhattan, the 69th stood
shoulder to shoulder with the predominantly
Irish Metropolitan Police to quell the New
York draft riots.

How then should we characterize the
actors and events of July 1863? Who took to
the streets? Workers? criminals? racists?
disaffected youth? What motivated participants? Justice? righteous anger? narrow self-
interest? bigotry? How can we sort out the
conflicting motives and varied participants
to make sense of what happened?

Look at some of the evidence. Consider
the different viewpoints of those who witnessed the events. Then join the historical
debate about what happened in New York
City during the week of July 13, 1863.

"THE IRRESPRESSIBLE CONFLICT."
In this cartoon from *Vanity Fair*, an Irish long-
shoreman tells a black worker seeking employment
on New York's waterfront: "Well, ye may be a
man and a brother, sure enough; but it's little
hospitality ye'll get out of yer relations on this dock,
me ould buck!" The sharp competition for
unskilled jobs contributed to the New York draft riots.

Vanity Fair, August 2, 1862. American Social History Project.

VOLUNTEERS WANTED! An 1861 recruiting poster
for an Irish-American regiment.

ICHi-22131. Chicago Historical Society.

An Editorial: "The Monster Grows More Dangerous"

In the Civil War era, New York newspapers usually had clear political affiliations. The then openly Republican New York Times *wrote the following editorial (Document Three) assessing the first two days of demon-strations and crowd activity during the anti-draft riots. On the same day, the* Times *also published a letter presenting a different view of the riot (Document Four).*

DOCUMENT THREE

The mob in our city is still rampant [out of control]....The monster grows more dangerous as he grows desperate....

It is too true that there are public journals who try to dignify the mob by some respectable appellation [name]. The *Herald* characterizes it as the people and the *World* as the laboring men of the City....The people of New-York and the laboring men of New-York are not incendiaries [arsonists], nor robbers, nor assassins. They do not hunt down men whose only offense is the color God gave them: they do not chase and insult and beat women; they do not pillage [loot] an asylum for orphan children, and burn the very roof over those orphans' heads. They are civilized beings, valuing law and respecting decency: and they regard with unqualified abhorrence [hatred] the doings of the tribe of savages...in their midst.

...You may as well reason with the wolves in the forest as with these men in their present mood....—*Give them grape* [grapeshot, cannonfire] *and plenty of it.*

OBJECT OF THE MOB. If this mob was originated in a passionate spirit of resistance to the Conscription law, it very soon changed its purpose, and assumed the character of merely a mob for robbery, plunder and arson. This is shown in the rifling of houses, hotels and stores, and the assaults and felonies upon the persons of unoffending citizens. Some of the ringleaders are noted thieves, who have served out several terms in Sing Sing and other penitentiaries and prisons. Hundreds of the workmen who joined with the crowd on Monday, were, of course, as honest as the average of us, but they were at once joined by all the knaves [dishonest men] of the City who saw...an opportunity for plunder....

LAW AND LIBERTY....A mob is un-American, anti-American. Every grievance can here be remedied, every wrong can here be righted by *law,* which has its power in the will of the people and "its fountain in the bosom of God." It will be a dark day for the liberties of America, for its honor, its greatness, its power, its glory, when this excrescence [ugly outgrowth] of European despotism fastens itself upon our free institutions and society. Every man who prides himself in the name of an American must use his determined efforts to drive back this black and deadly tide of human depravity.

—*Editorial in the* NEW YORK TIMES, *Wednesday, July 15, 1863*

A Letter to the Editor: "A Poor Man, But a Man for All That"

DOCUMENT FOUR

You will no doubt be hard on us rioters tomorrow morning, but that 300-dollar law has made us nobodies, vagabonds [drifters] and cast-outs of society, for whom nobody cares when we must go to war and be shot down. We are the poor rabble, and the rich rabble is our enemy by this law. Therefore we will give our enemy battle right here, and ask no quarter. Although we got hard fists, and are dirty without, we have soft hearts and have clean consciences within, and that's the reason we love our wives and children more than the rich, because we got not much besides them, and we will not go and leave them at home for to starve....Why don't they let the nigger kill the slave-driving race and take possession of the South, as it belongs to them.

—*Letter to the editor of the* New York Times, *signed*
"A POOR MAN, BUT A MAN FOR ALL THAT,"
dated Monday night, July 13; pulished July 15, 1863

Examining the documents

•*In the* New York Times *editorial (Document Three), what specific language is used to describe those who participated in crowd actions on the streets?* •*What does the* Times *see as the "object of the mob"?* •*On what basis does the editorial argue that the "mob is un-American, anti-American"?* •*What is "European despotism"?* •*What does it mean to say that mobs are an outgrowth of this despotism?* •*In what sense would mob rule undermine "our free institutions and society"?* •*Who is the* Times *calling a "tribe of savages…in our midst"?* •*Do you think that "tribes of savages" is an accurate description?* •*How does the viewpoint of the letter to the* Times *(Document Four) differ from the viewpoint of the paper's editorial?* •*How would the* Times*'s editorial board and the letter writer respond to one another's arguments?*

Suggested Activities for Draft Riots

LANGUAGE: THE ROLE OF DICTION

Divide into small groups and make a group list of all the words and phrases used by the *Times* editorial, "The Monster Grows More Dangerous," to describe the mob. Analyze the list. What mental pictures of the participants in these events do the words create? Are these words and images accurate or inaccurate? Discuss.

VISUAL IMAGES: THE USE OF EXAGGERATION

Illustrators and cartoonists often use exaggeration to make a point. But when does exaggeration cross the line into distortion and bias?

Find a historical or contemporary cartoon or illustration that you think crosses the line in depicting a particular race, nationality, religion, or grouping of people. Compare it to the illustration of the draft riot on page 91. Present your cartoon or illustration and your observations in small groups or in a report to the whole class. In groups or as a full class, discuss when exaggeration crosses the line into bias and distortion.

QUICK TAKES

Drawing on as much evidence as you can, write a response to any one of the following arguments. Then, in class, discuss your response with classmates who have written on the same issue.

1. The claim by protesters that the Civil War was a "rich man's war/poor man's fight."
2. The *Anglo-African*'s argument (Document Two) that "the protection of the feeblest of your fellow beings is the only guarantee you have of the protection for your own liberty in this or any other land."
3. The contention by the *New York Times* (Document Three) that a "mob is un-American, anti-American" and that just grievances can be remedied by law.

DISCUSSION

Was Fernando Wood's campaign rhetoric (pages 92) racist? Do any contemporary politicians play on racial divisions? Discuss. In developing positions on these questions, consider whether or not you have sufficient evidence to support your points. Where necessary, do some research for evidence to deepen the discussion and analysis.

CROSSTALK

You are the writer who signs his letter "A Poor Man, But a Man for All That." For homework, write a response to the *Times* editorial "The Monster Grows More Dangerous." Discuss.

Put yourself in the place of the *Times* editorial writer and write a response to the poor man's letter. Read it to your group. Then discuss why the editorialist and letter writer see things so differently. Could these differences be settled? If so, how?

The Richmond Bread Riot

Throughout the Civil War, food riots rocked several southern cities from Mobile and New Orleans on the Gulf Coast to Savannah and Richmond in the middle and upper South. There were a series of insurrections in the spring and early summer of 1863, the biggest of which occurred on April 2 in Richmond, the capital of the Confederacy. Rioters in all these cities were mostly women, many of them working-class wives or mothers of Confederate soldiers.

By briefly taking public action in these uprisings, rioters contradicted many of the myths about southern white womanhood. The image of white women promoted in pre- and postwar southern literature was one of gentility, obedience, and wholesome morality. Women were expected to remain behind the scenes, loyal to and supportive of their husbands and fathers and brothers.

The war transformed the role of women, particularly in southern cities. In Richmond, large numbers of white women worked in war-related industries. Many managed family households in the absence of husbands and fathers who had gone off to battle. Necessities of life, particularly food and clothing, grew scarce as resources were diverted for military purposes. Women found

How did the war conditions change the role of white women in the South?

GENTILITY—upper-class status; proper social conduct

"FAMILY WORSHIP IN A PLANTATION IN NORTH CAROLINA."
Among the few images emerging from the South, where paper and ink were in short supply, were engravings published in the *Illustrated London News* based on the sketches of its correspondent Frank Vizetelly. Vizetelly, espousing the Confederate cause, presented to British readers a serene scene of slavery on the southern home front.

Frank Vizetelly, *Illustrated London News*, December 5, 1863. American Social History Project.

food not only difficult to get but outrageously expensive. Newspapers like the *Richmond Whig* railed against "heartless extortioners and official rogues" who speculated in food and provisions, driving up prices and creating incredible hardship.

By 1863, the population of Richmond had swelled from 38,000 at the beginning of the war to approximately 100,000. Refugees, job seekers in war industries, and government officials poured into the city once it became the capital of the Confederacy. More than 14,000 inmates—most of them war prisoners—packed Richmond's jails. Wartime Richmond was a classic case of too many people chasing too few resources.

Under these conditions of war and scarcity, tensions between Richmond's governing and working classes sharpened. Working people were forced to scrounge for even the basic necessities of life. A Richmond woman, claiming that most people did not have "food enough to preserve life," begged the government to "devise some means to reduce the prices of meat and bread so as to prevent starvation." But such pleas went unheeded. On April 2,

Why were the prices of food and other necessities in the Confederacy so high?

Why did Richmond's population increase so dramatically during the war? How did this population growth affect social and economic conditions in the city?

"SOWING AND REAPING." The northern *Frank Leslie's Illustrated Newspaper* presents an unflattering portrait of southern womanhood in a May 1863 illustration. The depiction contrasts sharply with the view promoted by plantation elites of virtuous southern white mothers and wives who obey and defer to men. The panel on the left shows southern women "hounding their men on to Rebellion." The panel on the right depicts them later "feeling the effects of Rebellion and creating Bread Riots."

Frank Leslie's Illustrated Newspaper, May 23, 1863. General Research Division, The New York Public Library, Astor, Lenox, and Tilden Foundations.

1863, a crowd of several hundred, mostly white women, converged on a ten- block area around the capital square. Armed with knives and hatchets, they called for "bread and blood," breaking into stores and taking bacon, bread, flour, clothing, and other items.

Who participated in the April 1, 1863, uprising in Richmond? Why? How did the authorities handle the insurrection?

The mayor of Richmond and the governor of Virginia summoned the public guard. When Jefferson Davis, president of the Confederacy, arrived on the scene, he stood on a wagon to address the rioters and announced that he was giving them five minutes to disperse before he ordered the public guard to fire. Davis confided to a colleague that "it was not bread they [the crowd] wanted…they were bent on nothing but plunder and wholesale robbery." The square quickly cleared and the insurrection was over.

What was the connection between the food riots and the establishment of local relief systems in the South?

Richmond authorities arrested sixty-eight people, the vast majority of whom were white women. According to court inventories, officials confiscated mainly food and clothing from the rioters, but also an occasional tub, broom, or candle. State and city leaders made an example of most of those arrested, winning convictions in court and imposing fines and prison terms. At the same time, the city moved to set up free markets to distribute food and provisions to Richmond's inhabitants.

[It is not known what if any role African Americans played in the Richmond riot. See the exercise that looks further into this question at the end of the chapter on page 106.]

As riots spread to other southern towns, officials hesitated to use troops to fire on crowds of women, whom they knew to be wives of soldiers. Unlike Richmond, there were few arrests in other southern cities. Instead, most towns set up relief networks to distribute food free of charge or at minimal cost. By taking public action, women in selected southern cities had moved initially unresponsive gov-ernments to do something. Throughout the South, local officials and elites began establishing a system of more equitable (although not always adequate) food and clothing distribution. These were modest but significant accomplishments. The women of the South had forcefully taken the public stage.

In what ways was the pattern of insurrection and government response in other southern cities similar to or different from that in Richmond?

research suggests that there were many participants, but fewer than a thousand and maybe only several hundred. Some of Tutweiler's more sensational details, such as the woman rioter who had several fingers cut off, have never been verified by other accounts. Nonetheless, Tutweiler's letter is important. Given the partial newspaper blackout of news about the riot, letters such as this and word of mouth became people's main source of information about the events in Richmond.

DOCUMENT FIVE

…Thursday morning I went to the Office as usual. A few minutes after I got in, I heard the most tremendous cheering, went to the window to see what was going on, but could not tell what it was about. So we all went down to the street. When we arrived on the scene we found that a large number of women had broken into two or three large grocery establishments, & were helping themselves to hams, middlings [grain by-products], butter and in fact every kind of eatable they could find. Almost every one of them were armed. Some had a belt on with a pistol stuck in each side, others had a large knife, while some were only armed with a hatchet, axe or hammer. As fast as they got what they wanted, they walked off with it. The men instead of trying to put a stop to this shameful proceeding, cheered them on and assisted them with all in their power. When they found that no one was going to stop them, they went back & begun to carry off everything they could lay their hands on, tubs, buckets, brooms, which are selling here for six dollars apiece, hats, shoes, boots, candles, & various articles too numerous to mention.…

I think there were more than 5,000 persons on Cary St., if not more, besides that many more on Main and Broad. This morning they began again, but they were told that if they did not disperse, they would be fired on. Have not been downtown since dinner, & I do not know whether they obeyed the order or not. One woman knocked a pane of glass out of a shop window, of which the door was fastened & put her arm in to steal something, but the shop man cut off all four of her fingers off. I was right in the middle of the row all the time. It was the most horrible thing I ever saw. A written description can give you but very little idea of it. I am very much afraid that this will encourage people to try the same thing all over the Confederacy. Gov. Letcher told them he'd give them five minutes to disperse [actually it was the president of the Confederacy, Jefferson Davis], & if they did not disperse, he would have them fired on by city guards. They immediately began to leave the streets and in five minutes they were completely vacant....

—*Excerpt from a letter from* H. A. TUTWEILER
to Netta Tutweiler, April 3, 1863

A Son Asks for Leniency for His Mother: "Don't Be Angry That a Poor Boy Troubles You to Read This"

Several letters of appeal were written to Governor John Letcher on behalf of Mary Duke, who participated in the riot and was serving six months in jail. Attached to her appeal were statements by doctors attesting to her poor health. Below is a letter to the governor from her fifteen-year-old son. On July 1, 1863, Letcher pardoned Mary Duke.

DOCUMENT SIX

I am a poor boy, the oldest of four children & I am only 15 years old. My father is in Genl Lee's army & my mother is in prison—and we are left to ourselves, dependent on my labor to support us. When my mother was first put in prison, a lady came to stay with us but she says that she cannot stay no longer—and these little children will be left alone.

Our poor Mother did very wrong, but she has suffered greatly—all the rioters that have been tried have been discharged from the prison but her—she is in a decline and suffers in mind & body.

Four little children appeal to your clemency and ask you for their sake & for their father's sake who is fighting for the country, to pardon our sick mother and let her come back to our humble home. My little sisters are 10, 7 and 2 years old.

I sell news papers to feed us & try to save a little to help pay her fine which by the help of friends I can do if you will show us mercy.

Do good Governor, and four little hearts will rise up and call you "blessed." I served 10 mos [months] under the good Jackson in Co. C, Irish batt. [battery]—as drummer.

Don't be angry that a poor boy troubles you to read this. He asks most respectfully mercy for his mother, Mary Duke who was imprisoned 12 May last.

—An undated letter to Governor John Letcher from
MARY DUKE'S SON ANDREW *asking for her pardon*

Free Markets and Poor Relief

Markets for the free distribution of food were established in Richmond within two weeks of the riot. There was a similar pattern in other southern cities and towns. In cities where insurrections occurred, officials usually set up food distribution networks. In other cities, the government and voluntary associations initiated free markets to prevent such riots.

Does the following article from a Richmond newspaper provide any clues as to why the free market was established in that city?

DOCUMENT SEVEN

The City Council have established a free market. All appropriations [public funds] for the poor, not in the Poor House, shall be placed in the hands of overseers of the poor, to provide for the said market, which shall be open one day each week, and all persons who have tickets may enjoy its benefits. A free fuel depot will also be established which will be regulated in like manner and both will be discontinued whenever the amount of appropriations shall be expended. Once a week the Board of Overseers is to assemble to hear and grant applications, make investigations into the character of the applicants and do other business connected therewith. No relief will be given unless the applicant be unable to procure subsistence or fuel, nor to any able-bodied man, nor to any person who had participated in a riot. An agent is appointed to purchase and superintend the distribution of supplies.

This is a step in the right direction. Free markets in Charleston and New Orleans have been found to operate most advantageously. In the former city, which is one of the best regulated in the Confederacy, there has never even been a symptom of such a disturbance which disgraced Richmond not long ago.

— Excerpt from an article in
the RICHMOND WHIG, *April 15, 1863*

A Soldier's Complaint: My Wife "Could Not Get Bread Enough for My Children"

DOCUMENT EIGHT

After an absence of ten months in the army, I obtained a furlough and what joy did I anticipate in once more pressing my wife and little ones to my bosom. But imagine my feelings when told by my wife that she could not get bread enough for my children. She said that she had been to five gentlemen and could get no corn [grain], while some in her immediate neighborhood had been known to ship corn to Augusta that they might get extortionate prices. Most of the time of my absence I have been on the march through Mississippi, Alabama and upper Georgia, many times with nothing but wet clay for my bed. I have seen my comrades fall on my right and my left, I have heard the whistling of bullets and seen them strike within a few inches of me; but all those hardships and dangers only nerved my arm to strike one more blow for my country and her honor. But, sir, when I am told that my little ones are suffering for want through the avarice of those for whom I stand as a wall between the enemy and their property, I feel this the greatest hardship of all. Why, Mr. Editor, the Beast Butler [a Union general] with all his refinements of cruelty could not serve them worse.

—*Letter to the* SAVANNAH REPUBLICAN, *February 23, 1864*

There was much bitterness in the Confederacy against those who speculated in food. Sometimes that bitterness took the form of bread riots. But whether it was expressed in militant action or angry words, there was widespread outrage directed at those who held food off the market or sold it only to the highest bidder at scandalously inflated prices. The following is typical of letters to southern newspaper editors on this subject.

Examining the documents

•*What is the attitude of H.A. Tutweiler to the uprising in Richmond?* *What specific phrases or words would you cite as evidence of her attitude?* •*In Andrew Duke's letter, are the key facts and phrases intended to move Governor Letcher to pardon Mary Duke?* •*In the* Richmond Whig *article on poor relief, why do you think the City Council denies riot participants access to free markets? What is the link between the City Council's free market policy and the riots that took place three weeks earlier? What specific parts of the article point to such a connection?* •*Why might the letter to the* Savannah Republican *have special impact on readers?*

Suggested Activities for Richmond Bread Riot

ROLE PLAY AND PERSUASIVE WRITING

You are an adviser to Governor John Letcher. He has just received an appeal for the pardon of Mary Duke from her son Andrew (Document Six). The governor has asked you to prepare a memo outlining two sets of arguments, one *for* and the other *against* a pardon. He wants you to consider not only what is best for Mary Duke, but what is best for the state of Virginia and the city of Richmond.

Discuss your memo and the issues raised with classmates.

CREATIVE WRITING

Write a story about one or both of the illustrations from *Frank Leslie's Illustrated Newspaper* on page 99. What do the stories you and other students have written tell us about the depiction of southern women in these illustrations?

STEREOTYPES

Look up the word *stereotype*. Then write a one-page analysis of two images or illustrations reproduced in this chapter that stereotype a particular group or groups of people (e.g., Irish Americans, African Americans, women).

THE MYSTERY OF THE MISSING AFRICAN AMERICANS

To date, with one possible exception, historians of the Richmond bread riots have not been able to uncover any information about the role of the city's African-American community during this event. There are bits and pieces of conflicting evidence suggesting that one of the women arrested in the riots might have been African American. Some things are known about African Americans, free and slave, in Richmond during the war—for example, that many labored in an important iron works, and that black defiance against Confederate rule grew as Union troops approached the city at war's end. Still, we know little about African Americans during the riots.

Assuming information becomes available, what would you want to know? In small groups, brainstorm what questions you would want to ask as a historian investigating the role of the African-American community during the period of the bread riots.

SOLDIERS' LIVES

BEFORE READING. *Harriet Tubman, the famous ex-slave who served as a conductor on the Underground Railroad, accompanied the Second South Carolina Volunteers on a raid of lush rice plantations along the banks of the Combahee River. Virtually all of the soldiers in the Second South Carolina Volunteers were themselves freed slaves. The following account is drawn from Tubman's testimony about the joyful scene of black soldiers liberating plantation slaves.*

After reading the document, write one *of the following journal entries:*

1. You are a Confederate planter and slavemaster. You are an eyewitness to the events described by Tubman. Write a paragraph or two in reaction to what you see.

2. You are an ex-slave who is one of the soldiers in the Second South Carolina Volunteers. Write a paragraph or two explaining your thoughts and feelings about what happened.

An Eyewitness Account: The All-Black Second South Carolina Volunteers Raid a Plantation to Free Slaves

Company E, Fourth U.S. Colored Infantry, stationed at Fort Lincoln in Dakota Territory.

DOCUMENT ONE

"I never saw such a sight," said Harriet; "we laughed, and laughed, and laughed. Here you'd see a woman with a pail on her head, rice smoking in it just as if she'd taken it from the fire, young one hanging on from behind, one hand hanging around her forehead to hold on, another hand digging into the rice pot, eating with all of its might; holding onto her dress two or three more; down her back a bag with a pig in it. One woman brought two pigs, a white one and a black one; we took them all aboard; named the white pig Beauregard, and the black pig Jeff Davis [two prominent Confederate officials]. Sometimes the women would come with twins hanging around their necks; appears like I never saw so many twins in my life; bags on their shoulders, baskets on their heads, and young ones tagging behind all loaded; pigs squealing, chickens screaming, young ones squalling." And so they came pouring down to the gunboats. When they stood on the shore and the small boats put out to take them off, they all wanted to get in at once. After the boats were crowded, they would hold onto them so that they could not leave the shore. The oarsman would beat them on their hands, but they would not let go; they were afraid the gunboats would go off and leave them, and all wanted to make sure [that they were on] one of these arks of refuge. At length Col. Montgomery [who commanded the unit] shouted from the upper deck, above the clamor of appealing tones, "Harriet you have to give them a song." Then Harriet lifted up her voice and sang:

Of all the whole creation in the east or the west,
The glorious Yankee nation is the greatest and the best.
Come along! Come along! don't be alarmed,
Uncle Sam is rich enough to give you all a farm.

—*An account of* HARRIET TUBMAN's *testimony about the raid of the Second South Carolina Volunteers on June 3, 1863*

Soldiers' Lives: Pain, Glory, Boredom, Excitement

All young soldiers seem to have the same fantasy about going to war. They expect it will be like the games they played as children: they imagine a nice sunny day, both sides standing proud in bright clean uniforms; at the appointed moment, a polite battle begins, and the enemy always cooperates by falling down dead at the right moment.

But childish illusions about war usually disappear after soldiers experience their first battle. The actual battlefield turns out to be a sea of blood and chaos, with opposing armies ruthlessly trying to wipe each other out.

New weapons turned Civil War battlefields into vast killing fields. In the first encounters of the Civil War, Union and Confederate soldiers marched in tight formation toward enemy lines. But powerful Enfield and Springfield rifles, brutally effective from as far away as a quarter of a mile, slaughtered huge numbers of blue (Union) and gray (Confederate) soldiers. By the middle of the war, infantry on both sides stopped marching in tight formations and began digging elaborate trenches and building heavy fortifications to shield themselves from rifle bullets and heavy mortar and artillery fire. These murderous weapons escalated the astounding number of casualties in the Civil War.

How were the early battles fought? By 1863, how did the battlefield and warfare change? Why? More than 600,000 soldiers, north and south, died during the war. Why were the casualties so extraordinarily high? What caused most of the fatalities?

"CALVARY CHARGE AT FAIRFAX COURT HOUSE, MAY 31, 1861." Early in the war, artists often drew highly romantic and very inaccurate pictures. Such feats as firing from the saddle were viewed with great amusement by soldiers in the field, who enjoyed seeing illustrations of their exploits almost as much as they criticized their inaccuracies.

Harper's Weekly, June 15, 1861. American Social History Project.

What happened on the battlefield decisively shaped the course of war. But so did everyday considerations such as sanitation, food, and medical care. Dirty, hungry, sick men are not happy warriors, let alone efficient soldiers. And for front-line infantry, daily life was unbelievably harsh.

Food was often contaminated. But even bad food was in short supply. Sometimes soldiers starved. Hungry fighters searched the belongings of dead enemy soldiers for scraps. Nightmarish conditions meant living in rain-soaked, mud-caked tents, or sleeping in freezing weather without blankets, or baking in the sweltering heat, or fighting off swarms of aggressive mosquitoes.

It was not uncommon to see soldiers go into battle in rags and shoeless. Thorny underbrush turned their feet into a mass of blood and sores. Added to this were the constant horrors of the war itself—the slaughter on the battlefield; the sight of broken and butchered bodies; the screams of the wounded; the terror of seeing close friends killed before their eyes.

Disease proved a more efficient killer than hostile soldiers. For every soldier who died as a result of battle, three died of disease. Measles, dysentery, and malaria became major killers. Polluted water, spoiled food, and exposure to bad weather threatened

How did everyday considerations such as sanitation, food, and medical care shape the course of the war?

"MARYLAND AND PENNSYLVANIA FARMERS VISITING THE BATTLE-FIELD OF ANTIETAM."
As the war progressed and artist-reporters experienced battle firsthand, their illustrations often became more realistic. F. H. Schell sketched the carnage after the battle of Antietam and the morbid curiosity of the local inhabitants.

F. H. Schell, *Frank Leslie's Illustrated Newspaper*, October 18, 1862. American Social History Project.

the health of virtually every soldier. Medical assistance, when any was available, was often primitive and inadequate. Many soldiers preferred death on the battlefield to the terror of the military hospital.

In the first two years of war, as food, sanitation, and medical care deteriorated, a huge number of Union and Confederate soldiers deserted. But in the summer of 1863, after a string of Union victories at Gettysburg and Vicksburg, a newly won confidence began to reappear in Yankee troops. As northern morale rose, Confederate gloom deepened, spreading from the battlefront to the homefront, undermining the rebel cause.

"A HARVEST OF DEATH, GETTYSBURG, JULY 1863." Photographers also covered the war, following the Union Army in wagons that served as traveling darkrooms. Their equipment was bulky and the exposures had to be long, so they could not take action photographs during battle. But photography was graphic; this picture taken on the morning of July 4 showed the northern public that dying in battle lacked the gallantry often represented in paintings and prints.

(Timothy H. O'Sullivan) Alexander Gardner, *Gardner's Photographic Sketch Book of the War*, vol. 1 (1866). Prints and Photographs Division, Library of Congress.

"WHEN A BULLET STRIKES." Photography during the Civil War could only capture the terrible aftermath of battle. It was left to artist-reporters to depict the moment of death. Charles W. Reed drew this sketch along a creek near Petersburg, Virginia, in February 1865.

Charles W. Reed, February 1865. Prints and Photographs Division, Library of Congress.

A Soldiers's Cry: "My God, Will No One Have Mercy and Kill Me?"

DOCUMENT TWO

For four hours I hurried forward on my way to the front of the wagon train and in all that time I was never out of hearing of the groans and cries of the wounded and dying. Scarcely one in a hundred had received adequate surgical aid....Many... had been without food for thirty-six hours. Their torn and bloody clothing, matted and hardened, was rasping the tender, inflamed and still oozing wounds. Very few of the wagons even had a layer of straw in them, and all were without springs. The road was rough and rocky....From near every wagon...came cries such as these:

"Oh my God, why can't I die?"

"My God, will no one have mercy and kill me?"

"Stop! Oh! For God's sake, stop just one minute, take me out and leave me to die by the roadside...."

No heed could be given to any of their appeals....On! on! We must move on....During this one night I realized more of the horrors of war than I had in the preceding two years.

—Letter from a CONFEDERATE OFFICER *about the retreat from Gettysburg, July 1863*

The most painful memories for soldiers were often associated with the aftermath of battle.

A Black Soldier Describes Battle: Grim But Exhilarating

Brief, intense spurts of warfare were often followed by long periods of inactivity. As soldiers waited between battles, they became—depending on the season—too hot, too cold, or too wet, and almost always bored. As Document Three shows, battles could be grim but also exhilarating. The writer is a black Union soldier fighting in a predominantly white unit, the Eighth Connecticut Infantry. He describes fighting around New Bern, North Carolina, a base which the Eighth Connecticut Infantry seized from the Confederates. Some of the slaves pressed into service by the Confederates would escape to New Bern once it came under Union control.

DOCUMENT THREE

March 13....Eleven o'clock, we succeeded in driving off the enemy's pickets [advance detachments]. We are moving on to New Bern. The rebels retreated from the first battery [set of heavy artillery] without discharging a gun. We are in hot pursuit of them; the roads are very muddy; it is raining. Seven and a half o'clock; a halt has been made for the night; we are exposed to a drenching rain. We expect hard work tomorrow.

March 14. Seven o'clock A.M.—We are engaging the rebels. They are behind water and sand batteries. The fight is waxing warm. Many brave souls have been sent to their last account; and a large number of traitors [Confederates] have been made to bite the dust....

Nine o'clock A.M.—The rebels are fighting like devils; they do not give an inch; *their slaves are working their guns*. I cannot stand that....We must win the day, although half our number are slain.

One o'clock P.M.—Thank God! the battle is ended; blood has ceased to flow. Victory perches on our banners, but we have paid dearly for it. At eleven o'clock we broke the enemy's ranks; their right wing gave way. The Eighth with the Fourth and Fifth Rhode Island and the Eleventh [Connecticut] drove their left. They retreated to a third battery which they held till twelve o'clock, when they were again driven from their position. Their flag came down and the stars and stripes were run up in its place, amid the almost deafening shouts of our brave and victorious army.

We have, for two days, fought them in their well constructed batteries and rifle pits covering a space of twelve miles in a dense forest of tall pines and obstinate underbrush...covered with a slippery mud and raining all the time. If it does not satisfy them [the Confederates] that Uncle Sam is in earnest...we will give them another turn....

— WILLIAM H. JOHNSON *recounting the battle
for New Bern, N.C., in a letter published in* Pine and Palm, *the official paper
of the African Civilization Society, April 3, 1862*

*Examining the
documents*

*•Compare and contrast the
descriptions in Documents
Two and Three with the
visual images in the
pictures and illustrations
in this chapter. Do these
descriptions and images
present a positive or negative view of soldiers' lives?
a realistic or exaggerated
view? •Which do you think
had a greater impact on
how people at home imag-
ined the battlefront—
soldiers' letters or magazine illustrations and
photos? Why?*

Soldiers Lives: Race and Freedom

While the first African-American army regiment was organized by abolitionist generals early in 1862, Lincoln did not permit the active recruitment of African Americans into the Union Army until after the Emancipation Proclamation in January 1863. The response was overwhelming. Almost 200,000 African Americans served in the Union Army by war's end; nearly eight out of every ten of these black soldiers were either escaped or liberated slaves. Black soldiers became central to the Union victory and to the course of events following the war.

Many free northern blacks and southern runaways eagerly joined the Union Army. But racism shaped how the Union Army enlisted African Americans, who were slower or reluctant to volunteer. In Union-occupied Louisiana and Mississippi, for example, army squads swept through plantation slave quarters and forced all able-bodied black men to join the military. African Americans throughout the South condemned these policies, which tore families apart and contradicted the spirit and principle of the Emancipation Proclamation.

In some cases it was difficult for African Americans to see any difference between the behavior and attitudes of their former slavemasters and the Union officers. For one thing, the ranks of the Union Army included not only abolitionists from Massachusetts but also slaveholders from Kentucky. Moreover, the Union Army segregated black soldiers into separate units under white leadership and then subjected them to some of the dirtiest, most difficult jobs in the military. In a letter to President Lincoln, a black soldier complained, "We are treated in a different manner....Instead of the musket, it is the spade, wheelbarrow and the axe."

How did racism affect the enlistment and recruitment of African-American soldiers by the Union Army?

"ASSAULT OF THE SECOND LOUISIANA (COLORED) REGIMENT ON THE CONFEDERATE WORKS AT PORT HUDSON, MAY 27, 1863." The bravery of black soldiers is extolled in the pages of *Frank Leslie's Illustrated Newspaper*.

F. H. Schell, *Frank Leslie's Illustrated Newspaper*, June 27, 1863. American Social History Project.

PRIVATE PRYOR MAKES THE NEWS. In 1864, T. B. Bishop photographed escaped slave Hubbard Pryor before and after he enlisted in the Forty-fourth U.S. Colored Infantry. By the time the photographs were transferred to woodblock, appearing in the July 2 edition of *Harper's Weekly* as "The Escaped Slave" and "The Escaped Slave in the Union Army," the "after" Private Pryor had changed. He had become the kind of romantic soldier of which the *Weekly*'s editor thought his readers would approve.

Freedmen and Southern Society Project, University of Maryland; T. B. Bishop, *Harper's Weekly,* July 2, 1864. American Social History Project.

"THE APPEARANCE OF THE DITCH THE MORNING AFTER THE ASSAULT ON FORT WAGNER, JULY 19, 1863." An illustration in a September issue of the *Illustrated London News* depicts the grim aftermath of the attack led by the Massachusetts Fifty-fourth Colored Regiment on the Confederate fort in Charleston Harbor. The engraving was based on an eyewitness sketch dispatched to England on a British ship that had managed to evade the Union Navy's blockade of southern ports.

Frank Vizetelly (F. J. Skill, del.), *Illustrated London News,* September 26, 1863. American Social History Project.

Frederick Douglass: "Fighting Rebels With Only One Hand"

In the first year of the war, northern blacks volunteered for military service only to have the army turn them away. Black and white critics argued that the Union's virtual ban on black participation was unjust and unwise. Among the loudest of these critics was Frederick Douglass, who wrote the following editorial at a time when the North had yet to win a single major battle.

DOCUMENT FOUR

What upon earth is the matter with the American Government and people? Do they really covet the world's ridicule as well as their own social and political ruin?...They are sorely pressed on every hand by a vast army of slaveholding rebels, flushed with success, and infuriated by the darkest inspirations of a deadly hate, bound to rule or ruin....

Our Presidents, Governors, Generals and Secretaries are calling with almost frantic vehemence for men.—"Men! men! send us men!" they scream, or the cause of the Union is gone; ...and yet these very officers, representing the people and the Government, steadily and persistently refuse to receive the very class of men who have a deeper interest in the defeat and humiliation of the rebels than all others....What a spectacle of blind, unreasoning prejudice....

Why does the government reject the Negro? Is he not a man? Can he not wield a sword, fire a gun, march and countermarch, and obey orders like any other....[T]his is no time to fight with one hand when both are needed;....this is no time to fight only with your white hand, and allow your black hand to remain tied....

— FREDERICK DOUGLASS,
"Fighting Rebels With Only One Hand," Douglass Monthly, *August 1861*

"Press Gangs" Raid Freedmen's Homes, Churches, and Schools

Beginning in 1863, squads of Union soldiers employed strong-arm tactics to recruit liberated slaves in occupied areas of the South. Often manned by black soldiers under white officers, these Union "press gangs" raided people's homes, churches, and schools in search of recruits.

Almost from the beginning of the impressment policy, there was vocal, strong protest. In response to the following letter, General Benjamin Butler conducted an investigation and ordered a halt to the practice in occupied Virginia and North Carolina.

DOCUMENT FIVE

To Major General Butler: The undersigned respectfully solicits the attention of the Commanding General to the following facts.

Soldiers stationed at Craney Island under Col. Nelson are daily making arrests of Colored Citizens, in and around Portsmouth and Norfolk, for the purpose of compelling them to volunteer in the U.S. Service.

That these men are taken from their ordinary and necessary avocations; from their houses, workshops, drays, churches and schools and carried to Craney Island against their will, where they are urged to enlist; and if they refuse [they are] subjected to a species of torture to compel them to do so. They are forced to carry a ball, supposed to weigh forty to fifty pounds for several hours in succession.

The undersigned would further represent that these outrages cause much suffering among the poorer families, dependent on the daily wages of these men for support.

—Excerpt from a letter to General Benjamin Butler
from WHITE NORTHERN MISSIONARIES
working in occupied Virginia, December 10, 1863

A Soldier from the Massachusetts Fifty-fifth Infantry Asks:"Why Are We Not Worth as Much as White Soldiers?"

Until late in the war, black soldiers were paid less than whites. After waves of protest, Congress passed legislation in June 1864 granting equal pay. Prominent among the protesters were the African-American troops of the Massachusetts Fifty-fourth and Fifty-fifth infantries. For more than a year, these soldiers refused to take any money at all rather than accept unequal pay from the federal government. Below is a public letter from a soldier of the Massachusetts Fifty-fifth Infantry.

DOCUMENT SIX

Why are we not worth as much as white soldiers? We do the same work they do, and do what they cannot....Just let them think of the charge at Fort Wagner, where the colored soldiers were cruelly murdered by the notorious rebels. Why is it that they do not want to give us our [just] pay when they have already witnessed our deeds of courage and bravery....If we had staid [sic] at home with our fathers and mothers, wives and sisters, and dear ones at home, we could have received from $1.00 to $1.50 per day [$30 to $45 per month from civilian jobs as opposed to a below-poverty wage of $7 a month offered to African-American troops].

—*Excerpt from a letter written by an* UNNAMED SOLDIER IN THE MASSACHUSETTS FIFTY-FIFTH INFANTRY, *published in the* Christian Recorder, *March 5, 1864*

Examining the documents

•What is Frederick Douglass's method of argument in Document Four? How might Douglass answer his own question "Why does the government reject the Negro"?
•In 1861, the Union rejected black soldiers (Document Four). After 1863, however, press gangs actually forced some blacks into service (Document Five). How do you account for the change? Are there any common elements in the policies of rejection and impressment? •In Document Six, is the soldier's argument for equal pay a moral one? an economic one? both?

Freedom

While conditions in the Union Army during most of the war were discriminatory, military service provided African Americans the means for their own liberation. Even though press gangs recruited some by force, the vast majority of slaves and ex-slaves who served in the Union Army did so voluntarily and enthusiastically. This was particularly true in Delaware, Kentucky, Maryland, and Missouri—the four slave states loyal to the Union. Because Lincoln's Emancipation Proclamation did not apply to slaves in these states, the only way slaves there could legally gain their freedom was to join the Union Army. Some slavemasters in these loyal states, doing everything in their power to prevent their slaves from enlisting, resorted to assault, intimidation, and even murder. Still, many thousands of African Americans enlisted, dealing the "peculiar institution" in the border states a blow from which it could never recover.

African-American soldiers quickly distinguished themselves in battle. In 1863, a high Union official wrote that "the bravery of the blacks in the battle of Milliken's Bend

[Louisiana] completely revolutionized the sentiment of the army with regard to the employment of Negro troops. I heard prominent officers, who formerly in private sneered at the idea of Negroes fighting, express themselves after that as heartily in favor of it."

Harper's Weekly, one of the most influential and widely read magazines in the North, commented on the key role of African-American troops in the 1863 assault of Fort Wagner at Charleston, South Carolina, and in battles that enabled the Union to take control of the entire Mississippi River in the western theater of war.

> *Why did so many slaves from Delaware, Kentucky, Maryland, and Missouri join the Union Army?*

At Helena [Arkansas] they bore the brunt of the fighting, and defeated a superior force of the enemy. At Port Huron [Louisiana] they led ... General [Nathaniel P.] Bank's unsuccessful attack on the place, and left half their number in the field. At Charleston, the colored regiment from Massachusetts ... was placed in the front, and sacrificed itself to make way for the white troops that followed. Wherever the Negroes have had a chance, they have given evidence of the most exalted gallantry.

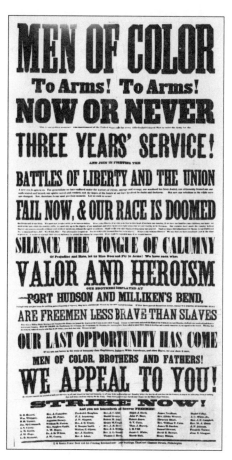

A recruiting poster directed to free African Americans in Pennsylvania, 1863.

The Library Company of Philadelphia.

Black Soldiers in Triumph: "The Colored Troops Were Wild with Joy"

The following account describes African-American soldiers in battle at Petersburg, Virginia, in June 1864.

DOCUMENT SEVEN

...The rebel cannon opened. The sons of Africa did not flinch, but took their positions with deliberation. They had been slaves; they stood face to face with their former master....The [Confederate] flag in front of them waving in the morning breeze was the emblem of oppression; the banner above them was the flag of the free....

The Rebels were on a knoll [a small hill] in the field, and had a clear sweep of all the approaches. The advancing troop must come out of the woods, rush up the slope, and carry it at the point of bayonet, receiving the tempest of musketry and canister [rifle and shells].

[General] Hinks deployed his line. At the word of the command the colored men stepped out from the woods, and stood before the enemy. They gave a volley, and received one in return. Shells crashed through them, but unheeding the storm with a yell they started up the slope upon the run. They received one charge of canister, one scathing volley of musketry. Seventy of their number went down, but the living hundreds rushed on. The Rebels did not wait their coming, but fled towards Petersburg, leaving one of the pieces of artillery in the hands of assailants, who leaped over the works, turned it in a twinkling, but were not able to fire upon the retreating foe, fleeing in consternation [confusion] towards the main line of entrenchments two miles east of the city.

The colored troops were wild with joy. They embraced the captured cannon with affectionate enthusiasm, patting it as if it were animate [alive], and could appreciate the endearment.

"Every soldier of the colored division was two inches taller for that achievement," said an officer describing it.

—*From* CHARLES CARLETON COFFIN,
Four Years of Fighting, *1866*

African-American women also played a role on the battlefield. One such woman, Lydia Penny, was known by Union soldiers as the "Mother of the Army." In a letter written in the winter of 1864, African-American quartermaster sergeant James H. Payne wrote:

> Many of our officers and men who were wounded at the battle of Deep Bottom will never forget the kind deeds of Sister Lydia Penny, who went among them and administered to their wants as they lay weltering in their blood on the banks of the James, near Jones Landing. There she could be seen, the only woman present, like an angel from above, giving words of cheer, and doing all in her power to relieve the suffering....

Death and Discrimination

African-American soldiers had to be courageous. If captured by the Confederate Army, they faced possible torture, enslavement, and death. The Confederate Army tried to intimidate black Union soldiers by its brutal treatment of prisoners. But some white Union generals responded in kind. In April 1863, upon hearing of a Confederate policy to execute captured black soldiers, Major General D. Hunter wrote to Jefferson Davis, the president of the Confederacy: "I now give you notice, that unless this order is immediately revoked, I will at once cause the

THE TABLES ARE TURNED. African-American troops under General Edward Augustus Wild liberate slaves on the Terrebee plantation in North Carolina in January 1864.

Harper's Weekly, January 23, 1864. American Social History Project.

execution of every rebel officer, and every rebel slaveholder in my possession."

Despite Hunter's protest, the murderous Confederate policy toward black Union troops continued. In April 1864, for example, black Union soldiers surrendered at Fort Pillow, Tennessee, only to have the Confederate commander, Nathan Bedford Forrest (future founder of the Ku Klux Klan), order their cold-blooded murder. By war's end, 37,000 black soldiers had died, but few in a manner as hideous and calculated as those at Fort Pillow.

While living and fighting conditions for white Union soldiers were harsh, they were far worse for African-American troops. The death rate for black soldiers was almost three times greater than for white soldiers. Subjected to harsher working conditions and more likely to die of disease, black soldiers did not get equal access to medical care or equipment.

Most black troops, while expecting Confederate soldiers to show them little respect or mercy, were not prepared for the bigotry they confronted in the Union Army. Discrimination took many forms: segregated camps, menial jobs, and racism in the officer corps. But the Union policy of unequal pay for white and black soldiers prompted the strongest and most outraged protests.

What encouraged African Americans to join the Union Army and fight? What discouraged such commitment?

A Struggle for Equality

In November 1863, African-American soldiers in the Third South Carolina Volunteers, unwilling to tolerate unequal pay in the Union Army, put down their rifles and refused to take orders. Union officers used force to end the revolt, executing its leader, African-American Sergeant William Walker. But protests continued until 1864, when the Union Army changed its policy and granted equal pay.

There were other demonstrations against racist treatment. For example, in December 1863, at Fort Jackson, Louisiana, African-American troops revolted when they saw an African-American drummer boy whipped by a white officer. A military court eventually put that officer on trial, found him guilty of "inflicting cruel and unusual punishment," and dismissed him from the army.

The struggle against slavery in the South and against racism in the Union Army transformed many African-American soldiers. They came to understand that the battle for equality would go on after the war and that it would be fought in the North as well as the South. Now steeled in military, political, and social combat, black Civil War veterans would play a critical role in future struggles for African-American rights.

In what specific ways did the Union Army discriminate against African-American recruits?

A Mississippi planter worried that the continued presence of black troops would turn his world of privilege and control upside down. In October 1865, he complained that the "Negro soldiery here are constantly telling our Negroes, that for the next year, the Government will give them lands, provisions, stock and all things necessary to carry on business for themselves." He warned defeated Confederates that the South was "resting upon a volcano—and that if Negro troops are not removed from our midst pretty soon... they will stimulate the Negroes to insurrection...."

Ex-slaves saw the same troops as liberators delivering them from bondage. In the following documents, consider the response to black soldiers as they led Union troops into Charleston, South Carolina, and Richmond, Virginia—two pillars of the Confederacy and all it represented.

DOCUMENT EIGHT

Although we are not allowed to remain in the city of Charleston, yet we claim the largest share in capturing it. On the day we entered the rebellious city, the streets were thronged with women and children of all sizes, colors and grades—the young, the old, the halt, the maimed, and the blind. I saw an old colored women with a crutch—for she could not walk without one, having served all her life in bondage—who on seeing us, got so happy that she threw down her crutch and shouted that the year of the jubilee had come.

—From a letter by SERGEANT J.H.W.N. COLLINS,
March 19, 1865, describing the February 1865 entry
of the Fifty-fourth Massachusetts Infantry into Charleston

DOCUMENT NINE

I have just returned from the city of Richmond; my regiment was among the first to enter that city. I marched at the head of the column, and I soon found myself called upon by the officers and men of my regiment to make a speech with which, of course, I readily complied. A vast multitude assembled on Broad Street, and I was aroused amidst the shouts of ten thousand voices, and proclaimed for the first time in that city freedom to all mankind. After which the doors to all of the slave pens were thrown open, and thousands came out shouting and praising God and Father, or Master Abe [Lincoln], as they termed him. In this mighty consternation, I became so overcome with tears that I could not stand up under the pressure of such fullness of joy in my own heart....

Some of the boys knowing that I lived in Ohio, soon found me and said, "Chaplain, here is a lady that wishes to see you." I quickly turned, following the soldier until coming to a group of retired ladies. I was questioned as follows:

> "What is your name, sir?" *"My name is Garland H. White."* "What is your mother's name?" *"Nancy."* "Where was you born?" *"In Hanover County, in this State."* "Where was you sold from?" *"From this city."* "What was the name of the man who bought you?" *"Robert Toombs."* "Where did he live?" *"In the state of Georgia."* "Where did you leave him?" *"At Washington."* "Where did you go then?" *"To Canada."* "Where do you live now?" *"In Ohio."* "This is your mother, Garland, whom you are now talking to, who has spent twenty years of grief about her son."

I cannot express the joy I felt at this happy meeting of my mother and other friends. But suffice it to say that God is on the side of the righteous, and will in due time reward them. I have witnessed several such scenes among the other colored regiments....

—*From a letter by* GARLAND H. WHITE,
chaplain of the Twenty-eighth U.S. Colored Infantry, April 12, 1865

Examining the Documents

•*Why do you think the presence of black troops (as described in Documents One, Eight, and Nine) excited such joyful celebration among slaves and ex-slaves?*
•*What was the importance of black troops being among the lead regiments as Union armies marched into Charleston and Richmond (Documents Eight and Nine)?*

Suggested Activities

INTERVIEW

Interview a combat veteran who fought in any war in this century about his everyday life as a soldier. First, brainstorm interview questions with classmates. Write a one-page summary of your interview. On a second page, compare and contrast your interviewee's experience with that of Civil War soldiers. Explain the similarities and differences. Compare interviews with classmates and discuss your conclusions.

ROLE PLAY

You are a free black living in Tennessee in an area liberated by Union forces. *Should you join the Union Army?* To help make the decision, draw up a two-column list of (1) positive factors and (2) negative factors for joining. Fill in both columns based on your reading of the text, the documents, and any other materials you have studied. Discuss, compare, and develop your list with classmates. Then write a page explaining your decision to enlist or not.

Arrange a debate between two students—one who decides to enlist, the other who does not.

CROSS TALK AND ROLE REVERSAL

You are a Confederate planter and slave-master. You are an eyewitness to the events described in Documents One, Eight, or Nine (choose one). Write a paragraph or two in reaction to what you see.

Now reverse roles. You are now Harriet Tubman, J.H.W.N. Collins, or Garland White, depending on the document you chose. Write two or three paragraphs in response to those you wrote as the Confederate planter.

Read and discuss your writing in small groups. Compare and analyze the points of view of planters and ex-slaves.

ESSAY

In 1928, historian W. E. Woodward argued that "the American Negroes are the only people in the history of the world so far as I know that ever became free without any effort of their own."

Is Woodward right, partly right, or wrong in his assertion that "American Negroes…became free without any effort of their own?" Write an answer in two pages. Present detailed evidence to support your argument.

IMAGES OF WAR

In small groups, discuss and analyze the illustrations and photographs of war in this chapter. Compare their accuracy and impact on the viewer. Which images do you think most accurately portray the war? least accurately portray the war? Why? What are the advantages and disadvantages of photographs in presenting the war's realities? of illustrations and line drawings? Does the point of view of the illustrators and photographers influence what they focus upon or leave out in an image? If so, give examples.

VIDEO OPTION: *DR. TOER'S MAGIC LANTERN SHOW*

Reread Documents One, Eight, and Nine. Then view *Dr. Toer's Magic Lantern Show* (one of the videos produced by the ASHP that can be used with this text). Pay particular attention to the section in the video featuring Noah Brave, an ex-slave and Union soldier.

After looking at the video and the documents, write a letter as Noah Brave. The letter is to your mother, with whom you and the rest of your family escaped from the Hubbard plantation in North Carolina in 1863. It is now 1865, and you have marched with troops into Charleston. The letter you write will tell your mother your observations and feelings as you enter Charleston. Try to make the letter as personal as possible, relating it to your experience as a son, an ex-slave, a runaway, and a soldier.

VIDEO OPTION: *GLORY*

What are the strengths and weaknesses of film in re-creating historical events and shaping our view of the past? Discuss this question after reading this chapter and then watching *Glory,* a Hollywood film based on the Civil War history of the Massachusetts Fifty-fourth Infantry. (*Glory* can be rented at almost any video store.)

CHAPTER SIX

RETREAT, ADVANCE, AND VICTORY: THE TRIUMPH OF THE UNION

BEFORE READING. *On January 6, 1865, Union General William Tecumseh Sherman issued Field Order Fifteen, one of the most dramatic government actions of the entire war. Having arrived in Savannah, Georgia, in December 1864, after leading his troops on a brutal march from Atlanta to the sea, Sherman announced that millions of acres of land along the Atlantic coast would be turned over to emancipated slaves, in lots of "not more than forty acres" per family.*

What led Sherman to take this dramatic step? What did he hope to achieve? What were the details of his plan? How would it affect the lives of

different groups of people who lived in this area— black and white, enslaved and free? Did the freed slaves get their forty acres? How did they respond to this sudden opportunity? And how did Sherman's action reflect and help shape the larger pattern of events taking place at the end of the Civil War?

Read the text of Sherman's field order and think about the questions listed above. And as you read this chapter, think about what Sherman's action meant in the context of the Union victory, the end of slavery, and the coming of freedom to millions of enslaved African Americans throughout the South.

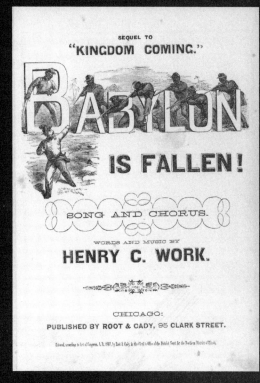

Illustrated sheet-music cover, 1863.
Lilly Library, Indiana University.

In the Field, Savannah, Georgia, January 16, 1865,
Special Field Orders, Number Fifteen, Issued by
General William Tecumseh Sherman

DOCUMENT ONE

I. The islands from Charleston [South Carolina], south, the abandoned rice fields along the rivers for thirty miles back from the sea, and the country bordering the St. Johns River, Florida, are reserved and set apart for the settlement of the negroes now made free by acts of war and the proclamation of the President of the United States.

II. ... [O]n the islands, and in the settlements hereafter to be established, no white person whatever, unless military officers and soldiers, detailed for duty, will be permitted to reside; and the sole and exclusive management of affairs will be left to the freedpersons themselves, subject only to United States military authority and the acts of Congress. By the laws of war, and orders of the President of the United States, the negro is free and must be dealt with as such. He cannot be subjected to conscription [draft] or forced military service, save by the written orders of the highest military authority of the Department [region], under such regulations as the President and Congress may prescribe.... [B]ut the young and able-bodied negroes must be encouraged to enlist as soldiers in the service of the United States, to contribute their share towards maintaining their own freedom, and securing their rights as citizens of the United States.... The bounties paid on enlistment may, with the consent of the recruit, go to assist his family and settlement in procuring agricultural implements, seed, tools, boots, clothing, and other articles necessary for their livelihood.

III. Whenever three respectable negroes, heads of families, shall desire to settle on land, and shall have selected for that purpose an island or a locality clearly defined, within the limits above designated, the Inspector of Settlements and Plantations will by himself, or by such subordinate officer as he may appoint, give them license to settle such island or district, and afford them such assistance as he can to enable them to establish a peaceable agricultural settlement. The three parties named will subdivide the land under the supervision of the Inspector, among themselves and such others as may choose to settle near them, so that each family shall have a plot of not more than (40) forty acres of tillable ground....

IV. Whenever a negro has enlisted in the military service of the United States, he may locate his family at any one of the settlements at pleasure, and acquire a homestead, and all other rights and privileges of a settler, as though present in person.

V. In order to carry out this system of settlement, a general officer will be detailed as Inspector of Settlements and plantations, whose duty it shall be to visit the settlements, to regulate their police and general management, and who will furnish personally to each head of a family, subject to the approval of the President of the United States, a possessory title in writing, giving as near possible a description of boundaries; and who shall adjust all claims or conflicts that may arise under the same, subject to the like approval, treating such titles altogether as possessory....

—*By Order of* MAJOR GENERAL
WILLIAM TECUMSEH SHERMAN,
January 16, 1865

1862–1863: Military Fortunes Shift

From the very beginning, the outcome of the Civil War was in doubt. The military advantage shifted dramatically from South to North during the first two and a half years. In 1862, the Union Army seemed on the verge of defeat. A year later, dispirited Confederate troops sustained huge casualties in battles at Gettysburg (Pennsylvania) and Vicksburg (Mississippi) that changed the course of the conflict.

But battles alone were not enough to determine the ultimate success of either side. Less dramatic factors—transport, food, clothing, and medical care—proved to be of critical importance. With a largely rural economy based on farming and slavery, the Confederacy could not solve these problems. The Union, on the other hand, had a stronger economy and a solid industrial base, and it enjoyed an immense logistical and economic advantage in transport. While the Confederate Army often relied on riverboats and horse-driven wagons to resupply their army, the North built railroads, which more efficiently moved troops, arms, food, and clothing to the battlefield.

Even with the advantage of a stronger economic and industrial base, the Union Army suffered one stunning defeat after another early in the war. But in July 1863, federal troops won two enormous victories, marking the beginning of the Union's military turnaround.

In the east, Robert E. Lee's Confederate Army suffered catastrophic losses at Gettysburg after launching a massive but unsuccessful attack on Union forces. When the battle was over, the Confederate Army counted its casualties: 28,000 men dead, wounded, or missing.

In the west, the Union Army, commanded by General Ulysses S. Grant, continued its assault on the strategic river port of Vicksburg. Since December 1862, Grant had tried to take this city without success. In spring of the following year, he tried a bold new strategy. Keeping his troops on the move before eventually surrounding the port, he cut off all its supplies. In July 1863, Grant finally captured Vicksburg.

Vicksburg was even more of a turning point than Gettysburg. Grant's army captured 30,000 Confederate soldiers, giving

How did the North's superior economic and industrial base give it a military advantage?

How did the battles of Gettysburg and Vicksburg change the military course of the war?

Confederate prisoners captured during the Battle of Gettysburg, photographed on Seminary Ridge by Mathew B. Brady on July 15, 1863.

Mathew B. Brady, stereo #2397, July 15, 1863.
Prints and Photographs Division, Library of Congress.

the Union control of the Mississippi Valley, the richest plantation region in the South. In addition, the North's victory at Vicksburg encouraged slaves to desert southern plantations in greater and greater numbers, many joining the Union's advancing forces.

1864: Lee Retreats, Grant and Sherman Advance

After the defeats at Gettysburg and Vicksburg, the momentum of the war shifted to the North. The northern policy of total war—blocking southern ports, destroying towns and cities, confiscating property, burning cotton, and offering freedom to slaves—was now paying off. By the middle of 1864, Robert E. Lee's famed Virginia army was in full retreat, its size shrinking as a result of massive desertions and deaths on the battlefield. Eventually, General Grant's superior Union Army pushed Lee's depleted troops back toward Richmond.

Meanwhile, Union troops led by General William Tecumseh Sherman invaded Georgia, forcing the Confederate troops under the command of General John Bell Hood to retreat to Atlanta in late August. Within two weeks, Sherman's army took Atlanta, one of the most important cities in the South. The morale of Confederate soldiers and civilians fell to a new low. Perhaps for the first time, many southerners saw the real possibility of

What tactics did Sherman employ in the march across Georgia and the Carolinas?

"CONTRABANDS ACCOMPANYING THE LINE OF SHERMAN'S MARCH THROUGH GEORGIA."
This illustration from a March 1865 *Frank Leslie's Illustrated Newspaper* depicts a stereotyped view of the men, women, and children who followed the Union Army's campaign through Georgia. But to northern readers, the engraving's significance lay in its unmistakable message about slaves' utter hatred of slavery. "The oft expressed fallacy that they preferred slavery to freedom," ran the picture caption, ". . . [has been] 'crushed to earth,' . . . never to rise again."
Frank Leslie's Illustrated Newspaper, March 18, 1865. General Research Division, The New York Public Library, Astor, Lenox, and Tilden Foundations.

SPOILING THE SPOILS OF WAR. Ruins of Richmond smolder on the morning of April 12, 1865. Evacuating southern forces set fires and detonated powder magazines, destroying more than nine hundred buildings in the defeated capital of the Confederacy.

Alexander Gardner, 1865 (ICHi-22115). Chicago Historical Society.

the Confederate Army's defeat and the end of a way of life.

Believing that only brute terror would persuade Confederates to give up the fight, Sherman and his army swept across Georgia, ruthlessly destroying almost everything in their path. As Sherman moved through Georgia, many slaves deserted their plantations and sought the protection of his troops. Ignored or turned away by Sherman's men, large numbers of black Georgians were caught and reenslaved by the marauding remnants of the Confederate Army. The callous action of Sherman and his army caused a scandal in Washington and major embarrassment for President Lincoln.

Lincoln sent Secretary of War Edwin Stanton to Georgia to investigate. Both Stanton and Sherman met with twenty African-American ministers in Savannah to hear their complaints. A few days later, as a result of the meeting, Sherman issued his famous Field Order Number Fifteen. The order set aside almost a half-million acres of captured Confederate land, dividing it into small plots for freed slaves.

What was Sherman's policy toward the slaves who followed his army across Georgia?

In desperation, Jefferson Davis, president of the Confederacy, now sought to make his own deal with black southerners. He called for the recruitment of slaves into the Confed-

"MARCHING ON!" The Fifty-fifth Massachusetts colored regiment sings
"John Brown's March" in the streets of Charleston, February 21, 1865.

Harper's Weekly, March 18, 1865. American Social History Project.

erate Army, offering them pay as well as freedom for themselves and their families. In
early 1865, the Confederate Congress passed
a law allowing African Americans to join its
army. The fact that the South was freeing
African Americans in order to save the Confederacy was one last bit of dramatic evidence
that its war to preserve slavery was all but lost.

Sherman's army left Georgia in February
1865 and moved through South Carolina
and North Carolina. With devastating results,
Sherman used the same slash-and-burn
tactics in these states that he had perfected
in Georgia, effectively destroying what
remained of the southern plantation system.
As Sherman's legions wreaked destruction
to the southeast, Grant's troops caught up
with Lee's staggering army in Richmond,
Virginia, and overpowered it.

Battle-hardened black soldiers under
Grant's command led the final assault on
Richmond. The citizens
of Richmond—both
black and white—
looked on with awe and
disbelief as black fight-
ers marched through
the city carrying the
Union flag and singing
the anthem of John Brown. The war had
come to a dramatic and symbolic climax.
In April 1865, the South conceded defeat.
Lee surrendered, and the most massive
bloodletting in American history was over.

*Why did Sherman
and Stanton meet
with black ministers in
Savannah in January
1865? Why was the
meeting important?*

The Second American Revolution

The Civil War was the nation's second revolution, the final act of a historical era that had begun more than eighty years earlier at the end of the American Revolution. During those eight decades, growing conflict between two economic systems shaped American history—one system based on slavery, the other on free labor. With the end of the war and the passage of the Thirteenth Amendment of the Constitution, slavery—and an oppressive way of life for millions of southerners—was destroyed. The Civil War

"JEFFERSON DAVIS AS AN UNPROTECTED FEMALE!" Union troops' capture of the former president of the Confederacy in May 1865 is caricatured in a *Harper's Weekly* cartoon. Whether Davis, who had eluded arrest for over a month, was actually wearing his wife's dress when he was caught is open to question. Nonetheless, the depiction of the captured Davis in woman's clothes was featured in many illustrations and cartoons in the northern press. These images—like earlier pictures of southern women rioting and sending their men to war—questioned the South's claims of courage and chivalry by showing its men and women reversing traditional sex roles.

Harper's Weekly, May 27, 1865. American Social History Project.

was a revolution that turned relations between races, classes, and sections (North/South/West) on their head. It marked the triumph of a system of free labor over slave labor, cleared the way for economic change in the South by destroying its 250-year-old plantation order, and created new markets, transportation links, and investment opportunities that would propel the development of U.S. capitalism into the twentieth century.

But these revolutionary changes came at great human cost. More than 600,000 Americans—white and black, southern and northern—died in the war. A week after Lee's surrender, President Abraham Lincoln became the final casualty of war, when, on April 14, he was assassinated by John Wilkes Booth, a Confederate sympathizer.

Even as Americans mourned their president and war dead, they faced unresolved questions about the future of the South and the nation. The struggle over these issues, in the historical period called Reconstruction, would determine the course of American democracy and race and labor relations for years to come.

In what sense was the Civil War a revolution?

"MUSTERED OUT." Alfred Waud sketched this scene showing the reuniting of returned African-American soldiers with their families in Little Rock, Arkansas, on April 20, 1866. It was published as an engraving in the May 19, 1866, issue of *Harper's Weekly*.

Alfred R. Waud, April 20, 1866, pencil and gouache. Prints and Photographs Division, Library of Congress.

The Savannah Agenda: A Blueprint for Freedom

As General William T. Sherman's Union troops marched through Georgia, African-American slaves flocked to follow them. Many slaves saw the Union troops as liberators, bringing freedom with fire and sword. Other slaves sought to satisfy more basic needs for food and clothing, for as the Yankees burned and pillaged their way to the sea, they made the area uninhabitable for slaves as well as their masters. By December 1865, when Sherman's army reached the port of Savannah, more than 50,000 refugees from slavery followed in its wake.

Sherman saw the refugees as a nuisance who slowed the furious onrush of his army. The general, a gruff, unsentimental career military man, was indifferent to the human costs of his scorched earth policy. He saw the plight of the refugees as a military issue. Until he could find a way to feed, clothe, and shelter the refugees, tens of thousands of black men, women, and children would clog the gears of his quick-striking war machine.

Sherman conferred with Secretary of War Edwin Stanton, who agreed to join him in Savannah. On January 12, 1865, Stanton and Sherman met with twenty leaders of the Savannah black community — all ministers — to enlist their help in solving the problem. Most of the ministers had been slaves; some had gained their freedom prior to the Civil War.

Sherman and Stanton asked the group as a whole many questions, including:

1. How "can you best take care of yourselves?" (In other words, how can you best provide food and shelter for your families?)

2. How "can you best assist the government in maintaining your freedom?"

3. Where would you rather live "scattered among the whites or in [settlements] by yourselves?"

The ministers answered the questions, and notes taken at the meeting have survived. Partly in response to this conversation, Sherman began preparing his famous Field Order Fifteen (see Document 1).

As you read the notes taken at this meeting, think about who these ministers were, how they answered Sherman's questions, and what this conversation reveals about the goals of freed slaves as the war came to an end.

DOCUMENT TWO

Garrison Frazier being chosen by the persons present to express their common sentiments upon the matters of inquiry, makes answers to inquiries as follows:

FIRST: State what your understanding is in regard to the acts of Congress and President Lincoln's [Emancipation] proclamation, touching the condition of the colored people in the Rebel States.

ANSWER: So far as I understand President Lincoln's proclamation to the Rebellious States, it is, that if they would lay down their arms and submit to the laws of the United States before the first of January, 1863, all should be well; but if they did not, then all the slaves in the Rebel States should be free henceforth and forever. That is what I understood.

SECOND: State what you understand by Slavery and the freedom that was given by the President's proclamation.

ANSWER: Slavery is, receiving by irresistible power the works of another man, and not by his consent. The freedom, as I understand it, promised by the proclamation, is taking us from under the yoke of bondage, and placing us where we could reap the fruit of our own labor, take care of ourselves and assist the Government in maintaining our freedom.

THIRD: State in what manner you think you can take care of yourselves, and how can you best assist the Government in maintaining your freedom.

ANSWER: The way we can best take care of ourselves is to have land, and turn it and till it by our own labor—that is, by the labor of the women and children and old men; and we can soon maintain ourselves and have something to spare. And to assist the Government, the young men should enlist in the service of the Government, and serve in such manner as they may be wanted....We want to be placed on land until we are able to buy it and make it our own.

FOURTH: State in what manner you would rather live—whether scattered among the whites or in colonies [settlements] by yourselves.

ANSWER: I would prefer to live by ourselves, for there is a prejudice against us in the South that will take years to get over; but I do not know that I can answer for my brethren. (Mr. Lynch says he thinks they should not be separated, but live together. All the other persons present, being questioned one by one, answer that they agree with Brother Frazier.)

FIFTH: Do you think that there is intelligence enough among the slaves of the South to maintain themselves under the Government of the United States and the equal protection of its laws, and maintain good and peaceable relations among yourselves and with your neighbors?

ANSWER: I think there is sufficient intelligence among us to do so.

SIXTH: State what is the feeling of the black population of the South toward the Government of the United States; what is the understanding in respect to the present war—its causes and object, and their disposition to aid either side. State fully your views.

ANSWER: I think you will find there are thousands that are willing to make any sacrifice to assist the Government of the United States, while there are also many that are not willing to take arms. I do not suppose there are a dozen men that are opposed to the Government. I understand, as to the war, that the South is the aggressor, President Lincoln was elected President by a majority of the United States, which guaranteed him the right of holding the office and exercising that right over the whole United States. The South, without knowing what he would do, rebelled. The war was commenced by the Rebels before he came into office. The object of the war was not at first to give the slaves their freedom, but the sole object of the war was at first to bring the rebellious States back into the Union and their loyalty to the laws of the United States. Afterward, knowing the value set on the slaves by the Rebels, the President thought that his proclamation would stimulate them to lay down their arms, reduce them to obedience, and help to bring back the Rebel States; and their not doing so has now made the freedom of the slaves a part of the war. It is my opinion that there is not a man in this city that could be started to help the Rebels one inch, for that would be suicide. There were two black men left with the Rebels because they had taken an active part for the Rebels; and thought something might befall them if they stayed behind; but there is not another man. If the prayers that have gone up for the Union army could be read out, you would not get through them these two weeks.

SEVENTH: State whether the sentiments you now express are those only of the colored people in the city; or do they extend to the colored population through the country? and what are your means of knowing the sentiments of those living in the country?

ANSWER: I think the sentiments are the same among the colored people of the State. My opinion is formed by personal communication in the course of my ministry, and also from the thousands that followed the Union army, leaving their homes and undergoing suffering. I did not think there would be so many; the number surpassed my expectation.

EIGHTH: If the Rebel leaders were to arm the slaves, what would be its effect?

ANSWER: I think they would fight as long as they were before the bayonet, and just as soon as they could get away, they would desert, in my opinion.

NINTH: What in your opinion, is the feeling of the colored people about enlisting and serving as soldiers of the United States? and what kind of military service do they prefer?

ANSWER: A large number have gone as soldiers to Port Royal [South Carolina] to be drilled and put in the service; and I think there are thousands of the young men that would enlist....They have suffered so long from the Rebels that they want to shoulder the musket. Others want to go into the Quartermaster's or Commissary's service.

TENTH: Do you understand the mode of enlistments of colored persons in the Rebel States by State agents [of the Union] under the Act of Congress? If yea, state what your understanding is. [NOTE: *African-American freedmen in the Confederate states liberated and occupied by U.S. military forces were recruited to serve in the Union Army. The recruitment, sometimes by force, was done by agents eager to fill the draft quotas of the northern states they represented. Ex-slaves recruited into the Union Army could be substituted for residents of a northern state to fill that state's draft quota.*]

ANSWER: My understanding is, that colored persons enlisted by State agents are enlisted as substitutes, and give credit to the [Union] States, and do not swell the army, because every black man enlisted by a State agent leaves a white man at home; and, also that larger bounties are given or promised by State agents than are [actually] given by the States. The great object [of the Union] should be to push through [crush] this rebellion the shortest way, and there seems to be something wanting in the enlistment by State agents, for it don't strengthen the army, but takes one away for every colored man enlisted.

ELEVENTH: State what, in your opinion, is the best way to enlist colored men for soldiers.

ANSWER: I think, sir, that all compulsory operations should be put a stop to. The ministers would talk to them, and the young men would enlist. It is my opinion that it would be far better for the State agents to stay home, and the enlistments to be made for the United States under the direction of Gen. Sherman.

In the absence of Gen. Sherman, the following question was asked:

TWELFTH: State what is the feeling of the colored people in regard to Gen. Sherman; and how far do they regard his sentiments and actions as friendly to their rights and interests, or otherwise?

ANSWER: We looked upon Gen. Sherman prior to his arrival as a man in the Providence of God specially set apart to accomplish this work, and we unanimously felt inexpressible gratitude to him, looking upon him as a man that should be honored for the faithful performance of his duty. Some of us called upon him immediately upon his arrival, and it is probable he would not meet the Secretary with more courtesy than he met us. His conduct and deportment toward us characterized him as a friend and a gentleman. We have confidence in Gen. Sherman, and think that what concerns us could not be under better hands. This is our opinion now from the short acquaintance and interest we have had. (Mr. Lynch states that with his limited acquaintance with Gen. Sherman, he is unwilling to express an opinion. All others present declare their agreement with Mr. Frazier about Gen. Sherman.)

Some conversation upon general subjects relating to Gen. Sherman's march then ensued, of which no note was taken.

Examining the document

•Why did General Sherman and Secretary Stanton meet with the black ministers?
•Given the content and tone of the questions asked by Sherman and Stanton, what do you think their main goals at the meeting were?
•How did Frazier contrast slavery and freedom?
•What did Frazier think was necessary for ex-slaves to enjoy and defend their newfound freedom?
•Did the ministers advocate integration or segregation for freedmen and women? Why?
•What arguments and evidence did Frazier present to show that ex-slaves would be loyal to the Union rather than the Confederacy?
•Look at question 10, including the explanatory note. Why did Frazier and the other ministers argue against the practice explained in the note? Did they think it important that freedmen fight in the Union Army? If so, why and how should they have been recruited? •Reread Sherman's Field Order Number Fifteen (Document One, pages 128–29). Does the order address all the concerns expressed by the black ministers to Stanton and Sherman at the January 12 meeting in Savannah?

Skidaway Island: "It Was Plymouth Colony Repeating Itself"

Four days after Sherman met with twenty African-American ministers in Savannah, he issued Field Order Number Fifteen. (See pages 128–29) By military decree, he allocated land to the refugees, provided for their defense, and encouraged their self-governance.

The order distributed more than 400,000 acres of land along the southeastern Atlantic coast from South Carolina to Jacksonville, Florida. More than 40,000 slaves settled on abandoned plantations, most of them on the islands and coast of South Carolina. The order called for possession of the land, but left the question of ownership unsettled.

Responsive to the ministers' argument for separation, Sherman's order prohibited all but a few whites from settlement on the abandoned plantations and promoted self-government by decreeing that "the sole and exclusive management of affairs will be left to the freedpersons themselves, subject only to United States military authority and the acts of Congress." The field order called on the ex-slaves to extend and defend their freedom, emphasizing that "young and able-bodied negroes must be encouraged to enlist as soldiers of the United States."

With the ink barely dry on Sherman's order, the Reverend Ulysses Houston, one of the twenty ministers who had met with Stanton and Sherman, led a band of black refugees to Skidaway Island off the Georgia coast. The settlement on Skidaway Island became a model of what the ministers meant when they argued that blacks wanted to set up their own self-governing communities. A northern reporter who accompanied the settlers to the island gave the following report about their pioneering, democratic zeal.

DOCUMENT THREE

Last Friday, a party with Rev. Mr. Houston, pastor of the Third African Baptist Church, went down to Skidaway Island to select their future homes. Mr. Houston (who was a slave until six weeks ago) is now forty years old. In his early years, he was a nurse in the marine hospital. He had an earnest desire to learn to read and by his kind attention to the sailors was enabled to do so.

He hired his time [bought the right to work for himself] paying his master fifty dollars a month, and establishing himself as a butcher. He went all over eastern Georgia, purchasing cattle, but employing all his spare hours learning to read, studying the bible and theology. He was ordained to preach by the Baptist Association of white ministers three years ago.

The questions raised by freedpeople on Skidaway Island about titles and land ownership would not go away. Within a month, Confederate planters were petitioning Union military authorities for return of their land on Skidaway Island. Eventually, President Andrew Johnson (who took office after Lincoln's death) pardoned the planters and returned their land, effectively ending this experiment in democracy on Skidaway Island.

He and his fellow colonists selected their lots, laid out a village, numbered the lots, put the numbers into a hat, and drew them out. It was Plymouth colony repeating itself.

"We shall build our cabins and organize our town government for the maintenance of order and the settlement of difficulties," said Mr. Houston....

In one day five thousand acres were assigned to the colonists eager to till them. A large party went down this morning with what provisions they could carry. They go out to commence life as citizens.

Yesterday, there was a meeting of these men at the old slave market. The room was crowded. They came together to hear remarks from Rev. Mr. French and Lieut. Ketchum [a Union officer], to ask questions and consult with each other. They wanted to know what title they would have to their land— what assurances they could have that it would be theirs after they had improved it. Their questions were plain, straightforward, and showed a shrewdness which I had not looked for.

—*Reported in the* NATIONAL FREEDMAN, *April 1865*

Examining the document

- *What do you think the reporter meant when he wrote that Skidaway Island "was Plymouth colony repeating itself"?*
- *What is the attitude of the reporter from the* National Freedman *toward what Houston and his followers were doing on Skidaway Island? What evidence would you give to support your answer?*

Suggested Activities

DISCUSSION

Consider what would have happened if President Andrew Johnson had not returned abandoned land on Skidaway Island to Confederate planters. What if, instead, he had given full ownership to Houston and his followers? What if the U.S. government, following the Savannah blueprint after the Sherman-Stanton meeting with black ministers, had established hundreds of separate, independent communities of African-American landholders in the area covered by Sherman's Field Order Number Fifteen? Would the history of race relations and prejudice in the United States since the Civil War have been different?

VISUAL IMAGES AND CREATIVE WRITING

Write a short story (one to two pages) or poem about one of the pictures in this chapter. Share and discuss what you wrote with classmates.

A Visit from the Old Mistress. In Winslow Homer's 1876 painting, an old plantation mistress visits the home of three of her former slaves. The coolness of the freedwomen's greeting, in sharp contrast to the reception the mistress would have received during slavery, suggests emancipation's impact on southern race relations.

Winslow Homer, *A Visit from the Old Mistress*, 1876, oil on canvas, 18 x 24 ⅛ inches. National Museum of American Art, Washington, D.C.

PART THREE

RECONSTRUCTION

1861	Union troops occupy the Sea Islands off the South Carolina coast in November.
1862	The Homestead Act, passed in May, provides western lands for pioneer farmers.
1862–90	Federal, state, and local governments distribute 180 million acres of free land to railroads, an area equal in size to New York and the six New England states.
1863	Lincoln announces a lenient plan to readmit occupied Confederate states to the Union. He promises to recognize governments in these states established by 10 percent of the 1860 electorate.
1865	General William Tecumseh Sherman issues Field Order Number Fifteen in January, authorizing ex-slaves to take possession of more than 400,000 acres of abandoned coastal plantations from South Carolina to Florida.
	In March, Congress establishes the Bureau of Refugees, Freedmen, and Abandoned Land, known as the Freedmen's Bureau. The Freedmen's Bureau promises to lease confiscated lands in forty-acre tracts to freedmen and "loyal white refugees."
	Lincoln is assassinated in April; Andrew Johnson becomes president. Congress passes and the states ratify the Thirteenth Amendment outlawing slavery.
	President Johnson offers amnesty in May to most Confederates. Under the amnesty plan, southern planters reclaim abandoned lands occupied by freedmen. Johnson establishes easy terms for readmission of seceded states.
	Southern states in the summer and fall establish "black codes" limiting the movement and controlling the labor of ex-slaves.
	In September, Congressman Thaddeus Stevens proposes confiscation and redistribution of southern plantation lands in a speech in Lancaster, Pennsylvania.
	"Colored Conventions" convene throughout the South in the fall to protest black codes and demand full civil rights.
	African Americans begin building hundreds of schools and independent churches throughout the South.
1866	In February, President Johnson vetoes the Civil Rights Act and legislation extending the life of the Freedmen's Bureau. Congress overrides both vetoes.

In February, Congress refuses to seat newly elected Senators and Representatives from southern states admitted under President Johnson's plan of Reconstruction and appoints a joint committee to investigate conditions in the South.

By June, the Fourteenth Amendment, granting freedmen citizenship and protecting their civil rights, passes both houses of Congress. The failure of the drafters of the amendment to address the right of women to vote prompts a split in the reform movement between supporters of black and female suffrage.

The (first) Ku Klux Klan is founded in Tennessee.

1867   By March, Congress passes a Reconstruction plan that divides the South into five military districts, calling for new constitutional conventions and giving the vote to freedmen.

Union Leagues throughout the South mobilize black and poor white candidates and voters for elections of delegates to state constitutional conventions.

1868   Radical Republican state and county governments are elected across the South.

By July, the Fourteenth Amendment is ratified, mainly with support from southern states, whose approval was required as a condition of readmission to the Union.

Stalwarts (moderates) gain control of the national Republican party as Radicals decline sharply in influence.

Ulysses S. Grant is elected president in November on the Republican slate; reelected in 1872.

1869   The Fifteenth Amendment is passed by Congress prohibiting states from denying the right to vote on "account of race, color or previous condition of servitude."

1870   States ratify the Fifteenth Amendment.

1870–71   Congress passes the Ku Klux Klan and Enforcement Acts.

1871   The U.S. government no longer recognizes Indian tribes as sovereign nations, and in the next thirty years confiscates sixty percent of their land.

1873–76   A nationwide depression weakens northern and Republican commitment to Reconstruction.

1875   Democrats launch the "Mississippi Plan," a successful campaign of intimidation and violence to regain control of the Mississippi state government.

1876   Democrats regain control of South Carolina, Louisiana, and Florida, using methods similar to those employed in Mississippi.

1877   Rutherford B. Hayes becomes president as a result of the Compromise of 1877 and ends Reconstruction.

Federal troops are removed from the South at the end of Reconstruction and used against labor in the nationwide railroad strikes of 1877.

1880–1900   Black and white sharecroppers become caught in a cycle of constant indebtedness. African Americans begin to lose their right to vote.

1# INTRODUCTION

"THE BOTTOM RAIL IS NOW ON TOP"

When the Confederate Army surrendered in April 1865, the planters who ruled the South had lost more than a war. Stripped of political power, their slaves now free, their land ravaged, and their investments in Confederate war bonds worthless, the planters stood naked before a world seemingly turned upside down. As one ex-slave put it, "The bottom rail is now on top."

The defeat of the planter class disrupted social, political, and economic relationships built over the previous 250 years of southern

"PARDON AND FRANCHISE." "Shall I Trust These Men?" Columbia, symbol of the Union, asks as she gestures toward former Confederate politicians and officers recently pardoned by President Johnson. In the second panel of this August 1865 *Harper's Weekly* cartoon, she presents a black veteran who has not yet received the right to vote, adding: "...And not this man?"

history. The future relationships between classes and races and the nature of politics, economics, and culture in the postwar South were open questions in 1865.

There were political issues. Who would rule the South? Who would have the right to hold political office? to vote? to participate as a full citizen of the United States?

There were economic issues. In an overwhelmingly agricultural economy, who would own the land? Who would work it, and on what terms?

What was meant by the phrase "the bottom rail is now on top"?

There were social issues with enormous significance for the future of race relations and everyday life in the South. Would that future be one of increasing equality, or continued inequality? What role would ex-slaves play in shaping their own freedom? in creating a New South? in building churches, schools, and independent African-American communities?

The future of American democracy hung on the answers to these questions. Reconstruction represented a dramatic moment in

What were the biggest issues in 1865 that would determine the future of the South?

U.S. history that opened possibilities for the realization of American democracy in the broadest sense— rule by the people. Ordinary men and women—ex-slaves, poor whites, black and white veterans of the Union Army—were poised to make history; to take control of their own destinies and that of the South; and to undo 250 years of slavery and inequality.

During Reconstruction, the struggle over the future of democracy in the South would have huge consequences for the next hundred years of relations between races and sections in the United States. The players in this historic drama represented a cross section of national and regional interests— the Republican and Democratic parties, northern businessmen, poor southern whites, abolitionists, missionaries, adventurers, and reformers. But none had a greater stake or impact than ex-slaves and ex-masters.

The African Americans who took the historical stage during Reconstruction were no longer slaves but rather free men and women who sought to carve out new lives for themselves free of their masters, independent of white supervision, and outside of the capitalist marketplace. For many

Who were the players in this historic drama? Which players had the greatest impact on what happened?

ex-slaves, freedom was a vision of emancipated men and women praying in black churches and learning in black schools; of reunited families removing women and children from field labor and rebuilding households battered by slavery; and of men working their own land as self-sufficient farmers and voting as citizens with full political rights. Reacting to generations of slavery and white domination, most freedpeople

PLAYERS—participants

CAPITALIST—one who owns a business (e.g., industrial, mining, agricultural, or service) and hires wage labor to produce goods for the market and profit

CAPITALISM—a system in which (1) most of the factories, mines, farms, and services are owned by capitalists; (2) profit determines what is produced; and (3) goods, services, and labor are bought and sold in the market

predictably wanted to be left alone. Given a little space, a piece of land, some learning, and a few political rights, they could take care of themselves and begin to work out the meaning of their freedom. It was a vision of freedom that included neither the planter and plantations nor the capitalist and his visions of economic expansion. The freedpeople knew plantation life and wanted nothing of it; they knew next to nothing of the capitalist marketplace and values, and therefore capitalism did not significantly influence their view of the future.

Freedmen and women now had a unique opportunity to shape their own history and that of the nation. But that history could only be made as a result of interaction with other historical actors. Planters, with diametrically opposed interests and a view of the South's future that looked a lot like its past, were the freedpeople's main antagonists. Ex-masters schemed to reinvent a plantation economy worked by black labor with restricted physical and economic mobility. What they proposed looked like slavery, sounded like slavery, and felt like slavery. But they gave it another name— a legal disguise called a "black code." In opposition, the freedmen and women looked away from the past and toward a future that would expand political rights and the ownership of land, enabling them to farm their own property and control their own labor.

DIAMETRICALLY—absolutely or totally

ANTAGONIST—opponent

BLACK CODES—laws intended to confine ex-slaves to plantation labor

DISENFRANCHISE—to deprive of the right to vote

AGENDA—program

Ex-masters, who had always ruled the South, had everything to lose by change; ex-slaves, who had always been the ruled, had nothing to lose and everything to gain. Of all the historical actors in Reconstruction, none defined their self-interest more clearly (and in reaction to one another) than the ex-slave and the ex-master. The history of Reconstruction moved back and forth between two opposing magnetic poles—one, the interests of the freedmen and women, and the other, the interests of the planter. In the middle, attracted to one side or the other, at times wavering in their allegiances, were poor white southerners and a host of northerners with varied political, economic, and social agendas.

What did ex-slaves want for themselves? How did they see the future of the South? What did the planters want?

Who had the most to gain by change? to lose? Why?

Disenfranchised poor white farmers could make common cause with disenfranchised poor black farmers on issues such as land redistribution, labor contracts, debtor protection, universal public education, and the right to vote; or, given the ugly but powerful legacy of more than two centuries of racism in the South, they could make common cause with the planters on the basis of white supremacy and the promise of a few political rights.

With whom did poor whites side—ex-planters or ex-slaves?

Abolitionists, radicals, and other northern Republican friends of the freedpeople were also pulled in different directions: on the one hand, there was the promise of equality in the South; on the other, there was the reality of existing and newly developing inequality in the North. Just how far could they push the agenda for racial and social justice in the South, when so many northern states after the Civil War still denied African Americans the rights of full citizenship, including the right to vote? How could they advocate equality in the South when corporations of heretofore unimaginable riches and power were creating new extremes in wealth and poverty in the North and West and changing the very face of the ruling Republican party? The more astute planters played on these racial and economic tensions. They courted northern investors while trying to isolate freedpeople from their northern Republican allies. As the alliances involving different races, different classes, and different regions shifted, advantage first swung to the planters, then to the freedpeople, and finally back to the former slaveholders. Reconstruction and the future of race relations teetered in the balance.

How did political decisions made in Washington, D.C., affect what happened in the South during Reconstruction?

The advantage shifted when either the president or the Congress of the United States took crucial actions affecting Reconstruction. Political decisions made in Washington, D.C., often determined what was politically possible in the defeated Confederacy. In turn, political power in the states, parishes, and counties of the postwar South largely decided the economic fate of ex-slaves and ex-masters. Former masters could not coerce African

Why was political power so important to the ex-slaves

Americans to work their plantations without the legal and police powers of the state. And without political power, the emancipated slave, as one southern editor put it, was "free, but only free to labor" on terms set by the planters. Federal intervention often proved decisive in determining which political alliance would rule the South—a Democratic party coalition led by planters and built on white racism, or a Republican party coalition that included northerners (who settled in the region after the war) and some poor southern whites, but that depended on the votes of ex-slaves as the solid core of its electoral support.

In the following chapter, focus on the political, social, and economic questions raised at the beginning of this introduction. How were these questions resolved? What did the struggle over these questions mean for the future of American democracy and race relations?

Consider the behavior of the men and women of different classes, races, and regions who had a stake in what was happening. What did the different actors in this historical drama want? How did they interact with one another?

Focusing on these historical actors—particularly the ex-slaves—weigh what others did to them, and what others did for them. But more important, evaluate what they did for themselves. How did they shape history, and how did history shape them?

ASTUTE—smart, clever

TEETER—to walk or move unsteadily

PARISH—a county, community, or local division of government

CHAPTER SEVEN

"NOBODY KNOWS THE TROUBLE I FEEL"

A Rehearsal for Reconstruction on the Sea Islands

BEFORE READING. *This chapter traces the stormy relationship between freedpeople and white northern reformers on the South Carolina Sea Islands between 1861 and 1866. While united in their hatred of slavery and support for the Union, the white northerners and black Sea Islanders sometimes clashed sharply over issues about land and labor. The differences involved questions of who should own land and under what conditions ex-slaves should work it. What makes this interaction so fascinating is that it took place during the Civil War and in the absence of southern whites. As a result, northern reformers and southern freedmen had a unique opportunity to reconstruct the slave plantation economy of the Sea Islands. That opportunity, while creating exciting possibilities for change, nonetheless exposed a negative as well as positive side to the relationship between northern reformers and ex-slaves.*

Invading the Sea Islands in November 1861, Union troops freed the slaves and occupied plantations abandoned by their fleeing Confederate masters. Union officials then took control of these lands, putting freedmen and women to work for modest wages. Edward Philbrick, a northern abolitionist who came to the Sea Islands, worked as a plantation supervisor for the United States government. He wanted to demonstrate that African Americans could produce more cotton as free  *wage labor than they did as slaves. But in his first encounter with the ex-slaves in April 1862 (Document One), Philbrick observed that they did not want to grow cotton, even for a wage.*

Almost two years later, in March 1863, Philbrick purchased the plantations he once supervised. The ex-slaves now worked directly for him. But they were not happy with Philbrick. In March 1864, they sent a petition to President Abraham Lincoln.

"CARVED FROM LIFE." This ivory bust was carved by a Union soldier in 1865. According to the inscription on its base, it is a sculpture of Nora August, Twenty- years old, "Purchased from the Market, St. Augustine, Florida[,] April 17th, 1860/ Now a Free Woman," living in St. Simon's Island, Georgia. August's hair is braided in a traditional West African style.

Sea Island Company, Saint Simon's Island, Georgia.

The first five paragraphs of the petition appear below, identified by the heading "We the undersigned." The entire petition is reprinted later in the chapter.

Read Philbrick's April 1862 observations (Document One) and the ex-slaves' March 1864 petition (Document Two). Why are freedpeople reluctant to produce cotton? Why doesn't Philbrick think that the freedpeople's "republican spirit" should "be encouraged at present"? Why are the ex-slaves so angry at Philbrick, a northern abolitionist who is paying them to work as free men and women? Why is there so much tension between Philbrick and the ex-slaves?

In a paragraph or two, answer these questions based on your reading of the excerpts below. As you read the text and see the story unfold, see if you were able to predict the nature of the conflict between Philbrick and the ex-slaves.

Ex-Slaves Ask: "What's the Use of Working for Our Driver or Massa"?

DOCUMENT ONE

People all start in the cotton field in good humor. Driver is called off by Mr. S. [the cotton agent from the U.S. Treasury Department] to furnish him with a crew; while he is absent from the field, the people mostly women and children say among themselves, "Here are twenty-four of our husbands and brothers gone to work for their own selves, what's the use of working for our driver or massa [the Yankee agent]—let's go to work for ourselves too," and away they scatter. The greater part go to work listing [choosing] ground in detached patches scattered all over 300 acres in a most republican spirit, but not in a way to be encouraged at present. Some go catching crabs; some go planting corn on their own hook. All leave the field early.

—*Letter from* EDWARD PHILBRICK, *April 11, 1862*

A Petition: "We The Undersigned"

DOCUMENT TWO

We the undersigned, believing that we are unfairly dealt with, are led to lay before you…our grievances… [and] our petition.…

OUR GRIEVANCES

Mr. Edward Philbrick (a northern man) has bought up all of our former masters' lands under false pretenses.

Before buying he promised to sell us again any amount of the land at one dollar per acre we wished to purchase. Said sale was to be made whenever the government sold the balance of its land [property abandoned by ex-masters] to people [ex-slaves] residing thereon.…

We have gone to Mr. Philbrick and asked him to sell us our land…[He] will not sell us one foot, and if he does sell to anyone he will charge $10 per acre. We have worked for Mr. Philbrick the whole year faithfully, and have received nothing comparatively, not enough to sustain life if we depended entirely upon our wages. He has stores charging us fearful prices for every necessary of life, and at last the people have become discouraged, almost heartbroken.

He will not pay us [in the form of] land [nor] pay us [enough] to work for him. And if we wish to work for others where we might make something, he turns us out of our houses. He says we will not live on his plantations unless we work for him.

—*Excerpt from a petition to President Abraham Lincoln signed by*
NINETEEN FREEDPEOPLE FROM
SAINT HELENA ISLAND,
March 1, 1864

Big Questions About Land and Labor

On November 7, 1861, early in the Civil War, a fleet of Union gunboats sailed into Port Royal Sound off the coast of South Carolina and bombarded the Sea Islands. Slaves on the islands later recalled it as the "day of the big gun shoot" when masters and overseers fled in panic. As they made hasty preparations to leave, Confederate planters ordered their field hands and house servants to accompany them. Those masters who believed their slaves to be loyal and obedient were rudely surprised when most not only remained, but hundreds participated in the sacking of luxurious town houses owned by the local planter aristocracy in Beaufort, the islands' main port. Others destroyed cotton gins, figuring if "King Cotton" couldn't be processed, cotton, the staple crop of the plantation slave economy, would no longer rule their lives. In just five days from the time of the first naval bombardment until the Union Army's occupation of Beaufort, slaves destroyed many of the symbols of a two-hundred-year-old plantation economy.

Why did ex-slaves target cotton gins for destruction?

Once the planters left, missionaries, schoolteachers, and Union officials, many of them abolitionists, descended upon the islands. What historian Willie Lee Rose has called a "Rehearsal for Reconstruction" began on the Sea Islands in late 1861,

EDISTO ISLAND, SOUTH CAROLINA, 1862. Freedpeople plant sweet potatoes.

H. P. Moore, 1862 (neg. 37628). Collection of The New-York Historical Society.

more than three years before the Civil War ended. The dramatic liberation of slaves, the sudden disappearance of southern planters, and the arrival of northern reformers led to positive changes of immense significance, and to bitter conflict as well.

On occasion, there were tensions between northerners and freedpeople. Nonetheless, Reconstruction in the coastal regions of South Carolina started earlier, lasted longer, cut deeper, empowered more ex-slaves than elsewhere, and raised more sharply the central question about the future of Reconstruction: Who would own land, who would work it, and on what terms?

STAPLE—a major crop of a region that is produced for the market

Philbrick Preaches Cotton and Free Labor

In March 1862, the first boatload of northern missionaries and schoolteachers arrived on the Sea Islands. Called "Gideonites," these northerners were antislavery crusaders who went South under wartime conditions to perform "good works."

The Gideonites were full of contradictions. Some did immense good, others did not. Some were condescending saviors who saw their mission on the Sea Islands as civilizing black "savages" by teaching them what they saw as the virtues of cleanliness, proper dress, self-denial, moral contentment, and hard

CONDESCENDING—acting with an air of superiority

The former slave quarters of a plantation in Hilton Head, South Carolina, 1862.

H. P. Moore, 1862. Collection of The New-York Historical Society.

work. Others treated the ex-slaves with respect as equals, learned from them, taught them the important skills of reading, writing, and arithmetic, and militantly supported their calls for the redistribution of abandoned plantations to the African-American men and women who worked them.

The Union government appointed a few of these northern antislavery reformers to manage the lands abandoned by the planters and to oversee the labor of ex-slaves. Motivated by both economic and moral goals, some abolitionists hoped to prove that free wage labor could produce more cotton at less cost than slave labor (and thereby help convince the North as early as 1861–62 to free all the South's slaves). Given this mix of economic and moral motives, there was frequently tension among the northerners teaching, preaching, and overseeing on the Sea Islands.

Most ex-slaves did not want to grow cotton or produce for the market. They generally refused to work in groups, or gangs, under white direction, even as wage earners. Sea Island freedpeople associated white supervision, gang labor, and cotton production with slavery.

In 1862, the first full year of Union occupation of the Sea Islands, African Americans showed much more enthusiasm for growing corn and potatoes than cotton. As one missionary superintendent observed, "the caterpillar got into the cotton and the negroes didn't."

Were freedmen more interested in (1) subsistence farming for themselves and their families; or (2) cotton production for the market? Explain. What is the evidence for your answer?

No one was more disappointed than Edward Philbrick, an abolitionist from Boston who came to the Sea Islands to demonstrate the superiority of free over slave labor in the cultivation of cotton. Over the next three and a half years, controversy swirled around Philbrick as northern superintendents and ex-slaves clashed over issues of land and labor.

When he first arrived on the Sea Islands, Philbrick took a position as a superintendent of ex-slave labor on a cotton plantation then under the control of the occupying Union Army. By year's end, Philbrick was supervising other superintendents and managing several plantations abandoned by their Confederate owners and seized by the U.S. Treasury Department.

A woman of the Sea Islands.

R. A. Holland, ed., *Letters and Diary of Laura M. Towne* (1912). American Social History Project.

Philbrick wanted to apply the principles of running a northern factory to southern agriculture. Using words and terms like *wage labor, investment, joint-stock company, marketplace,* and *profit,* he spoke the language of capitalism—a language unfamiliar to Sea Island freedpeople. Early in 1863, convinced that only a system of wage labor could make freed slaves productive and cotton production profitable, Philbrick organized a company of sixteen partners. On March 9, 1863, Philbrick's enterprise purchased 8,000 acres of eleven confiscated plantations from the U.S. government at the absurdly low price of less than a dollar an acre. Leasing two other estates, Philbrick and his associates controlled one-third of St. Helena Island, an area comprising thirteen plantations inhabited by 1,000 ex-slaves.

But the road to profit was full of obstacles, one of which was the stubborn resistance by ex-slaves to the cultivation of cotton and plantation labor. In March 1863, Philbrick wrote a letter describing the situation.

> We found them [to be] a herd of suspicious savages who regarded their change of condition with fear and trembling. [They were] looking to the cotton-field as a life-long scene of. . . [unending] toil, and hailing with delight the prospect of "no more driver, no more cotton, no more lickin." They had broken up the cotton-gins and hidden the iron-work, and nothing was more remote from their shallow pates [heads] than the idea of planting cotton for "white folks" again.

Philbrick observed that freedmen and women would rather hunt, fish, and farm their modest plots of vegetables. In this way, they could both provide for their families

CAPITALIST/CAPITALISM—see definitions on page 148

and enjoy their new liberty free from the backbreaking labor of the cotton fields. Since Philbrick wanted to produce cotton, this created a dilemma.

He responded in two ways: One, he compromised, and two, he let his superintendents carry guns. At the Coffin Point plantation, Philbrick recognized that the hands would not work the cotton fields as gang labor. He gave in, assigning each family land to grow their own vegetables and organizing a modified task system in the cotton fields. Instead of paying a set daily wage, he gave a fee for each task performed (e.g., planting, hoeing). But if that carrot didn't work, maybe the stick would. Philbrick allowed superintendents under his supervision to openly display their pistols, which they sometimes waved to threaten particularly stubborn field hands.

What does Philbrick's language tell us about his attitudes toward the emancipated slaves? What particular words or terms show these attitudes?

Documents two, three, and four, which follow, continue this story of conflict between Philbrick and the ex-slaves working land under his supervision.

Freed People Petition the President

The recently emancipated slaves on Philbrick's lands were not happy with the situation. A number of them sent a petition to President Abraham Lincoln.

A Petition

This is a fuller version of a document excerpted in the prereading exercise.

PRETENSE an outward appearance

DOCUMENT TWO

We the undersigned, believing that we are unfairly dealt with, are led to lay before you…our grievances…[and] our petition.…

OUR GRIEVANCES

Mr. Edward Philbrick (a northern man) has bought up all of our former masters' lands under false pretenses.

Before buying he promised to sell us again any amount of the land at one dollar per acre we wished to purchase. Said sale was to be made whenever the government sold the balance of its land [property abandoned by ex-masters] to people [ex-slaves] residing thereon.…

We have gone to Mr. Philbrick and asked him to sell us our land… [He] will not sell us one foot, and if he does sell to anyone he will charge $10 per acre. We have worked for Mr. Philbrick the whole year faithfully, and have received nothing comparatively, not enough to sustain life if we depended entirely upon our wages. He has stores charging us fearful prices for every necessary of life, and at last the people have become discouraged, almost heartbroken.

He will not pay us [in the form of] land [nor] pay us [enough] to work for him. And if we wish to work for others where we might make something, he turns us out of our houses. He says we will not live on his plantations unless we work for him.

If we go to General Saxton [the Union military commander for the Sea Islands], he tells us if Mr. Philbrick sees fit he will sell us the land according to [the] agreement. If not, then we must go on government land where we can buy as much as we please. But the [government] tax commissioners [who are supervising the sale] say they cannot sell to us unless we are living on the plantations now selling.

[When] we go to the superintendent general of the island, Mr. Tomlinson [who administers the lands abandoned by Confederate planters], he says work for Mr. Philbrick for whatever wages he sees fit to pay. If we do not, Philbrick may drive us off the land and we shall not take our houses with us. He says Mr. Philbrick bought everything: houses, lands and all.

Why did the government sell all of our masters' land for so trifling a sum? We are ready and willing, of truth anxious, to buy all of our masters' land and everything upon them; and pay more than he did for them.

We will not attempt to lay all our grievances before you as it will take much too long. We will only mention one case which exceeds anything mentioned in our masters' time. Charles Ware, an agent of Mr. Philbrick's, turned the clothes of a colored girl over her head [and then] turned her over a barrel and whipped her with a leather strap. She had been confined [given birth] but two days before and although the case was reported to Mr. Tomlinson, superintendent general, the agent still retains his place. This is shameful. We blush [to] write or send it [to] you, but the truth must be told. But you may ask what we would have done.

If possible, we pray for either one of these two things:

First. Either let Mr. Philbrick be compelled to live up to his promises with us, and sell us as much land as we want for our own homes at a reasonable price, giving us clear deeds for the same.

Second. Otherwise we pray [the] government to repurchase the land of Mr. Philbrick and then let us farm it giving one half of all that is raised to the government. We would much rather this and will furnish everything ourselves and will warrant that there will be but few feet of ground idle. As Mr. Philbrick has broken his part of the contract, is government bound to keep theirs?

And we will mention that many of us told Mr. Philbrick not to buy the land as we wanted it ourselves.

Third. And we furthermore beg that an agent may be sent us who will see not wrong, but right.... We do not want a master or owner... [or] a driver with his whip. We want a friend.

Trusting that this may be looked upon kindly, begging an immediate answer that we may know what to do. We are with very great respect your most humble and obedient servant.

—*A petition to President Abraham Lincoln*
signed by NINETEEN FREEDPEOPLE FROM
SAINT HELENA ISLAND, *March 1, 1864*

GULLAH — African-American Sea Islanders spoke the Gullah dialect, a mix of English and African languages. The isolation and almost totally African-American population of the islands explains the survival of strong African traditions and customs. Most planters on the islands were absentee owners even before the Civil War. Hence, unlike the mainland, white planter culture was not dominant.

Below are examples of common Gullah words that trace their origins to West African languages and in some cases have been adapted into the English language. (The African language of origin is in parentheses.)

GOOBER — peanut (Kimbundu)
GUMBO — okra (Tshiluba)
HEH — yes (Vai)
HOODOO — bad luck (Hausa)
YAMBI — yam (Vai)
CHIGGER — small flies (Wolof)
NANA — grandmother (Twi)
TOTE — to carry (Kongo)
BIDDY — small chicken (Kongo)
BUCKRA — white man (Ibo)

Lincoln Sends a Judge to Investigate

In response to the freedpeople's petition, President Abraham Lincoln sent a federal judge to the Sea Islands to conduct an inquiry. Some of the abolitionist missionaries and teachers sided with the ex-slaves in this dispute; others with Philbrick. The two letters that follow present Harriet Ware's version of the inquiry. Ms. Ware was an abolitionist from Boston teaching on the islands, a close associate of Philbrick, and the sister of Charles Ware, who was accused by the petitioners of abusing a freedwoman. These ties may have influenced her interpretation of events.

Two Letters From Harriet Ware

PALPABLY—obviously

DOCUMENT THREE

April 18, 1864. At night came Mr. Soule [a plantation superinten- dent] from Beaufort with an account of an investigation going on there concerning the tax commissioners before Judge Smith, an agent sent by the President for the purpose.... [Judge Smith] had been commissioned to look into the affairs of our "concern," as the Fripp Point men had sent a petition to the President to be relieved of Mr. Philbrick's oppression!...Whoever drew up the petition (of course it had been done by a white man, but we could not tell [who he was] because his name as witness had been omitted in the copy given Judge Smith) had so overshot the market that it was palpably absurd to all who knew the facts, and happily Mr. Soule had found Judge Smith to be a fair-minded, able, clear-sighted person, who could not have dust thrown in his eyes.

DOCUMENT FOUR

April 21, 1864. ...C[harles Ware] was not questioned at all....
[Al]though the judge was satisfied that Mr. Philbrick was not a
scoundrel and [that] all of us [were not] aiders and abettors of his
iniquities, we knew the [freed]men would never be satisfied [unless
they had a hearing before Judge Smith]....Poor things, they are
much more sinned against than sinning....[T]he session of the
Court began by the examination of John Major....John Major is a
discontented, conceited fellow, who has never worked for Mr.
Philbrick, though his wife and children have, and he headed the petition. It was splendid to see how quickly the Judge saw through him,
when he [the judge] has been only a week in the Department [the
Sea Islands]...but he showed the man pretty plainly what he
thought of him, telling him...that if he thought Secesh [Confederate
slavery] times were so much better, the Government loved him so
well that it would let him go back to his old master!...

[The testimony of Pompey, a freedman working on one of
Philbrick's plantations, was described]. Pompey's great difficulty
seemed to have arisen from a misunderstanding of statements made
by Mr. Philbrick, in which he considered that Mr. Philbrick took
back his word...[S]o [Pompey]...lost confidence in him....He says,
and all the men say so too, that Mr. Philbrick promised when he
bought the land to sell it to them when the war was over for...[a dollar per acre], and that when he was here last he told them he should
ask them ten dollars an acre. [Philbrick originally bought the land
from the government for a dollar an acre]. This [version of what
Philbrick promised] they all stand to, and cannot be convinced that
they made a mistake...[W]e have lost their faith because [they claim
Philbrick] has broken his word,—and outsiders have fanned the
flame telling them that if they did not work for Mr. Philbrick, for
what he chose to pay them,—and that he was going to pay them
nothing,—he would turn them out of their homes, and more to the
same effect. It was a most interesting occasion, and it was pleasant to
feel that there was a man [the judge] of so much sense in the Department. He tried to pacify the men, and then privately told Mr. Soule
that he should advise Mr. Philbrick to pay the fifty cents [rather than
the forty cents a day he had been paying].

ABETTOR — one who
aids in a crime

INIQUITY — sin or
wickedness

*What were the grievances
of the petitioners?
To what extent should
we accept Harriet Ware's
account as evidence of
what happened in the
hearing before Judge
Smith? Based on Ware's
account, do you think
Judge Smith addressed the
main concerns of the petitioners? Was he fair?*

*Much, but not all, of the
written record of these
events was left by
Philbrick, his associates,
and other northerners
on the islands. Do these
documents have a point
of view? If so, to what
degree should we accept
them as evidence of
what happened?*

*On whose side is Harriet
Ware? What is the
evidence for your answer?*

Philbrick Opposes Free Land for Ex-Slaves

Philbrick and his associate William Gannett justified their land purchases and wage policies as good economics and good moral policy. They cautioned against charity and free land for ex-slaves. Instead, they urged competition and the pursuit of economic self-interest in the marketplace. According to this line of reasoning, freedpeople could profit by selling their labor on the open market—that is, working for the best wages they could find—just as Philbrick and Gannett

Why did Gannett and Philbrick argue that it was not in the freedman's interest to get land free or at a price below market value? Do you agree with their position? Why, or why not?

EXERTION—effort

could profit by selling cotton. By working hard and saving their wages, the argument went, ex–slaves could eventually buy their own land, cultivate cotton, and sell it at a profit on the world market.

"[G]ive them land and a house" now, Gannett commented, "and the ease of gaining as good a livelihood as they have been accustomed to would keep many contented with the smallest exertion. I pity some of them very much, for I see that nothing will maintain their energy but suffering" [i.e., they will become lazy unless they learn the habit of hard work].

Philbrick claimed that:

I can say honestly that I do not believe in the success of a system of selling to any people any property whatever for less than its market value with a view to confer a lasting benefit upon them....I think that they would be better off

Emancipated slaves on the James Hopkinson plantation on Edisto Island pose for a photographer. The woman on the left carries a heavy hoe used for the planting of cotton.

H. P. Moore, 1862. Collection of The New-York Historical Society.

for paying ten dollars an acre for land, if the land is worth it, rather than one dollar, because they would use the land for which they had paid full price more economically, would be likely to get more out of it, and would be taught a feeling of independence more readily than being made the recipients of charity.

Some northern abolitionists, missionaries, and teachers on the Sea Islands, like Harriet Ware, rallied to Philbrick's support. Many others, however, were highly critical of Philbrick's policies and attitudes toward the freedpeople. James Thompson, a reporter, longtime abolitionist, and frequent critic of Philbrick, wrote in the *Beaufort Free South* on March 26, 1864, "Mr. Philbrick says...that negroes would be demoralized by obtaining land at $1.25 per acre. We ask, has Mr. Philbrick been demoralized by obtaining land at that price [actually, he paid less]? Also in what time would a negro be able to buy a farm at $25 per acre [or $1,000 for forty acres] if he worked for Mr. Philbrick at 55 cents per working day [up from 40 cents in 1863]?"

Squatters Seize Philbrick's Land

By 1864, discontent on Philbrick's plantations had taken an organized form. At mass meetings, freedmen and women complained about their status as landless field hands cultivating cotton at low wages. By late spring, a number of African Americans on the Coffin Point plantation were squatting on Philbrick's cotton lands, planting corn, and refusing to leave. When told by one of Philbrick's superintendents that they had no right to the property, a freedman responded: "Man! Don't talk about Mr. Philbrick's land. Mr. Philbrick's no right to the land."

Philbrick's experiment in agriculture, organized according to northern business principles, failed to transform discontented slaves into a happy army of wage laborers producing cotton for international sale. The bitter experience of slavery had taught African Americans what freedom was, and was not. Growing cotton under white management, even as wage labor, looked too much like slavery. Field hands who, under threat of the whip, once submitted to forced plantation labor now demanded "no more master, no more cotton." For them, freedom meant independence from planters, ex-masters, owners, foremen, employers, northern do- gooders, and anybody else with schemes for growing cotton with African-American labor. Like so many other nineteenth-century Americans, these ex-slaves believed that only land ownership could guarantee such independence. Their vision of land was not one of riches (particularly if that meant growing cotton) but of subsistence. They wanted land for survival. With their own farm or homestead, freedmen and women could provide their families the necessities of life and enjoy their newly won liberty free of white control.

Philbrick gave up his experiment in 1865, selling his land for five times the price he originally paid. But on January 16, 1865, the history of the south Atlantic coast took a sudden dramatic turn—a turn that promised land and independence to thousands of ex-slaves on the Sea Islands.

SQUATTING—settling land or occupying property without legal title to it

The Union Redistributes Abandoned Plantations

The dramatic turn was the announcement by General William Tecumseh Sherman of Field Order Number 15, described in detail in chapter 6, which authorized ex-slaves to take possession of more than 400,000 acres of plantation land in an area extending thirty miles inland along the Atlantic coast from South Carolina to Jacksonville, Florida. More than 40,000 slaves settled on plantations abandoned by their Confederate owners, most on the Sea Islands.

Field Order Number Fifteen called for the possession of the land, but was deliberately unclear on the question of title. That lack of clarity prompted a range of responses from freedpeople. Many assumed that possession meant ownership; others understood that possession guaranteed nothing without a title. But with or without a title, possession excited the hopes of ex-slaves for land ownership.

Two months later, in March 1865, Congress passed a bill creating the Bureau of Refugees, Freedmen, and Abandoned Land, known subsequently as the Freedmen's Bureau (chapters 9 and 11 will discuss the role of the Freedmen's Bureau during Reconstruction). What the land provision of that bill stated follows below.

TITLE —legal paper or evidence of property ownership

The Freedmen's Bureau: Forty Acres to Every Freedman?

DOCUMENT FIVE

...To every male citizen, whether refugee [southern whites loyal to the Union] or freedman, there shall be assigned not more than forty acres of such land and the person to whom it was so assigned shall be protected in the use and enjoyment of the land for three years. At the end of said term, or at any time during said term, the occupants of any parcels so assigned may purchase the land and receive such title thereto as the United States can convey.

—*Instructions by the* U.S. CONGRESS
*to the Freedmen's Bureau to set aside land
for freedmen and loyal white refugees, March 1865*

Why did Field Order Number Fifteen and the Freedmen's Bureau Bill generate so much excitement? Did either document guarantee land ownership for the emancipated slaves? How, and why, were the freedmen's hopes for land dashed?

President Johnson Dashes Freedpeople's Hopes for Land

In response to Field Order Number Fifteen and the land provisions of the law establishing the Freedmen's Bureau, thousands of African Americans on the Sea Islands occupied lands that had been abandoned by Confederate planters or seized by the Union. But on May 29, 1865, less than two months after the war ended, Andrew Johnson (who had become president upon Lincoln's assassination) dealt a devastating blow to the freedpeople's dream of land ownership. He announced a sweeping amnesty, which granted most planters and Confederate leaders full political rights and title to their abandoned and confiscated lands.

Under the terms of President Johnson's amnesty proclamation, planters returning to the Sea Islands had legal title to their abandoned lands. But the fact of the matter was that ex-slaves held the land and were not about to give it up. The mood of these former slaves was militant and determined. In the summer of 1865, Major Martin Delany, a fiery black military officer who was now an official of the Freedmen's Bureau, addressed 600 freedpeople in a church on Saint Helena Island. He called upon ex-slaves to defend their rights and land with military force. Unknown to Delany, the speech was recorded by a white officer from his own regiment.

AMNESTY — a general pardon for crimes or political offenses

Martin Delany: We Have 200,000 Men Well Drilled in Arms

DOCUMENT SIX

Now I look around me and notice a man, barefooted, covered with rags and dirt. Now I ask what is that man doing, for whom is he working. I hear that he works for that and that farmer, "for 30 cents a day." I tell you that must not be. That would be slavery over again. I will not have it, the Government will not have it and the Government shall hear about it. I will tell the Government. I tell you slavery is over, and shall never return again. We have now 200,000 of our men well drilled in arms and used to warfare and I tell you it is with you and them, that slavery shall not come back again, and if you are determined it will not return again.

— MAJOR MARTIN R. DELANY,
military officer and agent of the Freedmen's Bureau, in an address to 600 ex-slaves on Saint Helena Island, July 24, 1865

What was Delany advocating? Do you think he was right?

Some Freedpeople Refuse to Surrender the Land

The ex-slaves' desire for land and the presence of armed African-American soldiers were an explosive combination. Throughout 1865, reports persisted across the South of African-American soldiers agitating among former slaves about land ownership and armed revolt. Agents of the Freedmen's Bureau on the scene hesitated to turn the land over to the original owners, and armed freedmen made clear their intent to defend their farms. Alarmed, the Department of War dispatched General Oliver O. Howard, the head of the Freedmen's Bureau, to pacify the freedmen on the Sea Islands.

When Howard convened a town meeting at a large Episcopal church on Edisto Island, freedpeople fully anticipated what was about to happen. Shouts and cries filled the room. Howard could not bring the meeting to order until, according to his own account, "a sweet voiced negro woman began the hymn 'Nobody knows the trouble I feel—nobody knows but Jesus.'" Howard then announced that they would have to surrender their farms. An emotional scene followed in which one freedman summed up the feelings of those assembled when he wailed, "Why, General Howard, do you take away our lands? You take them from us who have always been true, always true to the Government! You give them to our all-time enemies! That is not right." A sympathetic Howard was left gasping for words, yet he had little

FREE-LABOR RULES. A work contract is read to a group of freedpeople on the former Grove plantation in Port Royal, South Carolina.

South Carolina Historical Society.

AUCTION. Freedpeople gather outside of a Beaufort, North Carolina, courthouse
as the Union Army auctions confiscated Confederate property.

Huntington Library, San Marino, California.

choice but to return the land to ex-planters under President Johnson's amnesty order.

But freedmen on the islands were not about to turn the other cheek and meekly surrender the land. Northern correspondent Sydney Andrews noted that "the negroes… almost universally believe that the islands have been given to them, and they are not likely to relinquish that belief….An attempt to force them from the islands at present, or to compel them to acceptance of the terms proposed by the planters, will overthrow their faith in the Government and there will be bloodshed." Within the month, a planter who returned to Edisto Island to assess the situation reported that "Negroes on the island are armed and have announced their purpose to allow no white man on it."

The militancy of the freedmen occupying the land is reflected in the following corre-spondence on page 168 between white Union officers, General William Beecher and Major General Rufus Saxton.

By 1866, some freedpeople had yielded their claims to the land and were working as contract labor for their former owners. But many fought sporadic battles over the next two years to keep the land they had cultivated and made productive. When an officer of the Freedmen's Bureau sent six Union soldiers in January 1867 to the Delta Plantation, one of the largest estates in the area, two hundred African Americans, waving pistols, muskets, clubs, and sticks confronted them. There was no mistaking the message of the freedpeople: they would not leave. The six soldiers retreated, only to return with an armed mili-tary force of fifty men and three days' rations. An even bigger army of African-American squatters stood up to the soldiers. One of the freedmen exclaimed, "We have one master now—Jesus Christ—and he'll never come here to collect taxes or drive us off." The leader of the freedmen ordered the squatters to "fall in!"; but before a shot was fired, the Union company withdrew.

DOCUMENT SEVEN

I went yesterday to [Mr. Nat Heyward's] plantation, called the people together and carefully instructed them in their rights and duties. They said that they had been assured by certain parties that Mr. Heyward would be obliged to lease land to them, and that they would not work for him at any price. They were perfectly good natured about it but firm. I then announced Mr. Heyward's offer:

That they were to retain their houses and gardens, with the privilege of raising hogs, poultry, etc. That he would pay for the full hands men $12, women $8 per month....

I am satisfied that no higher wages will be offered this year. Therefore I told the people they could take it or leave it, and that if they declined to work the plantation the houses must be vacated. I proceeded to call the role of all the able bodied men and women, each of whom responded "no." I then notified them that every house must be vacated on or before the 18th....I propose to remain and see everyone outside the plantation lines on that date.

Today, I have pursued the same course on another large plantation, with the same results. Of course I anticipated this. It could not be otherwise considering the instructions which people have received. I do not blame them in the slightest degree, and so long as they show no violence, shall treat them with all possible kindness. But it is better to stop the error they are laboring under at once.

— Letter to Major General Saxton from
GENERAL BEECHER, *January 9, 1866*

The struggle at Delta Plantation and on lands throughout the Sea Islands was in sharp contrast to the rest of the South (to be explored in chapter 11). Unlike those on the mainland, most black farmers on the islands became landowners. Forty years later, according to the 1910 census, long after Reconstruction and the restoration of white supremacy, more than sixty percent of the African Americans who worked the land on the Sea Islands owned it.

The events on the Sea Islands raised key questions about land ownership and the conditions and terms under which freedpeople would work the land. Throughout the entire South, these questions framed the struggles of African Americans for freedom and independence over the next decade, the period of Reconstruction. It is in this sense that the Sea Islands staged a rehearsal for Reconstruction from 1861 to 1867.

While the rehearsal foretold what was to come, it was in important ways unique to a particular time and place. Unlike the population on the mainland, the people of the Sea Islands were overwhelmingly

ALLIES. Calling themselves Gideon's Band, many northern reformers went to the Sea Islands to live with and assist the freed population. Abolitionist Laura M. Towne, shown here with three of her students, ran a school on St. Helena Island.

R. A. Holland, ed., *Letters and Diary of Laura M. Towne* (1912). American Social History Project.

African American. White planters were noticeable by their absence from November 1861 to April 1865. Nowhere else in the South were so many abandoned plantations occupied and cultivated by freedmen. Nowhere else in the South did the presence of so many northerners— military officers, government officials, teachers, missionaries, reformers— raise expectations for land ownership. But with high expectations came mixed results: many got land, many did not. White northerners and black southerners forged complex relationships—sometimes intense, mostly positive, but on a few occasions ugly, distrustful, and contentious. The rehearsal on the Sea Islands dramatized these connection and contradictions between reformers and ex-slaves. But most important of all, it showed possibilities for radical change in the coming period of Reconstruction.

Suggested Activities

MOCK JURY

Divide into several juries of five or six students each. The juries debate the following questions:

Should Judge Smith order Edward Philbrick to sell his land to the ex-slaves working it? If so, at what price per acre?

Each jury will try to reach a consensus, basing its decision on the evidence presented in Documents One, Two, Three, and Four and any relevant quotations from the text. A jury can decide (1) in favor of Philbrick or (2) in favor of the petitioning freedpeople, or (3) that there is insufficient basis to make a decision. If a jury chooses option (2), it must then decide a fair price per acre.

Each jury reports its decision, and the reasoning behind it, followed by discussion and analysis.

DEBATE

Who has the right to the land on the Coffin Point plantation—Philbrick or the squatters who took possession of the land?

Divide into two groups for a debate. One group will develop arguments and prepare two people to play Philbrick and one of his associates. The other group will prepare debating points for two people who take the role of squatters.

After a ten-minute debate, analyze (1) the different points of view, (2) the merits of the opposing arguments, and (3) the different approaches of Philbrick and the squatters. What factors influenced the thinking of the opposing parties?

IMAGES OF WOMEN

Study two pictures: "Carved from Life" on page 151 and "A Woman of the Sea Islands" on page 156. Based on your reading, write a paragraph or two explaining which picture best captures the character of women on the South Carolina and Georgia Sea Islands during this period. Share and discuss your conclusion with the class.

CHAPTER EIGHT

EMANCIPATION AND THE MEANING OF FREEDOM

BEFORE READING. *After emancipation, there were remarkably few acts of violence or retribution by ex-slaves against people. Property, however, was a different matter. Many freedpeople felt justified in taking or destroying property belonging to their one-time masters. Consider the following examples.*

"THE EMANCIPATION OF THE NEGROES, JANUARY, 1863—THE PAST AND THE FUTURE."
A celebration of the Emancipation Proclamation published in *Harper's Weekly*.

Who Gets the Handsome Mahogany Bedstead—
The Plantation Mistress or the Ex-Slave?

DOCUMENT ONE

…[T]hey broke into our well furnished residences on each plantation and stole or destroyed everything therein. Nor was there a soli-
tary instance in either plantation of any one of our Negroes preserving for us a single thing whatever.…A negro woman [Peggy] seized
as part of the spoils my wife's large and handsome mahogany bedstead and mattress and arranged it in her own Negro house on which
she slept for some time.

Frederick [the driver] was the ringleader [at the Marshland planta-
tion].…He encouraged all the Negroes to believe that the Farm, and
every thing on it, now since emancipation, belonged solely to them,
and that their former owners had now no rights or control there
whatever.

—*South Carolina planter* CHARLES MANIGAULT, *1865*

*In Document One,
did the mahogany bedstead
rightfully belong to
Mrs. Manigault, or was
Peggy justified in seizing
it? In Document Two,
who should get the kitchen
in the big house, Emma
Mordecai or Cyrus?
Write a paragraph or two
explaining your position.*

An Ex-Slave: "The Kitchen of the Big House Is My Share"

DOCUMENT TWO

Seems like we do all the work and [only] get a part. There
ain't going to be no more master and mistress, Miss Emma.
All is equal. I done hear it from the courthouse steps. All the
land belongs to the Yankees now, and they're going to divide it
out among the colored people. Besides, the kitchen of the big
house is my share. I helped build it.

— CYRUS, *a freedman, to his former mistress,
Emma Mordecai, after the fall of Richmond, April 1865*

First Freedom

In just four years, the Civil War turned two and a half centuries of southern history on its head. Emancipation severed old connections and changed the way black and white southerners interacted, thought, and even talked. Normally, habits of behavior and mind do not change easily. Nor do rhythms of everyday life created over 250 years. But in 1865, one word made southern life very different: *freedom.*

Emancipation happened in different ways and came in different forms. Some slaves seized freedom by sabotaging plantation production, escaping to Union lines, and joining the Union Army to fight for the liberation of their people. For others, freedom had to wait for Lincoln's January 1863 Emancipation Proclamation, for liberating northern armies, or for the ratification of the Thirteenth Amendment abolishing slavery in January 1865.

But once emancipation came, African Americans took the measure of freedom's boundaries, constantly pushing them outward. At freedom's first coming, they defied the physical and psychological barriers created by years of slavery. Discarding the symbols of their enslavement, many rejected names forced

How did ex-slaves gain their freedom?

upon them by slavemasters and took new ones. Casting aside the drab garments of slavery, they wore new badges of freedom—brightly colored outerwear, fancy hats, ornate parasols, elegant veils.

They held meetings without white permission, supervision, or presence—that is, without the probing eyes of a master or overseer. In everyday encounters, they challenged former masters, mistresses, and overseers. Such defiance was expressed in a variety of encounters—looking an ex-master straight in the eye, talking back to a plantation mistress, refusing to tip a hat or give way to whites on a sidewalk.

In a world turned upside down, slaves found their defiance exhilarating. But masters, like one South Carolina planter, saw such behavior as "excessively insolent." "Utterly disgusted" by scenes he saw daily in Charleston, the planter complained in a letter to a friend: "It is impossible to describe the conditions of the city— it is so unlike anything we can imagine—negroes shoving white persons off the walk— Negro women drest [sic] in the most outré style, all with veils and parasols, for which they have an especial fancy."

Why did so many ex-slaves take new names?

In what sense did their clothes and behavior become badges of freedom?

TRAVELING. African Americans exercised their new freedom in many ways; one of them was traveling where and when they chose. This engraving is from Edward King's *The Great South*, one of many postwar surveys of southern life. Northerners were curious to learn about the region that they had defeated in war.

(J. Wells Champney [W.L. Sheppard, del.]) Edward King, *The Great South*…(1875). American Social History Project.

OUTRÉ—outrageous

Who Survives on Government Handouts?

Ex-masters ridiculed the behavior of freedpeople upon emancipation. But could masters survive without their ex-slaves? Consider how this African-American soldier would answer the question.

DOCUMENT THREE

I take the liberty of writing to you a few facts that have come under my observation respecting the freedmen....The enemy of emancipation cries that the negroes will not work, that the government will have to support them, or they will become pests to the country.... Any one who has been where he can observe the working of emancipation can see the fallacy of such cant [false, insincere language]. Through the parishes where I have been I think I never saw the [black] laboring class more industrious. Many seem to vie one with each other in making a living, and saving something for a future day....Those who feel so badly because the Government feeds a few negroes should be with me on ration day and see their white brethren and sisters, those who for the last four years have been trying to destroy the nation, come for their food that the Government has to give to save them from starving....

— CORPORAL RICHARD T. HENRY
writing from Donaldson, Louisiana, 1866

Planters could not understand a world in which ex-slaves looked and acted very differently than they had just five years earlier. In the summer of 1865, freedmen and women seemed on the move. They tested pre-emancipation restrictions on their freedom of movement by walking the streets of cities such as Charleston and by moving back and forth between farms, plantations, and villages. This uncontested mobility was an everyday demonstration of the joy of freedom.

Often, the journeys of ex-slaves across county and state lines were missions of hope, urgency, and love. They searched for family members and friends sold by a master before the war or scattered by the chaos of four years of sectional conflict and slaughter. A northern reporter poignantly described meeting a freedman who had already traveled 600 miles on foot. "Plodding along, staff in hand, and apparently very footsore and tired," the emancipated slave seemed driven by sheer, willful determination to continue until he located his wife. It was a scene repeated thousands of times as freedpeople moved across the South desperately attempting to complete the work of their personal emancipation by reuniting their families.

Building Free Communities: The Family

The family, together with churches and schools, became the bedrock upon which ex-slaves built free African-American communities.

From the beginning of recorded history, men and women with common interests have banded together in communities. In turn, communities have created institutions that provide meaning, organization, connections, and structure to people's daily lives, transmitting culture and values from one generation to the next. In modern society, these institutions often take the form of kin and family networks, schools, churches, synagogues, mosques, clubs, teams, self-help societies, and political organizations.

Some institutions in African-American communities only took hold with the coming of freedom—particularly schools, political organizations, and self-help societies. Others, notably family and church, had a long history of development under slavery.

Family and kin networks had enabled Africans to survive the horrors of slavery, to teach children survival skills, and to develop a uniquely African-American culture. Under slavery, African Americans struggled to maintain these ties, and once emancipated, they moved quickly to make their families whole. Where possible, they reconnected with parents, spouses, children, and siblings separated by the inhuman slave trade or uprooted by Civil War. When this was not possible, larger kin networks adopted children, took care of the elderly, and provided support for separated spouses.

Couples whose unions survived the emotional damage of plantation life and war often sought legal and religious approval for their slave marriages. Between 1865 and 1866, husbands and wives by the thousands renewed sacred wedding vows before ministers and registered their marriages with Union authorities. By giving their slave marriages new meaning under freedom, they demonstrated the enduring importance of the family in African-American life.

Why was it so important for ex-slaves to (1) be on the move and (2) journey across state lines?

There was both continuity and change in the role of women in the family. Under slavery, it was common for women to plow,

WEDDING. A chaplain marries an African-American couple in the offices of the Vicksburg Freedmen's Bureau.

Alfred R. Waud, *Harper's Weekly*, June 30, 1866.
American Social History Project.

BEDROCK—foundation

COMMUNITY—a body of people having common organization and interests

INSTITUTION—any association or group of relationships organized by society (e.g., a school is an educational institution; a church a religious institution; the family a social institution)

KIN—relatives, and/or friends who act like family

SIBLING—a brother or sister

hoe, and harvest fields for twelve hours a day. A freedwoman, a mother of twelve, told a northern reporter what it was like: "I had to nurse my children four times a day and pick 200 pounds of cotton beside.... I have a heap of a better time now than when I was in bondage."

Small wonder that with freedom many African-American women left the fields to work full-time raising children and managing households. But as this happened, planters like Henry Watson of Alabama complained bitterly: "The female laborers are almost invariably idle, [they] do not go to the field, but desire to play the lady and be supported by their husbands 'like the white folks do.'" While Watson protested about "idle" women, mothers nursed and reared children, cooked, cleaned, cultivated gardens, tended chickens, preserved food, and made clothes.

Why did Henry Watson characterize freedwomen who refused to work the fields as "idle"? Is his characterization accurate?

The real issue was that Henry Watson and plantation masters like him no longer controlled the labor of black women. Every time freedwomen abandoned the cotton fields, they asserted independence from the Henry Watsons of the South and took a practical step that strengthened African-American families and households. The family now asserted control over the labor of its members, a power that had once been the province of the plantation master.

Building Free Communities: Schools

Shortly after the war, a freedman in Mississippi vowed that "if I never does do nothing more while I live, I shall give my children the chance to go to school, for I considers education the next best thing to liberty." By linking freedom and schools, he expressed a sentiment dearly held by many nineteenth-century Americans: that education and democracy went hand in hand.

"THE FIRST SCHOOLHOUSE BUILT FOR THE INSTRUCTION OF FREED MEN." Black soldiers from the Port Hudson, Louisiana, "Corps d'Afrique" pose with textbooks in front of their school.
Chicago Historical Society.

"'ZION' SCHOOL FOR COLORED CHILDREN, CHARLESTON, SOUTH CAROLINA." An 1866 engraving shows one of the many schools organized and run by freedpeople. "It is a peculiarity of this school," ran the accompanying caption, "that it is entirely under the superintendence of colored teachers."

Alfred R. Waud, *Harper's Weekly*, December 15, 1866.
American Social History Project.

SECOND READER.			35

LESSON XV.

cock	wash	pig	too
crows	dawn	dig	two
food	bound	hoe	scrub
wake	clean	plow	bake
home	know	noise	eyes
cheer	knives	kneel	school

What letter is silent in hoe? in clean? Say just, not *jist*; catch, not *cotch*; sit, not *set*; father, not *fader*.

THE FREEDMAN'S HOME.

SEE this home! How neat, how warm, how full of cheer, it looks! It seems as if the sun shone in there all the day long. But it takes more than the light of the sun to make a home bright all the time. Do you know what it is? It is love.

READING, 'RITING, AND ROLE MODELS. The textbooks prepared by northern reformers for freedmen and women contained more than practical lessons. Besides instructions on spelling, reading, and pronunciation, this page from *The Freedman's Second Reader* presents a "model" black household that exhibits the gentility of the northern middle-class ideal of the family.

American Tract Society, *The Freedman's Second Reader* (1865).
American Social History Project.

But the thirst for education also reflected the particular history of slavery and emancipation. In the nineteenth century, southern law prohibited the teaching of reading and writing to slaves. Before the war, the old master class understood that an educated slave was a dangerous slave. What was dangerous to the slaveholder, however, was liberating for the slave. After the war, emancipated slaves by the hundreds of thousands armed themselves with reading, writing, and arithmetic.

Once they understood written words and numbers, freedpeople could protect themselves in the world of free labor and signed contracts. A Louisiana slave knew that "leaving learning to your children was better than leaving them a fortune, because if you left them even five hundred dollars, some man having more education than they would come and cheat them out of it."

An elderly freedman sought education "because I want to read the word of the Lord." Another added that the "old missus used to read the good book to us on Sunday evenings, but she mostly read them places that said 'servants, obey your masters....'"

Do you agree with the nineteenth-century view that education and democracy go hand in hand? Why, or why not?

For whom was an educated slave dangerous? Why?

What power did knowledge give former slaves? What evidence in the text shows that they equated knowledge and power?

Black colleges established after the Civil War include Fisk (1866), Howard (1867), Morgan State (1867), Morehouse (1867), Hampton (1868), Dillard (1869), Tougaloo (1869), Alcorn (1871), Southern (1880), Spelman (1881), and North Carolina Agricultural and Technical (1891).

In 1865 and 1866, ex-slaves all over the South acted on a basic understanding: knowledge is power and ignorance is bondage. At great personal and financial sacrifice, they formed self-help societies all over the South to raise money for land for schools, school construction, and the hiring of teachers both black and white. Missionary societies from the North set up hundreds of schools in the former Confederacy. Even more remarkable, freedpeople established hundreds more schools using their own scant resources. The African-American schools and colleges created during Reconstruction trained generations of future black leaders. A century later, students of a different generation at these same historically black colleges spearheaded sit-ins and voter registration drives in the South during the civil rights movement in the 1960s and early 1970s.

Eager to Learn, Ready to Defend

The following documents provide a sense of obstacles confronted and overcome by ex-slaves in their quest for schooling. The first document was written by a white northern journalist touring the South after the war, the second by a teacher for the Freedmen's Bureau (race unknown), and the third by a northern African-American educator who taught in the Union-occupied South Carolina Sea Islands during the war. The final document tells about the defense of a Florida freedpeople's school against attacks by white terrorists.

"Many of the Negroes…Were Supporting Little Schools"

DOCUMENT FOUR

Many of the negroes…common plantation negroes, and day laborers in the towns and villages, were supporting little schools themselves. Everywhere I found among them a disposition to get their children into schools, if possible. I had occasion very frequently to notice that porters in stores and laboring men in warehouses, and cart drivers on the streets, had spelling books with them, and were studying them during the time they were not occupied with their work. Go into the outskirts of any large town and walk among the negro inhabitants, and you will see children and in many instances grown negroes, sitting in the sun alongside their cabins studying.

— SYDNEY ANDREWS *quoted in the* Joint Report on Reconstruction, *39th (U.S.) Congress, 1st Session, 1866*

"A Pile of Books Is Seen in Almost Every Cabin"

DOCUMENT FIVE

It is surprising to see the amount of suffering which many of the people endure for the sake of sending their children to school. Men get very low wages here…and a great many cannot get work at all. The women take in sewing and washing, go out by day to scour, etc. There is one woman who supports three children and keeps them at school; she says, "I don't care how hard I has to work, if I can only send Sally and the boys to school looking respectable." Many of the girls have but one decent dress; it gets washed and ironed on Saturday, and then it is worn until the next Saturday.… One may go into their cabins on cold, windy days, and see the daylight between every two boards, or feel the rain dropping through the roof; but a word of complaint is rarely heard. They are anxious to have their children "get on in their books," and do not seem to feel impatient if they lack comforts themselves. A pile of books is seen in almost every cabin, though there be no furniture except a poor bed, a table and two or three broken chairs.

— MISS M. A. PARKER,
the American Freedmen, *April 1869*

DOCUMENT SIX

...I never before saw children so eager to learn, although I had several years experience in New-England schools. Coming to school is a constant delight and recreation to them. They come here as other children go to play. The older ones, during the summer, work in the fields from early in the morning until eleven or twelve o'clock and then come to school, after their hard toil in the hot sun, as bright and anxious to learn as ever.

...The majority learn with wonderful rapidity. Many of the grown people are desirous of learning to read. It is wonderful how people who have been so long crushed to earth...can have so great a desire for knowledge, and such a capacity for attaining it....

— CHARLOTTE FORTEN,
"Life on the Sea Islands," Atlantic Monthly, *March 1864*

DOCUMENT SEVEN

Freedmen Defend
Their School
Against a Mob

*Examining the
documents*

•*What specific evidence do these documents provide about the importance of education for ex-slaves?*
•*What obstacles did freedpeople have to overcome to get schooling?*
•*Who were the "respectable rowdies" referred to by Captain C. M. Hamilton, and why do you think they would attack a school?*

The night school has been frequently disturbed. One evening a mob called out of the school house, the teacher, who upon presenting himself was confronted with four revolvers, and menacing expressions of shooting him, if he did not promise to quit the place, and close the school.

The freedmen promptly came to his aid and the mob dispersed.

About the 18th or 19th of the month, I was absent...when a formidable disturbance took place at the school. The same mob threatened to destroy the school that night, and the freedmen, learning this, assembled...at their place of instruction in a condition of self-defense.

I understand that not less than forty colored men armed to protect themselves, but the preparation becoming known to the *respectable rowdies,* they only maneuvered about in small squads, and were wise enough to avoid a collision.

— CAPTAIN C. M. HAMILTON *in a letter to the Office of the Adjutant General in Washington, D.C., 1866*

Building Free Communities: Churches

African-American freedom songs have echoed across the generations from secret religious meetings held under cover of darkness on slave plantations, to independent African-American churches built after the Civil War, to black congregations in southern towns like Montgomery, Birmingham, Atlanta, Albany, Selma, and Meridian during the civil rights era beginning in the 1950s. The legacy of freedom established after the Civil War by African-American churches and, as we have seen, educational institutions, extended far into the twentieth century.

LEGACY—something handed down from the past

In the 1860s and 1870s, the independent black church rapidly became the moral, cultural, and political center of the African-American community. Preachers emerged as community and political leaders. As early as 1865–66, they played a central role in organizing black political conventions in virtually every southern state. These conventions demanded civil and political rights for African Americans, rights that over the next five years became part of American law.

Consider a scene that was the forerunner of similar meetings in churches all over the South a century later during the civil rights era of 1955–1975. On May 25, 1865, one thousand men and women, singing and praying, crowded into the Bute Street African Methodist Church in Norfolk, Virginia, to mobilize a "freedom ballot."

FIRST AFRICAN CHURCH. The interior of a Richmond, Virginia, church during Sunday services in 1874.

W. L. Sheppard, "The First African Church, Richmond, Virginia," *Harper's Weekly*, June 24, 1874. American Social History Project.

The provisional governor of Virginia, appointed by President Andrew Johnson, had called for state assembly elections on that day. The governor took for granted that only white males could vote.

But on election day, several hundred African-American men, in groups of ten, went to the city's fourth ward to submit contested ballots. The remainder cast their contested votes in the church.

The very act of voting—even if the ballots were challenged—gave the congregation a new sense of its power. It used the contested ballots to question the election results and to inspire political activism by African-American churches across the state. Eventually, the leaders of the "freedom ballot" met with President Andrew Johnson, and within months they gained voting rights for black men in Virginia.

The roots of these independent black churches went back to the secret, nighttime religious ceremonies organized by African Americans during slavery. On the bigger plantations, the master or his chosen preacher conducted services for slaves and cited chapter and verse from the New Testament to justify the "peculiar institution." But late at night, slaves often would retreat to nearby woods to conduct their own services. Independent of white supervision, they practiced a religion that merged the Old Testament with African culture.

How did voting, even if the votes were challenged, give the Bute Street Congregation a new sense of its power?

Why did most ex-slaves want to worship in separate churches? What role did these churches play in the African-American community

CONTESTED BALLOT—a vote challenged as illegal

"A NEGRO REVIVAL MEETING." The emotional quality of southern black religious services startled many white observers accustomed to more subdued observance.

W. L. Sheppard, *Frank Leslie's Illustrated Newspaper*, August 9, 1873. General Research Division, The New Public Library, Astor, Lenox, and Tilden Foundations.

After emancipation, churches in the South attended by both whites and blacks were typically dominated by whites. White or white-dominated multiracial churches tended to be more subdued than black ones and more centered on the New Testament rather than the Old. To many freedpeople, these churches had the sound and feel of the Christianity preached by the master on slave plantations before the Civil War.

Ex-slaves pooled meager resources to form their own congregations and build churches. In doing so, they took control of their religious lives. Out from underneath white supervision, emancipated slaves created religious institutions that were largely democratic in structure, enthusiastic and highly emotional in worship, and politically connected to the African-American community as a whole. For generations to come, the sounds of freedom, in words and music, would ring loud and clear from independent black churches.

Building Free Communities: Social and Political Organizations

On July 4, Independence Day, and January 1, Emancipation Day (the anniversary of Lincoln's 1863 proclamation), the religious, educational, social, and political institutions of the southern black community were on parade. Joyous men and women—dressed in bright colors, some wearing the uniforms of churches, schools, fraternal organizations, self-help associations, benevolent societies, and political clubs—marched in celebration of freedom and independence. In a city such

as Richmond, Virginia, where by the 1870s there were more than 400 such organizations (Masonic lodges, debating associations, drama clubs, equal-rights leagues, fire companies, temperance organizations, burial and welfare societies, and others), the parade would stretch for many city blocks.

African-American community life was rich and varied, with a wide range of voluntary associations providing life insurance and death benefits, organizing charitable and good works, and creating a climate of good fellowship and sisterhood. In 1865, throughout the South, African-American mutual-aid societies created networks of orphanages, relief agencies for the poor, employment societies, and soup kitchens.

To survive, flourish, and organize, African-American communities needed not only strong social, religious, educational, and self-help institutions, but also political organization. From the end of the Civil War to the last gasp of Reconstruction in 1876, there was a tremendous surge from the grass roots of African-American political activity. As we shall see in chapters 9 and 10, Republican clubs, "colored conventions," Union Leagues, and armed militia added an essential political and even military dimension to African-American life as the reconstructed black community struggled to protect hard-won rights and to gain new ones.

In the new era of emancipation, family, religion, politics, self-help, and education became the steel that forged independent African-American communities. Soon, however, political decisions made in Washington would put free men and women in those communities to the test of fire.

A Merging of African Culture and the Old Testament

As a continuing source of strength for the African-American community, the black church expressed a rich spirituality that sustained slaves and freedpeople through hard times. Anglo-American Protestantism was only one of several significant influences on the culture and philosophy of the black church. Scholars have found that African-American Christianity also drew on the forms and remembered rituals of African religion and on the language of the Old Testament. The result was a powerful religious culture, full of faith and exhilaration, that contrasted with the more repressed Christianity of many white northerners.

Slave owners, drawing mainly on the New Testament, had taught their slaves to be Christians. But many slaves found significant meaning in the Old Testament with its images of David versus Goliath, of Hebrews liberated from Egyptian slavemasters, of Jonah escaping the body of a whale, and of Daniel delivered from the lion's den. As historian Lawrence Levine has suggested, slaves used the Bible to express their fervent hopes for a new and better world by identifying with Old Testament morality tales that told of struggles against injustice and for freedom.

Another historian, Sterling Stuckey, has uncovered many African influences on African-American religious rituals and songs. In West Africa, the Yoruba, the Ibo, and other peoples affirmed their religious faith through music and collective dance, particularly movement in a large circle or ring. The ring symbolized the circle of life — the bonds that linked members of the community with their ancestors. The dance was a distinctive merging of spiritual, physical, musical, and emotional expression.

African Americans in slavery and freedom created Christian "ring shouts," which drew on collective memories of African culture. Ring shouts took the form of dancing, clapping, chanting, and improvised music similar to that found in West and Central African circle ceremonies. The spontaneity and improvisational nature of the music and dance meant that it could be modified and adapted to the realities faced by African Americans in both slavery and freedom in the United States.

While still celebrating the wholeness of life, the ring ceremony during slavery also served a practical purpose. It drew together slaves who came from many different parts of Africa and joined them into a single community. The participatory dance helped enslaved Africans, who often spoke different African languages, build a sense of unity and common purpose. What evolved was a life-affirming blend of African and Christian religion.

During slavery, many aspects of African-American religious life were hidden from the master. With the arrival of freedom, African-American religion came out into the open, as the freedpeople refused to be directed any longer by whites, whether they were former masters or northern missionaries.

In many, but not all, instances, the circle disappeared in the United States in the late nineteenth and twentieth centuries. But what remained and developed—sometimes taking new forms in the confined physical space of the church building—were the sacred values and continuity, the spontaneity, the music, the improvisation, and the active physical, emotional, and spiritual participation by the entire religious community.

Several historians have traced links between the soulful and improvisational nature of the music from West and Central African circle ceremonies and the development of African-American spirituals, gospels, blues, and jazz.

As you read the first-person accounts below, consider: (1) the historical roots and role of the African-American church, culture, and life from slavery through Reconstruction to the present; (2) the different notions of religion embraced by freedpeople and their northern allies.

An Ex-Slave: "It Wasn't Cold and 'Proper' Like in the White Folks' Church"

The first document is a statement recorded by folklorist William John Faulkner as it was spoken by Simon Brown, an ex-slave and famous teller of African-American folktales.

DOCUMENT EIGHT

I use to drive my Massa's family in town to church, in the "two horse surrey," on a Sunday. I had to sit upstairs with the other slaves. We acted like we enjoyed the services, but we didn't.... But the slaves had Christian religion too, and it wasn't cold and "proper," like in the white folks' church....

The [black] folks would sing and pray and "testify" and clap their hands just as if God was right there in the midst of them. He wasn't way off up in the sky: He was a-seeing everybody and a-listening to every word and a-promising to "let His love come down." My people would be so burdened down with trials and tribulations and broken hearts, that I see them break down and cry like babies.... Yes sir, there was no pretending in those prayer meetings. There was a living faith in a just God who would one day answer the cries of his poor black children and deliver them from their enemies. But they never say a word to the white folks about this kind of faith.

—*Ex-slave* SIMON BROWN *speaking to folklorist William John Faulkner, in* The Days When the Animals Talked, *1977*

A Union Officer Describes the Ring Shout: "Drums Throb.... the Circle Enlarges, Louder Grows the Singing"

DOCUMENT NINE

All over the camps, the lights glimmer in the tents, and as I sit at my desk in the open doorway, there come mingled sounds of stir and glee. Boys laugh and shout,—a feeble flute stirs somewhere in the tent, not an officer's,—drums throb far away in another…and from a neighboring cook-fire comes a monotonous sound of that strange festival, half pow-wow, half prayer meeting, which they know only as the "shout." These huts are usually enclosed in a little booth, made neatly of palm-leaves and covered in at top, a regular native African hut….This hut is now crammed with men, singing at the top of their voices, in one of their quaint, monotonous, endless-negro Methodist chants, with obscure syllables recurring constantly, and slight variations interwoven, all accompanied with a regular drumming of the feet and clapping of the hands, like castanets.

Some "heel and toe" tumultuously, others merely tremble and stagger on, others stoop and rise, others whirl, others caper sideways, all keep steadily circling like dervishes [whirling dancers]; spectators applaud special strokes of skill; my approach only enlivens the scene; the circle enlarges, louder grows the singing, rousing shouts of encouragement come in…and still the ceaseless drumming and clapping in perfect cadence, goes steadily on. Suddenly there comes a sort of snap, and the spell breaks, amid general sighing and laughter …. And this not rarely and occasionally, but night after night.

— THOMAS WENTWORTH HIGGINSON,
Army Life in a Black Regiment, *1869*

White and black missionaries visiting African-American churches in the South after the Civil War were frequently appalled when they first witnessed the "shout," with its ecstatic, expressive dancing, singing, chanting, drumbeating, and hand-clapping. When some northerners tried to halt the practice, congregations of freedpeople resisted. As they saw it, the missionaries were robbing Christianity of its joy, celebration, and emotion. The "shout" reflected unmistakable cultural differences between the forms of Christianity practiced by the missionary and ex-slave.

Most of the missionaries who criticized the "shout" were white.

But consider this exchange between two devoutly religious Afri-can-Americans, Bishop Daniel Alexander Payne of the African-American Episcopal Church and a participant in a ring shout.

RING SHOUT PARTICIPANT: Sinners won't get converted unless there is a ring.

BISHOP PAYNE: You might sing till you fell down dead, and you would fail to convert a single sinner, because nothing but the spirit of God and the word of God can convert sinners.

RING SHOUT PARTICIPANT: At camp meeting there must be a ring here, a ring there, a ring over yonder, or sinners will not get converted.

African influences made southern black religion very distinct from that practiced by white northern mission-aries, and even that of Bishop Payne. This theme runs through Document Ten and perhaps explains why ex-slaves wanted to hear their own preachers in their own churches, as noted in Document Eleven.

A Freedwoman: "Not Make Noise!"

DOCUMENT TEN

I go to some churches, and I see all the folks sitting quiet and still like they don't know what the Holy Spirit is. But I find in my Bible, that when a man or a woman gets full of the Holy Spirit, if they should hold their peace, the stones would cry out; and if the power of God can make the stones cry out, how can it help making us poor crea-tures cry out, who feel to praise Him for His mercy. Not make noise! Why we make a noise about everything else; but they tell us we must not make noise to praise the Lord. I don't want such religion as that. I want to go to Heaven in the good old way. And my brothers and sisters, I want you all to pray for me, that when I get to Heaven I won't never come back again.

—*Comments made by* A FREEDWOMAN
at a religious meeting, 1865, as reported by northern white visitors

A White Missionary: "Their Long-Silent Preachers Want to Preach & the People Prefer Them"

DOCUMENT ELEVEN

They [blacks] feel that religion is something they possess—they do not feel their need of religious instruction from the pulpit—for they always had it here—they have been obliged to listen to white min-isters provided, or placed over them by their masters, while they have men among themselves whom they believe were called of God to preach, who were kept silent by the institution from which they are now freed—& to have white preachers still placed over them, is too much like old times to meet with their approval. Their long-silent preachers want to preach & the people prefer them.

— LOUISE A. WOODBURY, *a white northerner representing the American Missionary Association, September 7, 1863*

"The Temple Rocked with the Power of God"

Compare the documents that follow with Thomas Wentworth Higginson's description of a "shout" in Document Nine. In an autobiographical novel, Go Tell It on the Mountain, *James Baldwin describes a church service in Harlem in the 1940s (Document Twelve). In Document Thirteen, jazz historian Marshall Stearns describes a ceremony he witnessed in South Carolina in the 1950s, and then links the "continued existence of the ring-shout" to jazz forms developed in the twentieth century.*

DOCUMENT TWELVE

...[The] Power struck someone, a man or woman; they cried out, a long wordless crying, and, arms outstretched like wings, they began the Shout. Someone moved a chair a little to give them room, the rhythm paused, the singing stopped, only the pounding feet and the clapping hands were heard; then another cry, another dancer; then the tambourines began again, and the voices rose again, and the music swept on again, like fire, or flood, or judgement. Then like a planet rocking in space, the temple rocked with the Power of God.

—JAMES BALDWIN, Go Tell It on the Mountain, 1952

A West African Circle Dance

DOCUMENT THIRTEEN

The dancers form a circle in the center of the floor, one in back of another. Then they begin to shuffle in a counter-clockwise direction around and around, arms out and shoulders hunched. A fantastic rhythm is built up by the rest of the group standing back to the walls, who clap their hands and stomp on the floor....Suddenly sisters and brothers scream and spin, possessed by religious hysteria, like corn starting to pop over a hot fire....This is actually a West African circle dance...a complicated and sacred ritual.

...[The] continued existence of the ring-shout is of critical importance to jazz, because it means that an assortment of West African musical characteristics are preserved, more or less intact, in the United States—from rhythms and blue tonality, through the falsetto break and the call-and-response pattern, to the songs of allusion and even the motions of African dance.

—MARSHALL STEARNS, The Story of Jazz, 1956

"And Once I Became That Me, I Have Never Let…Go"

*What are the links°
between the black churches
of the nineteenth century
and the freedom communi-
cated in song and struggle
in the twentieth century?
In the interview below,
Bernice Johnson Reagon,
a Georgia-born civil rights
activist, tells how her
voice came from a feeling
deep within. Her voice
and her vocal style, which
had roots in black church
music, played a powerful
role in the militant freedom
struggles against
segregation in Albany,
Georgia, during the civil
rights movement of the
early 1960s.*

DOCUMENT FOURTEEN

Now, the singing tradition in Albany was congregational. There were no soloists, there were song leaders.

When you ask somebody to lead a song, you are asking them to plant a seed. The minute you start the song, then the song is created by everybody there. It's almost like a musical explosion that takes place.…

After this first [civil rights] march, we're at the Union Baptist Church, Charlie Jones [another leader of the Albany civil rights movement] looks at me and said, "Bernice, sing a song." And I started "Over My Head I See Trouble in the Air." By the time I got to where "trouble" was suppose to be, I didn't see any trouble, so I put "freedom" in there. And I guess that was the first time I really understood what I'd been given in terms of songs. I'd always been a singer but I had always, more or less, been singing what other people taught me to sing. That was the first time I had an awareness that these songs were mine and I could use them for what I needed them for. This sort of thing was important because I ended up being arrested in the second wave of arrests in Albany, Georgia. And I was in jail. And when we got to jail, Slater King was already in jail and he said, "Bernice, is that you?" And I said, "Yeah." And he said, "Sing a song."

The voice I have now, I got the first time I sang in a movement meeting, after I got out of jail. Now I'm past that first meeting in Union Baptist, I've done "Lift Every Voice and Sing." I am a song leader, I lead every song in jail, but I did not lead the songs in jail in the voice that I have now. The voice I have now I got that night and I never heard it before in my life. At that meeting they did what they usually do. They said, "Bernice, would you lead us in a song." And I did the same first song, "Over My Head I See Freedom in the Air," but I never heard that voice before. And once I became that me, I have never let that me go.

— BERNICE JOHNSON REAGON *in an interview
quoted in* The Eyes on the Prize Civil Rights Reader, *1986*

Examining the documents

•According to Simon Brown, in Document Eight, how was the Christianity of slaves different from that of the "white folks' church"? Why did slaves want to worship separately from whites? •What is the "shout," as described by Higginson in Document Nine? Is Higginson's description of the shout positive? negative? both? What leads you to this conclusion? •In Document Ten, how do you think the freedwoman would respond to the white missionaries and Bishop Payne who were so critical of the shout (introduction to the document)? Why are their points of view on this matter so different? •Why does Louise Woodbury (Document Eleven) feel that ex-slaves much prefer black preachers over white? •What similarities and differences do you see in the ceremonies described in Documents Nine, Twelve, and Thirteen? What links do you see between the West African circle rituals, the nineteenth-century African-American ring shout, and the Harlem church service described by James Baldwin? •What was so special about the new voice that Bernice Johnson Reagon found at the movement meeting after getting out of jail (Document Fourteen)? Where does she say that voice comes from?

Suggested Activities

CREATIVE WRITING

In the first document in this chapter, South Carolina planter Charles Manigault writes:

> A negro woman [Peggy] seized as part of the spoils my wife's large and handsome mahogany bedstead and mattress and arranged it in her own Negro house on which she slept for some time.

Imagine that Mrs. Manigault has returned with her husband to the plantation they abandoned during the Civil War. She finds Peggy with her "handsome mahogany bedstead" and other property taken from the Manigault's big plantation house. What do you think the two women would say to one another? Develop a page or two of dialogue between them.

POSITION PAPER

Reread the first two documents. Then write a two-page paper taking a position on the following: *Were ex-slaves right when they seized or destroyed the property of their former masters?*

LETTER WRITING

You are a student at the Florida night school attacked by a mob in Document Seven. Write a letter to a friend explaining why it is so important to defend the school. Exchange the letter with a classmate.

DISCUSSION

Based on your reading of the documents on African-American religion and any other material you find relevant, examine and discuss the issues and themes that are consistently reflected in the black church from slavery to the present.

IMAGES OF RELIGION

Does the illustration titled "A Negro Revival Meeting" present a positive or negative picture of African-American religion? Is your response based on your point of view? the illustrator's point of view? Explain your answer.

IMAGES OF FREEDOM

Which picture or illustration in the chapter do you think best captures the meaning of freedom for emancipated slaves? Write a one-page paper explaining your choice. In your analysis, make clear how the image captures a sense of what freedom meant.

ANOTHER VIEW OF EMANCIPATION

Former slavemasters reacted differently to the loss of their slaves and way of life. At war's end, they no longer owned slaves, some lost their land, and many were in debt. Some could not cope with a world in which there were no slaves. Others schemed, made adjustments, and tried to reassert control over their former labor force.

In small groups, discuss and compare in detail the reactions of former slavemasters in the two documents that follow.

DOCUMENT FIFTEEN

As my grandfather sat on the piazza of his house at the Watersee, his former slaves stopped on the way to the station to bid him goodbye. All they said was that they were going home, and would look for him soon. He never returned to the Combahee [River valley in South Carolina] and did not see them again. Broken in health and staggered by his losses, Charles Heyward could never recover under the final blow. The emancipated slave could look forward to a better day for himself and his descendants, but the old slaveholder's day was done. He soon went to his grave and his traditions and his troubles were buried with him.

— DUNCAN CLINCH HEYWARD,
Seed from Madagascar, *1937*

DOCUMENT SIXTEEN

Our place is to work; take hold and persevere; get labor of some kind; get possession of the place; stick to it; oust the negroes and their ideas of proprietorship [land ownership]; secure armed protection close at hand on our exposed River, present a united and determined front; and make as much rice as we can....Our plantations will have to be assimilated [integrated] to the industrial establishment of other parts of the world, where the [capitalist] owner is protected by labor tallies, time tables, checks of all kind, and constant watchfulness. Every operator [worker] will steal time and everything else.

—*Georgia rice planter* ALLEN S. IZARD *in a letter to Mrs. William Mason Smith, September 15, 1865*

Examining the documents

•*In Document Fifteen, what "traditions" and "troubles" does Duncan Cinch Heyward see his grandfather taking to his grave? In Heyward's view, why could the exslave look forward to a "better day," but not the ex-slaveholder?* •*In Document Sixteen, how does Izard propose to regain control of his land and labor force? What adjustments does he plan to make to the new postwar realities? Since he no longer owns slaves, how does he plan to supervise his workforce?* •*How do the responses to the end of slavery differ in these two documents?*

CHAPTER NINE

RECONSTRUCTION OR RECONCILIATION: CONGRESS VS. THE PRESIDENT

BEFORE READING. *Examine the first two sections of the Fourteenth Amendment on the following page. Who, according to Section 1 of the amendment, is a citizen? Do emancipated slaves qualify as citizens under Section 1? do women? What protection does the section guarantee all citizens?*

Does Section 2 of the amendment guarantee the right to vote? How does it penalize states that restrict the right to vote? Under Section 2, can states restrict the rights of women to vote without penalty? of emancipated male slaves? Can states restrict the right to vote by age?

RECONSTRUCTION TOBACCO. An advertisement for a postwar southern brand probably financed by northern investors.

Tobacco Label Collection, Library of Congress.

The Fourteenth Amendment

aver rules Drey Scott

SECTION 1. All persons born or naturalized [granted full citizenship] in the United States, and subject to the jurisdiction [authority or control] thereof, are citizens of the United States wherein they reside. No State shall make or enforce any law which shall abridge [reduce] the privileges or immunities [protections] of citizens of the United States; nor shall any State deprive any person of life, liberty, or property without due process of law; nor deny to any person within its jurisdiction the equal protection of the laws.

SECTION 2. Representatives shall be apportioned among the several States according to their respective numbers, counting the whole number of persons in each State, excluding Indians not taxed. But when the right to vote at any election for the choice of electors for President and Vice-President of the United States, Representatives in Congress, the Executive and Judicial officers of a State, or the members of the Legislature thereof, is denied to any of the male inhabitants of such State, being twenty-one years of age and citizens of the United States, or in any way abridged, except for participation in rebellion, or other crime, the basis of representation therein shall be reduced in the proportion which the number of such male citizens shall bear to the whole number of male citizens twenty-one years of age in such State. [In other words, the number of a state's representatives in Congress and the number of its electoral votes in a presidential election will be reduced if it denies any male adult citizens the right to vote.]

he kinda smells BAD

— *The first two sections of the*
FOURTEENTH AMENDMENT,
approved by Congress, June 13, 1866;
ratified by the states July 28, 1868

The South's Uncertain Future

In 1865–66, free men and women all over the South grabbed liberty by the horns. They shouted hallelujah songs from newly built independent churches. They reunited families. And by the tens of thousands, men, women, and children of all ages learned reading, writing, and arithmetic. Their everyday lives became a testament to the meaning of freedom. But without political rights, and without a measure of political and economic power, emancipated slaves could not continue to enjoy the fruits of their newly gained freedom. The future of liberty in the South rested as much upon political decisions made in Washington, D.C., as upon what happened in the South.

The Thirteenth Amendment of the Constitution, passed by Congress and ratified by the states in 1865, removed any vagueness about the legal freedom of slaves. It abolished slavery everywhere in the United States—in the South, in the border states that fought on the Union side, in the North, and in the western territories. But while slaves were technically free, were they citizens? Could they vote? Could they exercise the freedoms guaranteed under the Bill of Rights? In 1865, the answer to these questions were unclear.

The future of freedom for African Americans in the South depended on the resolution to these questions, and on the response to similar issues about the political status of ex-masters and top Confederate leaders. Should the Union treat the largest slaveholders, secessionist leaders, and Confederate generals as traitors? Should the government strip them of citizenship? Should it deny them the right to vote and the right to hold office?

Congress and the President: Conflicting Reconstruction Plans

Powerful men in Congress and the White House were the only ones who could resolve these unanswered questions about the rights of ex-slaves and ex-masters. Their decisions set the terms for Reconstruction in the South. But the president and Congress were increasingly at odds over what course to pursue. Their differences escalated into a tense, bitter confrontation between President Andrew Johnson and the Republican-controlled Congress.

Were ex-slaves legally citizens in 1865? Could they vote?

The confrontation between Johnson and the Republicans went back to the beginning of the Civil War and the debate over war aims. At the start of the war, Lincoln's primary goal was the preservation of the Union. Radicals in his own party, however, called for a war to destroy slavery. Disagreements over how to conduct the war were later reflected in sharply contrasting approaches to peace and Reconstruction.

In his 1865 inaugural address, after his reelection as president, Lincoln made a plea for unity. Have "malice towards none," he counseled. Let us "bind up the nation's

SECESSIONIST—Confederate

MALICE—will to harm or injure

In 1860, Andrew Johnson was a Democratic party senator from Tennessee. When his state seceded in 1861, he defied the Confederacy by remaining in his U.S. Senate seat, the only southern senator to do so. President Abraham Lincoln, a Republican, rewarded the loyalty of Johnson, a Democrat, by making him his vice-presidential candidate when he ran for reelection in 1864.

wounds." As early as 1863, in this same spirit of reconciliation, Lincoln had established guidelines to bring Confederate states already occupied by northern armies back into the Union. As soon as ten percent of those voting in 1860 pledged to support the U.S. Constitution and to abolish slavery, a state could return to the Union. Since slaves, free African Americans, and many poor whites could not vote in 1860, that date is very important. In effect, Lincoln was restoring rights to selected southerners on one condition: that they abolish slavery. But his plan said nothing about empowering all those who couldn't vote in 1860: African Americans and poor whites.

There is alot of evidence to suggest that Lincoln saw his wartime "ten-percent" plan as a starting point and not as a firm and final plan for Reconstruction. In his last speech, Lincoln endorsed the right of emancipated slaves to vote. Couched in cautious language, the endorsement seemed to apply only to educated freedmen and former soldiers. What's important, though, is that it showed movement in Lincoln's thinking about Reconstruction. Just as Lincoln had changed his war aims, there are indications that his plans about Reconstruction were also evolving.

ENDORSED — supported

How were differences between the president and the Radicals over Reconstruction linked to the debate over war aims?

How did Johnson's approach to Reconstruction differ from Lincoln's?

PARDONED. A *Frank Leslie's* cartoon portrays Andrew Johnson with a basket overflowing with pardons to be distributed to former Confederate officials. "Look here, Andy," says a recently reinstated southerner, "if you want Reconstruction, you had better set me over the whole thing down in our state."

Frank Leslie's Illustrated Newspaper, August 1865. American Social History Project.

Under the Constitution, Vice-President Andrew Johnson became president upon Lincoln's death. Lincoln had chosen Johnson to run with him in his 1864 reelection campaign. The choice of Johnson—a pro-Union southerner and Democrat from the state of Tennessee—was in keeping with Lincoln's desire to heal wounds that divided the nation between North and South and between Democrats and Republicans. But when he became president, Johnson took Lincoln's ten-percent plan and turned it into an inflexible formula for bringing the South back into the Union on terms that would return power to the planters and would deny political rights to emancipated slaves.

In sharp contrast to Johnson, Radical Republicans saw Reconstruction as the logical outgrowth of a war for freedom. The whole point of the war, they argued, was not reconciliation but the destruction of slavery. And the destruction of slavery, as they saw it, had to go beyond the Thirteenth Amendment, that is, beyond basic emancipation. According to this line of reasoning, you could only destroy slavery in the defeated South by building new political and economic structures in its place; hence the term Reconstruction.

While there were some internal differences among them, the Radicals generally pushed the following agenda: First, take away the political power of the slaveholders, restrict their rights, and deny them the privilege of voting; second, give that power to ex-slaves and poor whites and guarantee them full rights as citizens, including the right to vote; recruit them into the Republican party; and third, dismantle the system of slave labor and create one built on free wage labor.

There was a practical problem with the Radical plan: the Radicals were a minority in their own party. But it was their good fortune to have a politically inept adversary, President Andrew Johnson. In just two years, Johnson succeeded in offending much of northern public opinion and virtually the entire Republican party— conservative and moderate Republicans as well as Radicals.

What was the difference in approach between Johnson and the Radicals?

Johnson's inflexible refusal to compromise played into the hands of the Radicals. They were the only ones with a clear, well-thought-out alternative to Johnson's plan. Moderate Republicans embraced a part of the radical plan. Since the Republicans commanded a majority in Congress, key sections of the radical agenda became Reconstruction policy by 1867.

Why, and how, did the Radicals want to reconstruct the South?

The Johnson Plan

Like Lincoln before him, Johnson argued that under the U.S. Constitution, no state had the right to secede. Taking this logic to the next step, he claimed that the eleven Confederate states had never legally left the Union. Johnson's critics cried foul. By such legal sleight of hand, they argued, he was erasing the four bloodiest years of American history. It was as if secession, the creation of the Confederate States of America,

RADICAL—someone who favors sweeping changes
INEPT—clumsy; incompetent
CONSERVATIVE—traditional
MODERATE—middle of the road

"ANDREW JOHNSON'S RECONSTRUCTION AND HOW IT WORKS." An 1866 Thomas Nast cartoon
presents Andrew Johnson as the famous theatrical villain Iago,
whose betrayal of Othello in Shakespeare's play was cloaked in noble words.

Thomas Nast, *Harper's Weekly*, September 1, 1866. Prints and Photographs Division, Library of Congress.

the Civil War, and the deaths of over 600,000 Americans had never mattered.

Consider the implications of Johnson's legal approach: If secession had never legally happened, then the federal government had no right to reconstruct any state as a condition for its readmission to the Union. As Johnson saw it, every southern state—as long as it obeyed the Constitution and punished traitors to the Union—had the right to choose its own leaders, run its own affairs, and select its own representatives to the U.S. Congress. States could exercise these rights based on the electorate before they seceded (illegally, Johnson would say) from the Union.

In the spring and summer of 1865, while Congress was out of session, Johnson moved quickly to restore southern states to their legal place in the Union. In May, his amnesty policy guaranteed full rights of citizenship to all white southerners who pledged loyalty to the Union. Initially, his amnesty excluded Confederate leaders, prominent slaveholders, and any others judged to have committed acts of treason against the U.S. Constitution. He then undid the exclusion by allowing these elite southerners to petition him for pardons— pardons that he granted with alarming generosity. When he set up interim state governments, he invariably chose conservative southerners to lead them. Once these state governments ratified the Thirteenth Amendment abolishing slavery and repudiated Confederate debts, they could return to the Union in good standing.

What were the implications for Reconstruction of Johnson's argument that southern states could not legally secede?

AMNESTY—a general pardon for offenses

TREASON—betrayal of one's country

INTERIM—temporary

REPUDIATE—disown

"SLAVERY IS DEAD?" The impact of Andrew Johnson's policies on the lives of freedpeople is evaluated in this January 1867 *Harper's Weekly* cartoon.

Thomas Nast, *Harper's Weekly,* January 12, 1867. American Social History Project.

Losing the War, Winning the Peace

Under Johnson's plan, the new southern state governments looked like the old ones. Confederate generals, cabinet officers, and legislators won election to state office and Congress. Alexander Stephens, vice-president of the Confederacy, claimed a seat in the U.S. Congress as a representative from Georgia.

Outraged editorial writers in northern newspapers fumed that the Confederacy had lost the war but won the peace. Just eight months after General Robert E. Lee had surrendered at Appomattox, Confederate leaders once again governed the southern states.

By the end of 1865, it seemed that the more things changed in the South, the more they stayed the same. Once again, black labor worked cotton, sugar, and rice fields for white planters. The governments set up under Johnson's plan instituted Black Codes, a system of labor control that looked suspiciously like slavery. In most states, the codes restricted freedpeople to agricultural or domestic labor. Usually this was accomplished by means of vagrancy acts that

Why did it appear in late 1865 that the Confederacy had lost the war but won the peace?

What were the Black Codes?

VAGRANT —a person with no visible means of support

"SELLING A FREEDMAN TO PAY HIS FINE." "Special artist" James E. Taylor
toured the South for *Frank Leslie's Illustrated Newspaper* after the Civil War, when the notorious Black Codes
were being enforced. He sketched this scene in front of the county courthouse
in Monticello, Florida, during the winter of 1866–67.

James E. Taylor, *Frank Leslie's Illustrated Newspaper,* January 19, 1867. American Social History Project.

empowered local law enforcement authorities to arrest and fine African Americans who had no visible means of support or who refused to sign long-term contracts to labor for whites. When freedpeople could not pay the penalties, officials would turn them over to local landlords to work off the fines. This meant hard labor from sunrise to sunset for bare-minimum wages. In some states, the Black Codes even permitted white employers to apprentice black children for indefinite periods of time without permis-sion from their parents.

Black Codes that resembled slavery mocked the Union's victory in a war in which hundreds of thousands of men gave their lives so that all Americans might be free. The very thought of the Confederate vice-president sitting in Congress infuriated radicals, exasperated moderates, insulted large segments of northern public opinion, offended Republicans, and even raised questions among some Democrats who had opposed the war.

African Americans Respond

In 1865–66, while President Johnson granted pardons in Washington, there was a surge of political activity by African-American communities throughout the South. As discussed in chapter eight, churches, such as the Bute Street African Methodist Church in Norfolk, Virginia, mobilized their congregations to demand the right to vote.

In turn, Black Codes drew a swift and remarkably political response from the African-American community. Understanding the necessity of political action, African-American leaders across the South called for state "colored conventions" to develop an agenda for freedom. Despite restrictions on travel imposed by Black Codes, over two thousand freedmen—representing virtually every nook and cranny of black South Carolina—crowded into the Zion Presbyterian Church in Charleston on the last Saturday of November 1865. In a petition to the U.S. Congress, the South Carolina Colored People's Convention eloquently argued its case against the Black Codes and for freedom.

> We simply ask that we shall be recognized as men; that there be no obstructions placed in our way; that the same laws that govern white men shall govern black men; that we have the right of trial by jury of our peers; that schools be established for education of colored children as well as white; and that the advantage of both colors shall, in this respect, be equal; that no impediments be put in the way of our acquiring homesteads for ourselves and our people; that in short we be dealt with as others are—in equity and justice.

The call of the South Carolina Colored People's Convention, and black conventions just like it across the South, anticipated the agenda of radical Reconstruction and encouraged Republicans in Congress to respond to the new Black Codes with a similar sense of urgency.

In this climate, Congress refused to seat Alexander Stephens and other former Confederates elected to the Senate and House of Representatives under Johnson's lenient plan of reconciliation.

What issues were raised by the black conventions? How did they anticipate radical Reconstruction?

IMPEDIMENT—obstruction

ANTICIPATE—to foresee

Johnson Unites the Republicans

Johnson had succeeded in uniting, if only temporarily and against himself, the rival radical, moderate, and conservative factions of the Republican party. Led by its Republican majority, and prodded by black political action in the South, Congress appointed a Joint Committee on Recon-struction to investigate conditions in the old Confederacy. The committee's final report in 1866 documented the grim legacy of Johnson's policies in the South: racism, violence, repression, and semislavery. The very appointment of the joint committee, not to mention its damning final report, challenged Johnson's authority and asserted the power of Congress to reconstruct the South.

The final report of the joint committee created a sense of urgency in Congress. Racial violence and Black Codes threatened the liberty of every freedman and woman in the South. Responding swiftly, Congress took three actions to protect the rights of southern African Americans.

First, Congress began drafting a new amendment—the Fourteenth Amendment —to guarantee freedpeople full rights as citizens.

Second, it extended the life of the Freedmen's Bureau, an agency of the federal government run mostly by white northerners and created by Congress in the last months of the Civil War in 1865 to help African Americans make the transition from slavery to freedom. As part of its charge from

Why did Congress refuse to seat senators and congressmen elected by southern governments under the Johnson plan?

How did Johnson unite the Republicans?

REPRESSION—the act of crushing or dominating

TRANSITION—change

THE FREEDMAN'S BUREAU! A racist Democratic broadside during the 1866 election campaign.

Prints and Photographs Division, Library of Congress.

Congress, the bureau was to establish schools, divide the confiscated lands of Confederate planters, supervise contracts between freedmen and their landlords, and mediate disputes between ex-planters and ex-slaves. Chapter 11 explores how the bureau sometimes intervened on the side of planters. Nonetheless, African Americans throughout the South saw the Freedmen's Bureau as an important line of defense against hostile local courts that enforced Black Codes and against coercive landlords who imposed harsh conditions of labor.

Third, Congress passed the Civil Rights Act of 1866. Under its provisions, ex-slaves became citizens, enjoying the "full and equal benefit of all laws." The bill gave federal courts the power to intervene when state and local governments denied freed-

people full protection under the law. In one sweeping act, Congress had cut the legs out from underneath the Black Codes and reversed the 1857 Dred Scott decision of the Supreme Court (see chapter 2), in which Chief Justice Roger Taney claimed that no black person in the United States enjoyed "any rights which the white man was bound to respect." Just nine years later, Congress declared that the Constitution respected the rights of all men—black and white.

The Civil Rights Act and the Freedmen's Bureau asserted the powers of the federal government over those of the southern states. In doing so, both pieces of legislation broke from the deeply rooted American tradition of states' rights. But even Republican moderates who advocated states' rights agreed that this was an exceptional circumstance.

CONFISCATE—seize or take away

MEDIATE—settle or resolve differences

IMPOSE—to force upon

COERCIVE—enforced agreement or obedience

"THE MASSACRE AT NEW ORLEANS." Thomas Nast's view of Andrew Johnson's role in the July 1866 riot.

Thomas Nast, *The Massacre at New Orleans*, 1867, oil on canvas, 7 feet 10 ¾ inches x 11 feet 6 ½ inches.
Prints and Photographs Division, Library of Congress.

Only the full power of the federal government, they concluded, could break the back of the Black Codes and racial violence in the South.

President Johnson didn't buy this argument. Outraged, he vetoed both the Civil Rights Act and the legislation extending the life of the Freedmen's Bureau. In doing so, he did more than just defend states' rights. His inflammatory language and actions rekindled fires of racial, sectional, and political division. In his veto message to Congress, Johnson claimed that the legislation both violated states' rights and "operate[d] in favor of colored and against the white race."

Why did Johnson veto the Civil Rights Act and the extension of the Freedmen's Bureau?

Democrats and ex-Confederates used Johnson's veto to play on racial fears and bigotry. One Democratic newspaper in the South cheered the president for standing "with our race [against] niggers, gipsies and baboons." Another Democrat railed at Congress because the Civil Rights Act of 1866 would grant African Americans citizenship. "How long will it be," he asked, "before it [Congress] will say the Negro shall vote, shall sit in the jury box, and intermarry with your families?"

What was the reaction of moderate and Radical Republicans to Johnson's vetoes?

Johnson's veto and the inflammatory rhetoric of Democrats and ex-Confederates angered moderate Republicans. In February 1866, they joined Radical Republicans in mobilizing a two-thirds majority vote in Congress to override Johnson's veto of the Civil Rights Act. A few months later, Congress drafted new legislation to preserve the Freedmen's Bureau. Johnson vetoed the new bill, but Congress overrode his veto, and the Freedmen's Bureau continued its work in the South.

By his actions, Johnson had declared war on Congress. He refused to enforce the Civil Rights Act and continuously sabotaged the work of the Freedmen's Bureau. His defiance only goaded congressional Republicans to take more militant action. They hastened preparation of the Fourteenth Amendment to the Constitution for ratification by the states.

The new amendment banned Confederate leaders from federal and state office, placed the full weight of the U.S. Constitution behind citizenship for African-American men, and insured that every state provided "equal protection of the laws." Where governments denied freedmen the vote, the amendment reduced representation to Congress in direct proportion to that state's black male population. But the amendment did not insure voting rights for African Americans, it simply reduced the power of those states that restricted black voting rights.

STATES RIGHTS—the principle that the states should control their own affairs without the interference from the federal government.

VETO—to prevent from becoming law. The president can veto legislation, but Congress can override the veto by a two-thirds vote of its members.

INFLAMMATORY—arousing strong emotion

RAIL—to use harsh language

RHETORIC—language used for effect

SABOTAGE—obstruct or undercut

GOAD—incite or prod

MILITANT—aggressive

Contested Turf:
The Fourteenth Amendment

The Fourteenth Amendment to the Constitution may have been the single most important political document of the Reconstruction era.

To move the amendment through Congress, Radical Republicans gave ground in 1866 to the moderate majority of their own party on the crucial issue of equal suffrage (the right to vote). The amendment did not grant the vote to adult citizens (universal suffrage), as advocated by the women's suffrage movement and other reformers. On the central issue of voting rights for black freedmen, it penalized states that denied the vote to any "male inhabitants" by reducing representation in Congress (Section 2). In sum, the amendment did not give African-American males the right to vote, but rather punished states that denied freedmen that right.

Nonetheless, the amendment had a huge impact on the political status of former slaves. Upon emancipation, freedmen and women under the law were neither slaves nor citizens. This created legal confusion, because technically they were free, but under the law they possessed no civil rights.

The first sentence of Section 1 of the amendment cleared the air, awarding citizenship to "anyone born [virtually all the emancipated slaves] or naturalized in the United States." The second sentence went on to proclaim "equal protection of the laws." The government could not deprive any "citizen of the United States" of "life, liberty, or property without due process of law."

The amendment represented an immense legal step forward for freedom and equality. But there were complications—one short-term, the other longer term.

In the short-term, the debate over ratification of the Fourteenth Amendment split the nineteenth-century reform movement.

For forty years, that movement had linked abolitionists and advocates of women's rights. Key leaders of the women's movement felt betrayed by abolitionist friends inside and outside Congress. The Fourteenth Amendment addressed racial discrimination, they argued, but not sexual discrimination. They pointed to the second clause of the amendment, which for the first time introduced the word "male" into the U.S. Constitution. Leaders in the fight for female suffrage made a decision at this point to sever forty years of ties with abolitionists and to create an independent women's movement. Susan B. Anthony and Elizabeth Cady Stanton felt that women would never get the vote if they waited for a male-dominated reform movement that was ready to push the rights of African-American men, but was often hesitant to do the same for women of all races. Following passage of the Fourteenth Amendment, the abolitionist-dominated reform movement and the women's movement generally went separate ways.

Over the long term, there was a second complication. From 1873 to 1954, the Supreme Court of the United States interpreted the Fourteenth Amendment in a way that narrowed the rights of African Americans. In fact, the Court used the "due process" and "equal protection" clauses more often to protect the rights of corporations than of individual citizens. (Under the law, a corporation is a legal person; the word person is used in the last clause of Section 1 of the Fourteenth Amendment.)

In 1954, however, in the landmark case of Brown v. Board of Education, the Supreme Court desegregated schools, reversing seventy years of interpretations that restricted the Fourteenth Amendment. During the late 1950s and throughout the 1960s, when millions of Americans struggled for civil rights, the courts used the Fourteenth Amendment to extend equal protection under the law to all citizens.

For almost 130 years, the Fourteenth Amendment has been contested turf. Conservatives and liberals, radicals and moderates, men and women, corporations and mass movements, courts and legislatures, and various ethnic and racial groups — particularly African Americans — have all struggled over the meaning and interpretation of the amendment.

The documents that follow examine a small but important piece of that contested turf: the tension between the women's movement and the old antislavery coalition over universal suffrage and the Fourteenth Amendment.

Here are four related documents: a petition sent to the abolitionist Gerritt Smith; a December 1868 letter from Smith to Susan B. Anthony explaining why he could not sign the petition; a reaction to Smith's argument from Elizabeth Cady Stanton, one of Anthony's co-leaders in the women's movement (and Smith's cousin); and finally, a piece written by Anthony four years later in 1872.

A Petition for Women's Suffrage

DOCUMENT TWO

To the Senate and House of Representatives in Congress Assembled:

The undersigned citizens of the State of _____ earnestly but respectfully request that, in any change or amendment of the Constitution you may propose to extend or regulate Suffrage, there shall be no distinction made between men and women.

—*One of many petitions drafted after the Civil War by*
ELIZABETH CADY STANTON *and* SUSAN B. ANTHONY, *leaders of the women's movement and also abolitionists*

Gerritt Smith: "I Cannot Sign the Petition"

DOCUMENT THREE

My Dear Susan B. Anthony: I this evening received your earnest letter. It pains me to be obliged to disappoint you. But I cannot sign the petition you sent me. Cheerfully, gladly can I sign a petition for the enfranchisement [granting the right to vote] of women. But I cannot sign a paper against the enfranchisement of the Negro man, unless at the same time woman shall be enfranchised. The removal of the political disabilities of race is my first desire, of sex my second. If put on the same level and urged in the same connection, neither will be soon accomplished. The former will very soon be, if untrammelled [unrestricted] by the other, and its success will prepare the way for the other.

—Letter to Susan B. Anthony from abolitionist and advocate of suffrage for ex-slaves GERRITT SMITH, *December 30, 1868*

Elizabeth Cady Stanton: Why Can't White Male Reformers See "the Wrongs to Women in Their Own Households"?

DOCUMENT FOUR

[Gerritt Smith] does not clearly read the sign of the times, or he would see that there is to be no reconstruction of this nation, except on the basis of Universal Suffrage, as the natural, inalienable right of every citizen to its exercise....

As the aristocracy of this country is the "male sex" and as Mr. Smith belongs to the privileged order, he naturally considers it important, for the best interests of the nation, that every type and shade of degraded, ignorant manhood should be enfranchised, before even the higher classes of womanhood should be admitted to the polls.

This does not surprise us. Men always judge more wisely of objective wrongs and oppressions, than of those in which they themselves are involved. Tyranny on a southern plantation is far more easily seen by white men...[in] the north than the wrongs of the women of their own households....

Again, Mr. Smith refuses to sign the petition because he thinks that to press the broader question of "Universal Suffrage" would defeat the partial one of "Manhood Suffrage"; in other words to demand protection for women against her oppressors would jeopardize the black man's chances for securing protection against his oppressors. If it is a question of precedence merely, on what principle of justice or courtesy should woman yield her right of enfranchisement to the Negro? If men cannot be trusted to legislate for their own sex, how can they legislate for the opposite sex, of whose wants and needs they know nothing! It has always been considered good philosophy in pressing any measure to claim the uttermost in order to get something.... Henry Ward Beecher advised abolitionists, right after the war, to demand "Universal Suffrage" if they wished to secure the ballot for the new made freedmen. "Bait your hooks," said he, "with a woman and perhaps you will catch a Negro." But their intense interest in the Negro blinded them, and they forsook principle for policy. In giving woman the cold shoulder they raised a more deadly opposition to the Negro than any we had encountered, creating an antagonism between him and the very element most needed, especially in the South, to be propitiated [won over] in his behalf....

...There is no other ground on which to debate the question. Every argument for the Negro is an argument for woman and no logician can escape it....

Although those who demand "Women's Suffrage" on principle are few, those who would oppose "Negro suffrage" from prejudice are many, hence the only way to secure the latter is to end all this talk of class legislation, bury the Negro in the citizen, and claim suffrage for all men and women as a natural, inalienable right.

— ELIZABETH CADY STANTON, *January 14, 1869*

Susan B. Anthony: "Being Persons, Then, Women Are Citizens"

DOCUMENT FIVE

Though the words persons, people, inhabitants, electors, citizens, are all used indiscriminately in the national and State constitutions, there was always a conflict of opinion, prior to the war, as to whether they were synonymous terms, but whatever room there was for doubts, under the old regime, the adoption of the Fourteenth Amendment settled that question forever in its first sentence:

> All persons born or naturalized in the United States, and subject to the jurisdiction thereof, are citizens of the United States wherein they reside.

The second settles the equal status of all citizens:

> No state shall make or enforce any law which shall abridge the privileges or immunities of citizens of the United States; nor shall any State deprive any person of life, liberty, or property without due process of law; nor deny to any person within its jurisdiction the equal protection of the laws.

The only question left to be settled now is: Are women persons? I scarcely believe that any of our opponents will have the hardihood to say that they are not. Being persons, then, women are citizens and no State has a right to make any new law, or to enforce any old law, which shall abridge their privileges and immunities. Hence, every discrimination against women in the constitutions and laws of the several States is today null and void, precisely as is every one against Negroes.

— SUSAN B. ANTHONY, *November 1872*

Examining the documents

• *Why won't Gerritt Smith sign the petition to Congress (Documents Two and Three)? In his view, what is the relationship between women and African-American men getting the vote? Why does he want to separate the two issues?* •*What is Elizabeth Cady Stanton's argument in Document Four in response to Smith? What does Stanton mean when she chides Smith for believing "that every type and shade of degraded, ignorant manhood should be enfranchised, before even the higher classes of womanhood should be admitted to the polls"? Is this argument consistent with the one that she makes for "universal suffrage as the natural, inalienable right of every citizen"? What does Henry Ward Beecher (quoted by Stanton), in arguing for African-American suffrage, mean by saying "bait your hooks with a woman and perhaps you will catch a Negro"?* •*What is Susan B. Anthony's argument (Document Five) for claiming that the Fourteenth Amendment guarantees women's rights?* •*Overall, why did the women's movement split with the old abolitionist movement over the Fourteenth Amendment?*

"THE PROMISE OF THE DECLARATION OF INDEPENDENCE FULFILLED."
A double-page engraving in the March 19, 1870, issue of *Frank Leslie's Illustrated Newspaper*
commemorates the passage of the Fifteenth Amendment to the Constitution.

Frank Leslie's Illustrated Newspaper, March 19, 1870. American Social History Project.

Johnson was furious. He saw the proposed amendment as one more humiliating attack on states' rights and presidential authority. Urging southern states to reject the amendment, he took his case to the nation by turning the 1866 congressional election into a referendum on Reconstruction.

Johnson campaigned for Democrats and against Republicans. He seemed on a mission to punish radicals, but his crusade backfired when antiblack violence escalated in the South. In the summer of 1866, white rioters murdered eighty African Americans in Memphis and New Orleans while local authorities looked on. Vivid newspaper accounts of these savage acts nauseated northern readers and turned public opinion sharply against Johnson's policies of reconciliation with the South. The majority of northern voters, by no means in a forgiving mood toward the South, gave Republicans, particularly Radicals, a resounding victory in the November congressional elections. With a commanding three-to-one majority in Congress, the Republicans reversed the course of Johnson's southern policies.

Why did Johnson fail so miserably when he took his case to the American people in the 1866 election?

Radical Reconstruction

Radicals were never able to gain support for their maximum program (land confiscation and distribution, massive federal funding for southern education, etc.). Even so, they shaped a Republican coalition in the House and Senate that made black voting rights the centerpiece of what came to be known as congressional or Radical Reconstruction. Just six months earlier, it seemed unimaginable that

moderates could have supported such a program. But in a sweeping mandate, Congress passed three Reconstruction Acts in early 1867 that launched an activist agenda by:

- providing for the replacement of the state governments established under Johnson's plan of reconciliation;
- dividing the South into five military districts;
- calling for the election of new state constitutional conventions by loyal black and white southerners under the protection of federal troops (and temporarily barring many former Confederate officials from voting or holding office);
- ordering these conventions to draft new constitutions, including provisions for black suffrage;
- decreeing the election of new state governments under the provisions of the recently drafted constitutions;
- requiring ratification of the Fourteenth Amendment as a condition for readmission of southern states to the Union.

The change in the course of events was stunning. The Reconstruction Acts of 1867 unseated Alexander Stephens and his fellow Confederates in Congress, dismantled the Johnson governments throughout the South, empowered freedmen, and ensured ratification of the Fourteenth Amendment.

How did the 1867 congressional legislation drastically alter the course of Reconstruction?

When Andrew Johnson continued to obstruct, an angry House of Representatives drew up charges of impeachment to be heard by the Senate. But Johnson had done nothing that was unquestionably illegal. In a more sober moment in the spring of 1868,

REFERENDUM — the submission of a measure or issue to the public for a vote

COALITION — an alliance of groups

with moderate Republicans casting the deciding votes, the Senate found Johnson not guilty. He served out the remainder of his term, but with greatly diminished power.

In 1870, two years after the Fourteenth Amendment was ratified, Congress and the states responded to another round of racial violence in the South by providing additional constitutional protection for the black electorate. The Fifteenth Amendment declared that the right of U.S. citizens to vote could "not be abridged or denied" by any state "on account of race, color, or previous condition of servitude." The Fourteenth and Fifteenth Amendments—sporadically enforced until 1876 (the end of Reconstruction), then rarely enforced until 1954 (the *Brown v. Board of Education* school desegregation decision by the Supreme Court)—provided the legal foundation for the civil rights movement of the 1950s, 1960s, and 1970s. They are part of the enduring constitutional legacy of Reconstruction.

In 1857, when Chief Justice Roger Taney announced the Dred Scott decision (see page 50 in chapter 2) and dismissed the very notion of legal and even human rights for African Americans, who could have imagined that in little more than a decade the Thirteenth, Fourteenth, and Fifteenth Amendments would change the U.S. Constitution? Radical Reconstruction did that and much more. With the passage of the Reconstruction Acts of 1867, Congress opened up new possibilities for American democracy. Over the next nine years, African Americans, poor whites, and others rose to the democratic challenge in the South.

IMPEACH—to charge a public official with misconduct. The House of Representatives can impeach a president. The Senate then hears the charges and conducts a trial. To convict a president and remove him from office, a two-thirds vote of the Senate is required.

SPORADICALLY—irregularly, but not continuously

"THE FIFTEENTH AMENDMENT ILLUSTRATED." A cartoon in an 1870 edition of *Die Vehme* (*The Star Chamber*), a short-lived St. Louis satirical weekly, supports woman's suffrage at the expense of African Americans, Chinese, and illiterate immigrants.

Joseph Keppler, Die Vehme, April 2, 1870. General Research Division, The New York Public Library, Astor, Lenox, and Tilden Foundations.

The NAACP Argues *Brown v. the Board of Education*

In 1954, in the case of Brown v. the Board of Education of Topeka, Kansas, *the Supreme Court desegregated public schools. This was not the first time that the Supreme Court spoke to the issue. In 1896, in* Plessy v. Ferguson, *the Supreme Court, applying the principle of "separate but equal," ruled that segregation was constitutional. Voting seven to one, the court upheld a Louisiana judge, John H. Ferguson, who had imposed a criminal sentence on an African American, Homer Plessy. Plessy's crime was that he rode in an all-white railroad passenger car instead of an all-black one, in violation of Louisiana's segregation laws.*

Schools set up under the Plessy *decision were separate and equal in name, but separate and grossly unequal in fact.*

From the time that it was established in 1939, the Legal Defense and Education Fund, Incorporated, of the National Association for the Advancement of

Colored People (NAACP) argued that segregation in general and the Plessy *decision in particular violated the Fourteenth Amendment to the Constitution. The NAACP Legal Defense and Education fund focused on the following portion of the amendment:*

> No state shall make or enforce any law which shall abridge the privileges or immunities of citizens of the United States; nor shall any state deprive any person of life, liberty, or property without due process of law, nor deny to any person within its jurisdiction the equal protection of the laws.

The Fund argued that the amendment clearly prohibited discrimination, and particularly segregation, based on color or race.

What follows is part of the brief, or legal argument, filed by the Fund in the Brown *case asserting that the original intent of the framers of the Fourteenth Amendment was to deny states the right to discriminate or segregate on the basis of race. In its 1954 desegregation decision, the Supreme Court drew heavily on the Fund's brief.*

DOCUMENT SIX

[The Supreme Court] requested enlightenment as to whether Congress which submitted, and the state legislatures and conventions which ratified, the Fourteenth Amendment contemplated [thought] or understood that it would prohibit segregation in public schools, either of its own force or through subsequent [later] legislative or judicial action. The evidence, both in the Congress and in the legislatures of the ratifying states, reflects substantial intent of the Amendment's proponents and the substantial understanding of its opponents that the Fourteenth Amendment, would of its own force, proscribe [forbid] all forms of state-imposed racial distinctions, thus necessarily including all racial segregation in public education.

The Fourteenth Amendment was actually the culmination of the determined efforts of the Radical Republican majority in Congress to incorporate into our fundamental law the well defined equalitarian principle of complete equality for all without regard to race or color. The debates of the 39th Congress and succeeding Congresses clearly reveal the intention that the Fourteenth Amendment would work a revolutionary change in our state-federal relationship by denying to the states the power to distinguish on the basis of race.

The Civil Rights Bill of 1866, as originally proposed, possessed scope sufficiently broad in the opinion of many Congressmen to entirely destroy all state legislation based on race. A great majority of the Republican Radicals—who later formulated the Fourteenth Amendment—understood and intended that the Bill would prohibit segregated schools. Opponents of the measure shared this understanding. The scope of this legislation was narrowed because it was known that the Fourteenth Amendment was in the process of preparation and would itself have scope exceeding that of the original draft of the Civil Rights Bill.

…The broad general purpose of the Amendment—obliteration of race and color distinctions—is clearly established by the evidence. So far as there was consideration of the Amendment's impact upon the undeveloped educational systems then existing, both proponents and opponents of the Amendment understood that it would proscribe all racial segregation in public education.

The evidence as to the understanding of the states is equally convincing. Each of the eleven states that seceded from the Union ratified the Amendment, and concurrently eliminated racial distinctions from its laws, and adopted a [new state] constitution free of requirement or specific authorization of segregated schools, and none enacted a school segregation law until after readmission.… [The] amendment required them to remove all racial distinctions from their existing and prospective laws, including those pertaining to public education.

—*Excerpt from the fall 1953* BRIEF OF NAACP LEGAL DEFENSE AND EDUCATION FUND, INCORPORATED, *submitted to the Supreme Court in* Brown v. the Board of Education of Topeka, Kansas

Examining the document

• *Why was it important for the NAACP Legal Defense and Education Fund to establish that Congress, when it drafted and passed the amendment, understood that it would forbid "racial segregation"? What arguments and evidence does the brief present that Congress and the states had this understanding?*

Suggested Activities

FOURTEENTH AMENDMENT In small groups, first discuss, then rewrite, how you would reword Sections 1 and 2 of the Fourteenth Amendment to guarantee Americans of every race and gender their full rights as citizens. Craft the language carefully, clearly, and briefly, so that there can be no confusion about how to interpret the amendment.

DISCUSSION

What is the debate about between Gerritt Smith and Elizabeth Cady Stanton (Documents Three and Four)? Who do you think is right, and why?

DISCUSSION

Look up the word *radical*. What was "radical" about the Radical plan of Reconstruction?

MOCK COURT

Do further research on the 1954 *Brown v. Board of Education* Supreme Court decision. Break intro three groups. One group will prepare a presentation by the NAACP calling for desegregation of schools. A second will develop arguments for the Topeka Board of Education defending the "separate but equal" doctrine. A third, playing the role of Supreme Court justices, will develop questions to ask both presenting groups. The NAACP presents first, the Topeka group second. After each presentation, the justices ask questions. The justices then deliberate and present their decision to the class the next day. Class discussion and analysis follows. (This may be done over several days.)

IN-DEPTH RESEARCH

Do a research paper on the women's suffrage movement from the time of the Fourteenth Amendment in 1868 to the 1920 passage of the Nineteenth Amendment, which granted women the right to vote.

"FIFTEENTH AMENDMENT ILLUSTRATED"

Look at the final picture in the chapter titled "Fifteenth Amendment Illustrated." What is its point of view and message? Who is the intended audience? How are African Americans, immigrants, and women stereotyped? After considering these questions, write a one-page letter reacting to the illustration to the editor of the satirical magazine that published it. Share and discuss letters with classmates.

ANALYZING A POLITICAL HANDBILL

Study carefully the political handbill titled "Freedman's Bureau" on page 202. Who put it out? why? when? where? Who is the intended audience? What is the message and purpose of the flyer? On what basis does it seek to appeal to its intended audience?

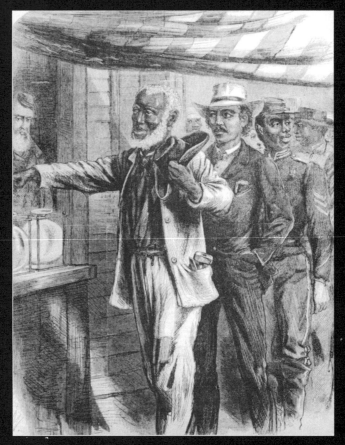

"THE FIRST VOTE." An 1867 *Harper's Weekly* illustration features three figures symbolizing black political leadership: a skilled craftsman, a sophisticated city dweller, and a Union Army veteran.

RECONSTRUCTION IN THE SOUTH: PUSHING FROM THE BOTTOM UP

BEFORE READING. *Consider these questions after reading the document below. Why was Yulee so upset about J. W. Toer's magic lantern show?* *What in particular concerned Yulee? Who was the audience was for the magic lantern show?*

Dr. Toer's Magic Lantern Show

A Georgia planter and lawyer, Elias Yulee, writes to the Freedmen's Bureau expressing his concern about the activities of a freed slave named J. W. Toer and his "magic lantern" show. (A magic lantern show was an early form of slide show, using hand-tinted glass slides.) While reading the document, try to imagine what Dr. Toer's show was about and its effect upon the audience. [NOTE: We will meet Mr. Yulee again in Document Two of the next chapter and Preacher. T. G. (Tunis) Campbell later in this chapter.]

DOCUMENT ONE

Walthourville, Liberty County, Georgia
April 23, 1867

Colonel G. G. Silby, Commanding
Colonel,

    ...I make known to you the proceedings of some colored itinerants [travelers] who are collecting money from [the freed slaves] under the pretense of securing their rights. A colored preacher named T. G. Campbell, a stranger, and a man named Toney Golden of this county have held several meetings.... These frequent meetings are preventing the people, unnecessarily, from working.... I was at a large meeting of the colored people yesterday, called by preacher Campbell and Toney Golden, and the spirit of the addresses was calculated to create a division into classes—Blacks against Whites.

A black man calling himself Professor J. W. Toer presided. He is travelling about with a magic lantern to exhibit what he calls the progress of reconstruction, which together with his harangue [noisy speech] during the exhibition, tend to the arousing of antagonistic feelings towards the whites. He had a scene, which he called "Before the Proclamation," another "After the Proclamation." ... If the whites were to meet [react to] the issues raised, disorder would result, but they are apathetic & submissive to the laws of the U.S., on which they depend for protection. I cannot see the sense of arraying the blacks against the whites under such circumstances. ...

Toney Golden announced ... it was now the black man against the white man ... [t]hat the blacks could have perfect control of the County, and could elect whom they pleased to all offices. That the Sherman Bill [the 1867 Reconstruction Act dividing the South into five military districts] had been appealed to the Supreme Court ... but no matter what the Court decided, the people of the North would rise as one man and compel its observance by force if necessary.

The whole spirit evoked by this meeting leads one to dread the probable increase of crime and outrage in this county, where the blacks are ten to one of the white population, and I would advise the stationing of a military force in this locality, for the protection of the whites and the repression of the lawless mass. ...

Very respectfully, your obedient servant

E. Yulee

— ELIAS YULEE *in a letter to the Freedmen's Bureau, April 23, 1867*

From 1865 to 1868, millions of African Americans in the South made a stunning political journey from slavery to citizenship, from being considered a piece of property with no legal rights to enjoying status of equal participants in a democratic society, with the right to vote, to serve on juries, to run for office, and to direct the affairs of government. By 1868, thousands of formers slaves were taking part in the writing of state constitutions, presiding over courts, and drafting legislation aimed at transforming the South and improving the lives of their communities. How did this remarkable transformation take place? And what did it mean for southern society and the lives of freed slaves?

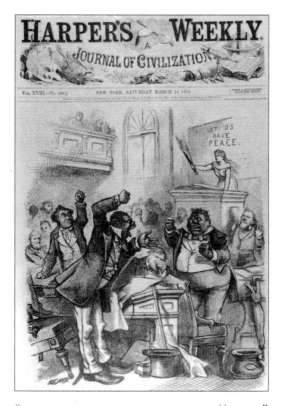

"COLORED RULE IN THE RECONSTRUCTED (?) STATE."
Although Thomas Nast was an ardent supporter of equal rights, he often resorted to racial and ethnic stereotypes in his *Harper's Weekly* cartoons. Questioning the actions of some southern black Republican legislators, Nast drew the figure of "Columbia," symbol of the nation, chiding: "You are aping the lowest whites. If you disgrace your race in this way you had better take back seats."

Thomas Nast, *Harper's Weekly*, March 14, 1874.
American Social History Project.

WHITE SUPREMACY FOREVER!
Anti-Union League handbill, 1867.

Prints and Photographs Division, Library of Congress.

The Political Education of a Free People

The political education of southern freedpeople began long before Reconstruction. As discussed in chapter 3, the actions of black men and women, slave and free, had a profound impact on the politics of the Civil War, helping to transform northern war aims from maintaining the Union to achieving freedom. As early as 1862, emancipated slaves on the Sea Islands (see chapter 7) organized against Union land policies, petitioned the federal government, and enlarged the boundaries of their freedom.

In the spring and summer of 1865, when the planter class in the South tried to snatch victory from the jaws of defeat, African-American communities answered politically. Thousands organized "colored people's" conventions (see chapter 9) in virtually every southern state to develop a civil rights agenda in response to Black Codes. And as described in chapter 8, churches mobilized their congregations to demand full rights as citizens, particularly the right to vote.

The Union Leagues

But it was the passage of the March 1867 Reconstruction Act (setting up five military districts and calling for new state constitutions) that excited the greatest outpouring of mass activity. By the tens of thousands, African Americans took the political stage in 1867. They struck, rallied, protested, and in South Carolina even refused to pay taxes to the planter-dominated government. Finding their political voice, they demanded economic justice and civil rights. Their organized intensity made the South a very different place after March 1867 than ever before.

Union Leagues gave this political energy an organized form. Founded during the Civil War, the goal of the Union Leagues was a patriotic one: "to preserve liberty and the Union" and "to secure equal and political rights to all men under the government." After the Confederate defeat, the Union Leagues became an active arm of Radical Reconstruction in the South. They functioned as combination Republican political clubs, civic groups, military organizations, and labor federations. With passage of the 1867 Reconstruction Acts, the leagues sent black and white organizers into the South, recruiting heavily among African Americans and poor whites. Southern chapters conducted political activity for the Republican party, built churches and schools, launched labor strikes and protests, trained black leadership, and created militia companies to defend African-American communities against planter-led violence. Many emancipated slaves identified with the Union Leagues, seeing them as organizations that aggressively championed their freedom. In the fall of 1867, the leagues played a highly visible role in mobilizing the African-American community to run candidates and participate in elections for delegates to state constitutional conventions.

Why was there such an outpouring of political activity by freedpeople with the passage of the March 1867 Reconstruction Act?

What were the Union Leagues? What role did they play in the African-American community during Reconstruction?

"Meeting at Night and Drilling"

The development of Union Leagues in the South dramatically changed the way ex-slaves and ex-planters related to one another. The planters became increasingly alarmed; the freedpeople became increasingly militant. A North Carolina planter, recalling the activities of the Union League in his county, explains why.

Why were North Carolina planters so alarmed by the Union Leagues?

DOCUMENT TWO

The Negroes in my county had three places where they were meeting at night and drilling. One place was their [Union] League-house. They were stationing their sentinels on the highways…and were halting white people on the roads, and…not allowing them to go by. In the extreme northern part of my county where the Republican vote is the strongest…the Negroes had another place of meeting; in the town of Shelby, in which I live, they had a place where they were meeting and drilling at night. The people were alarmed….They did not know with what object the Negroes were meeting and carrying on these operations. They thought that the lessons which the Negroes were being taught in the league were leading them on.

—*Unidentified* NORTH CAROLINA PLANTER, *1868*

The Church and Politics

Some organizers used black churches to establish multiracial Union Leagues. In July 1867, Reverend Henry M. Turner described his efforts to preach and organize in Macon, Georgia.

Do black churches play a role in politics today as they did in Reverend Turner's time?

DOCUMENT THREE

I have just returned from the southwest portion of the state. Have travelled through that hill-charged section under the garb of a presiding elder, preached at each place, lectured politically and formed Union Leagues….At Fort Valley, Rev. Isaac Anderson is doing good work. At Americus, they have a strong league and the colored people and poor whites are pretty well Republicanized.

(Turner subsequently became a member of the Georgia state legislature. Many years after the defeat of Reconstruction, he advocated that American blacks return to Africa.)

— REVEREND HENRY M. TURNER, *July, 1867*

Drafting New Constitutions

The Reconstruction Acts of 1867 required southern states to create new state constitutions as a condition of readmission to the Union. In an astonishing outpouring of participatory democracy, hundreds of thousands of black males—many of them slaves as recently as 1865—voted in elections for delegates to the conventions that would draft the constitutions. In some states, up to ninety percent of the eligible African-American voters cast ballots. Together with white voters, they elected over one thousand delegates, including 265 African Americans.

In what way were the conventions a landmark in the history of U.S. democracy?

The conventions represented a landmark in the history of U.S. democracy. Never before had black and white delegates met together to create constitutions that would form the basis of state governments. One Texas newspaper saw the work of the constitutional conventions as the final chapter in "the equal rights revolution." The constitutions broke new ground, protecting the civil rights of African Americans, instituting universal manhood suffrage, establishing public schools for all races, and overturning a century-old tax system that had burdened the poor and benefitted the rich.

PARTICIPATORY DEMOCRACY—active, mass involvement in politics

"THE NATIONAL COLORED CONVENTION IN SESSION AT WASHINGTON, D.C."
An illustration shows a political meeting organized by African Americans in 1869.
Theodore R. Davis, *Harper's Weekly*, February 6, 1869. American Social History Project.

Document Four is an excerpt from the official record of the convention. Before the age of tape recorders and stenographic typewriters, individuals wrote down the debates by hand. In the process, they may have produced an accurate record. But they may also have missed words, substituted new language, or polished old language. In addition, participants in the debate (or others) may have corrected or changed the transcript.

Think about all of these possibilities as you read Document Four, a part of the constitutional debate on compulsory schooling. Every African-American delegate to the convention supported universal public education. But they differed, as shown by the comments of the four African-American delegates below, on whether or not that education should be voluntary. In the end, the convention established South Carolina's first public education system open to all children, but did not require attendance or demand integration.

DOCUMENT FOUR

R. C. DELARGE: The schools may be open to all, but to declare that parents shall send their children to them whether they are willing or not is, in my judgment, going a step beyond the bounds of prudence [caution, good judgment]. Is there any logic or reason to step beyond the bounds of prudence? Is there any logic or reason in inserting in the constitution a provision which cannot be enforced.

A. J. RANSIER: I am sorry to differ with my colleague from Charleston on this question. I contend that in proportion to the education of the people so is there progress in civilization. Believing this, I believe that the committee has properly provided for the compulsory education of all children in the state....

J. A. CHESTNUT: Has not this convention the right to establish a free school system for the poorer classes? Then if there be a hostile disposition among the whites, an unwillingness to send their children to school, the fault is their own, not ours. Look at the idle youth around us. Is the sight not enough to invigorate every man with a desire to do something to remove this vast weight of ignorance that presses man down? I have no desire to curtail [limit] the privileges of freedmen, but when we look at the opportunities neglected, even by the whites of South Carolina, I must confess that I am more than ever disposed to compel parents, especially of my own race, to send their children to school. If whites object to it, let it be so.

F. L. CARDOZO: Before I proceed to discuss the question, I want to divest [strip] it of all false issue of the imaginary consequences that some gentlemen have illogically thought will result from the adoption of this section with the word compulsory. They affirm that it compels the attendance of both white and colored children in the same schools. There is nothing of the kind in the section. It simply says that all children should be educated; but how, it is left to the parents to decide. It is left to the parent to decide whether the child should be sent to a public or private school. There can be separate schools for white and colored. It is left so that if any colored child wishes to go to a white school, it shall have the privilege of doing so. I have no doubt, in most localities colored people will prefer separate schools, particularly until some of the present prejudice against their race is removed.

—*Debate on compulsory schooling,* SOUTH CAROLINA
CONSTITUTIONAL CONVENTION, *1868*

From *Freedom Road* by Howard Fast: "Damn It, I Say Educate"

Howard Fast's 1944 best-selling novel Freedom Road *looks at Reconstruction in South Carolina through the eyes of ex-slaves and poor whites. The excerpt below tries to capture the democratic flavor and language of the debate about education among freedmen and poor white delegates at the 1868 constitutional convention.*

While Fast did extensive historical research and examined the transcript of the 1868 convention, he nonetheless used his creative imagination to reconstruct the debate. Creative imagination can enlarge our understanding of the past or distort it. As a novelist, Fast had the freedom to do what the official recorder of the convention could not do. He could go behind the scenes of the convention, explore dramatic tensions between participants, capture the dialect and emotion of their language, and create new dialogue. Keep this in mind as you read the excerpt (Document Five).

The character named Gideon, until recently a slave and now a delegate to the convention, is the central figure in the novel.

DOCUMENT FIVE

Together, they set their shoulders for a single object, in a sense the basis for the whole new state Constitution—universal compulsory education. They had good support; they had opposition, on the other hand, that pleaded with them:

"Compromise—conciliate! You cannot force education on a whole population of illiterates."

"Why?"

"They won't stand for it."

"Then we will make it law."

"Where will you find field hands if you educate a population to be lawyers?"

"Not all men are lawyers, even in New England where literacy is so high. An educated man can work as well in the field as an uneducated man."

"The whites won't go to school with the colored."

"Then we will build separate schools for those who want them. But all children, black and white, must go to school."

"This is insanity. There has never been such a law before in this country."

"Then we will begin. It has to begin somewhere."

"And can Carolina niggers do what the smartest folk in the world haven't done?"

"We can try."

Finally the committee brought their bill to the floor, and for hours the debate raged hotly and stridently [in harsh tones]. Gideon noticed that they found support where they least expected it, from white southern delegates, the poor white trash that the newspapers had raged at even more fiercely than they condemned Negroes, the despised Scalawags [white southern Republicans], the tall, lean, slow-spoken, straw-haired men elected by that shadow race of the poor and landless, men from the swamps and lonely piney woods. Anderson Clay, who rose and yelled, "Damn it, yes! If the only way is schools where black and white go together, then sure enough, I'm for schools! If I can sit in a Convention hall with niggers, then my son can sit in a schoolhouse with them!"

And Claire Boone, from the Pee Dee Swamp, "I fought in this war. I fought three years before I got enough learning to read a newspaper, or a book. Two brothers of mine, they're dead—for what? A war to keep a few damned slave operators in power! We didn't know, by God, we couldn't! Damn it, I say educate—educate and to hell with the consequences! We sit here, the elected representatives of the people of this state, and we chew our fingernails about the consequences of every word we say."

Gideon spoke shortly. "No man stays free," he said. "I know a little history, and the little I know makes it a fight for freedom, all along. There is one big gun for freedom—education. I say, arm ourselves."

—*From* Freedom Road *by* HOWARD FAST, *1944*

•Which document—the official record or the excerpt from the novel—do you think gives you a better historical understanding of the debate over schools at the constitutional convention? Why? Which gives you a better sense of the style, language, and content of the debate? Why?
•In Document Four, what are the similarities and differences in the positions of the four delegates?
•In Document Five, how would you describe the interaction between poor white delegates and freedmen at the convention? Do they like one another? Do they respect one another? Do they share common goals and interests? What are they debating? What are their arguments? Do the delegates fit any of the stereotypes presented in Document Eight (an excerpt from The Clansman *at the end of this chapter)?*

A JURY OF PEERS. One of the startling new sights in the postwar South, as recorded by a visiting "special artist" in November 1867: an integrated grand jury.

James E. Taylor (Albert Berghaus, del.), *Frank Leslie's Illustrated Newspaper,* November 30, 1867. Prints and Photographs Division, Library of Congress.

Taking Control of State Governments

The political energy that characterized the 1868 conventions spilled over into the elections for new state governments in the South. The Republican party swept state elections in 1867–68. At the center of the Reconstruction coalition built by the Republican party—and the vital key to its electoral success—was the African-American voter. The enormous black vote for the Republican party was consistent and enthusiastic. During Reconstruction, six hundred black Republicans took seats in state legislatures, fourteen in the U.S. House of Representatives, and two in the U.S. Senate. Another six served as lieutenant governors, and thousands more influenced everyday life in the South as mayors, town aldermen, magistrates, sheriffs, deputies, justices of the peace, voter registrars, and school board members. African Americans so identified with the Republican Party that, together with churches and schools, it became a central institution of the postwar southern black community.

Why was the Republican party so central to the African-American community?

Republicans, Democrats, and the Black Vote

Today, the African-American community tends to vote overwhelmingly Democratic. But after the Civil War, the black vote was just as solidly Republican. What explains this shift of party allegiance over the last century?

During Reconstruction, African Americans identified the Republican party with emancipation and political empowerment. But as chapter 12 reveals, African-American ties to the party loosened as the national GOP deserted Reconstruction. Still, until the 1930s, African-American voters were more likely to cast ballots for Republicans than Democrats.

During the Great Depression of the 1930s, the "New Deal" economic programs of President Franklin Delano Roosevelt provided financial relief to millions of African Americans, who suffered a higher rate of unemployment and poverty than other Americans. The black vote began to shift to the Democratic party. In response to grass-roots movements in the 1960s, the Democratic Congress passed, and a Democratic president signed, sweeping legislation that greatly expanded the civil rights of African-American citizens and protected their right to vote. Literally millions of new African-American voters went to the polls to elect black and white Democratic candidates.

Will African Americans continue to vote Democratic? Will large numbers shift back to the Republican party? Or will African Americans explore new political alternatives?

GOP—"Grand Old Party," a nickname for the Republican party

Built on the foundation of a nearly solid African-American vote, southern Republican state governments varied in makeup, duration, character, and political emphasis. Only in the lower house in South Carolina did African Americans constitute a majority of the legislature. Reconstruction in South Carolina touched the lives of hundreds of thousands of poor blacks and whites, lasted longer (until 1877), attracted more national attention, and distributed more land than in other southern states. In most states, Republican Reconstruction extended into the early and mid-1870s. By contrast, in Virginia and Tennessee, Reconstruction was over almost before it began, ending in 1869 when conservative, white-dominated governments took power. But even though the Republican party lost control of every southern state by 1877, it continued to attract as much as forty percent of the vote through the 1890s.

While from state to state Reconstruction was uneven in duration and content, it had a striking impact on the entire South—expanding education, extending political and economic rights, promoting economic development, and building a modern legal system. Inheriting underdeveloped state economies with primitive transportation networks and no public schools, the southern Republican party began modernizing the South. Thomas Miller, a former South Carolina legislator, summed up the record of good black and white Radical Republican government:

> We were eight years in power. We had built schoolhouses, established charitable institutions, built and maintained the penitentiary system, provided for the education of the deaf and dumb, rebuilt the jails and courthouses, rebuilt the bridges and reestablished the ferries. In short, we had reconstructed the State and placed it upon the road to prosperity. . . .

Yet, despite its considerable accomplishments, the party was tugged internally and pulled in many different directions by whites, blacks, the poor, the rich, northerners, and southerners. In the short run, the very size and diversity of the Republican party enabled it to gain power in the South. In the end, however, its enemies played upon tensions in the party to defeat it.

The Republican Party Coalition

While black Republicans were key to the growth of the southern GOP, they did not act alone. There were many Republicans in the South with many different political agendas—business Republicans, landed Republicans, poor white Republicans, "carpetbagger" Republicans. Sometimes their agendas overlapped, sometimes they diverged. What the different wings of the Republican party shared in common was a commitment to free labor. But free labor meant different things to different Republicans.

In reality, the Republican party in the South was a coalition, and a very fragile one at that. Historians studying this period have used conflicting terms to describe the coalition—progressive, democratic, efficient, inefficient, opportunistic, corrupt. All the words are probably accurate. If we examine the different blocs of the Republicans in the South, and how they pulled their party in different directions, we can begin to understand three key factors: (1) what unified the Republicans into a Reconstruction coalition; (2) what freedmen could and could not accomplish in the party; and (3) what factors split the Republicans and eventually undercut the party's commitment to freedom and equality in the South.

Was the Republican Reconstruction coalition united? divided? both? Explain.

The southern Republican party attracted African Americans, some poor whites, and a handful of northern abolitionists (who moved South) because it had a radical agenda for political freedom and economic justice. It attracted a small group of planters and support from northern corporations because it had an ambitious agenda for economic development. It also attracted the inevitable opportunists, tiny in number but highly visible, who went south in search of political spoils and personal economic gain.

African-American Republicans reflected this diversity of interests and motives. Urban, educated African Americans, who had been

CARPETBAGGER—a northerner who went South to participate in Reconstruction

OPPORTUNISTIC—taking advantage of circumstances regardless of principles or consequences

SPOILS—benefits, rewards

born free, tended to be much more cautious than officeholders who were ex-slaves from rural districts. When drafting new state constitutions, some were not as ready as their rural counterparts to confiscate land abandoned by Confederate planters or to extend the vote to all adult males, including illiterate ex-slaves. Freed slaves from rural areas pushed hardest for new laws protecting poor farmers and agricultural workers, particularly those in debt. African Americans from cities and from families that had been free before the war were much more hesitant to provide protection for indebted farmers or to support land reform that involved significant redistribution of property.

Creating Myths—Scalawags and Carpetbaggers

Confederate opponents of Radical Reconstruction pinned a scornful, undeserved name on white, southern Republicans, calling them "scalawags," which is southern slang for rascal. The mocking label of scalawag presented a distorted picture of white southerners drawn to the Republican party.

A few southern white Republicans were wealthy planters who understood that the South's future would not be like its slave past. They wanted to be part of a diversified, modern southern economy that, like the North, would promote agriculture, mining, transportation, and industry based on a

RADICAL MEMBERS. A composite photograph portrays the men who composed the radical coalition in the South Carolina legislature.

Prints and Photographs Division, Library of Congress.

system of free or wage labor. These planters saw the Republican party as their ticket to northern markets and investment money.

Most white Republicans, however, were poor farmers from the more mountainous regions of the South. During the Civil War, the mountains of West Virginia, Tennessee, Georgia, and Alabama had been strongholds of Unionist sentiment. White, southern hill farmers had long resented the big slaveholders because they took the best land and dominated the southern economy. After the war, many of these farmers fell into debt, sometimes to these same planters. Three things in particular attracted them to the Republican Reconstruction platform: (1) the promise of political action to protect both white and black farmers from debtor courts and jails; (2) public education for their children; and (3) political rights for themselves.

One reality, however, made some white farmers hesitant to enlist in a party so identified with African Americans: their racist attitudes toward black people.

What do the labels "scalawag" and "carpetbagger" mean? Are these positive or negative terms? What is the origin of these terms?

Given these contradictory interests and feelings, it is not surprising that poor whites responded to the Republican party in so many different ways.

CARPETBAG—a small suitcase made of carpet material, widely used in the nineteenth century

"THE WOLF AND LAMB IN POLITICS." Two of the resilient stereotypes of Reconstruction politics are portrayed in this contemporary illustration: the corrupt Radical politician and the ignorant and malleable black voter.

(J. Wells Champney) Edward King, *The Great South*…(1875). American Social History Project.

Many, overcoming racial attitudes solidified by the previous two hundred years of southern history, joined with freedmen to create a powerful multiracial Republican coalition to reconstruct their region. But other poor whites, seduced by calls for white supremacy, traveled a different road (discussed further in chapter 12).

What attracted poor whites to the Republican party? What made some hesitant to join?

The same people who gave us the word *scalawag* also created the myth of the northern carpetbagger. Like scalawag, carpetbagger was an inaccurate label that the defeated Confederate elite cleverly stuck on Republicans—in this case northern Republicans who moved south after the war. The image promoted by the enemies of the Republican party suggested that hordes of no-good northerners, packing all their earthly possessions into small carpetbags, were heading south to get rich from the spoils of political office.

The northern opportunist who fit the carpetbagger stereotype was the rare exception. Most northerners (mostly men, but also women) who settled in the region and became active in the Republican party had first gone south as Union soldiers, Freedmen's Bureau agents, religious missionaries, or schoolteachers. Some started businesses; others worked as farmers. Most were white, some were black, and almost all these northerners were driven by a commitment to rebuild the South as a democratic society.

Who were the northern Republicans who moved south after the Civil War? What were their motives for going south and joining the Radical Republican coalition?

Northern investors, too, looked south and to the Republican party. Their capital promoted needed economic development in the nation's poorest region. It also greased the palms of Republican, and later Democratic, politicians in the South.

The Black Electorate and Northern Capital

In the end, two major forces shaped the agenda of the southern Republican party: the black electorate and northern businessmen. The majority of Republican officeholders were white, but the party's electoral base in the South was predominantly black. Republican African-American voters became the major force for political, social, and economic democracy in the South. They agitated for more political rights, more efficient government, more schools, more hospitals, more land, and more debtors' relief. By pushing from the bottom up, they gained rights and benefits for the vast majority of southern free labor, both black and white.

Northern businessmen, on the other hand, operated from a narrower base of self-interest. Corporations, particularly railroads, were ready to invest in states starved for capital. Railroads held out the promise of economic development that could benefit the white and black constituencies of the Republican party all over the South. But the reality of economic development championed by the railroads never matched the promise. In the end, railroad corporations undermined Republican-controlled Reconstruction governments by draining funds from state treasuries and placing an immense burden on ordinary southern taxpayers. As state governments became financially strapped, Republicans lost important voter support.

What attracted railroad corporations to the South in the first place was the prospect of big profits and low-wage free labor. But investments came with a high price: Railroads wanted subsidies and grants of land along their line from state and local governments. The railroads and the northern promoters became the source of much corruption; some were also fleecing state treasuries north of the Mason-Dixon line as well as the U.S. Treasury. Some legislators in the South, both black and white, willingly took bribes. Others lacked the experience necessary to protect reconstructed states and their voters from corporations on the take.

CONSTITUENCY—any group of supporters

FLEECE—to defraud or swindle

MASON-DIXON LINE—Pennsylvania's original boundary with Maryland and Virginia (now West Virginia) dividing the North from the South

How did the black electorate and northern business shape the Republican party? In what ways were their agendas for the Republican party in the South the same? different?

The enemies of Reconstruction—including some who participated in large-scale graft when Democrats took power after Reconstruction—had a stake in exposing corruption in Republican governments. Much like the Democratic bribe taking that would

ELECTIONEERING IN THE SOUTH. *Harper's Weekly,* 1868.
W. L. Sheppard, *Harper's Weekly,* July 25, 1868. American Social History Project.

precede and follow Reconstruction, Republican corruption had a familiar look. Northern-born white Republican governors in Louisiana and South Carolina got fabulously rich from bribes involving railroads and fraudulent land schemes. In Georgia, in return for a $30,000 loan from the Harper Brothers publishing house, a white Reconstruction official pushed the state's new public school system to purchase the New York-based firm's textbooks. In Texas, railroads bought the votes of African-American legislators necessary to push legislation favorable to their lines. An outraged and disappointed freedman wrote that "our leading men sold themselves for gold."

To some, the corruption of a highly visible few might seem an ongoing fact of American political life. Bribery in southern legislatures could not begin to match the enormous corruption that routinely took place in the U.S. Congress, in northern legislatures, and at city halls. But as one Republican paper put it at the time, "We cannot afford to bear the odium of profligates in office." Even the hint of corruption in the South played into the hands of the opponents of Reconstruction.

HIRAM REVELS. In 1870, the Boston firm of Louis Prang and Company published a chromolithograph (an inexpensive type of colored print) portrait of the the first African-American United States senator. One prominent admirer of the portrait was Frederick Douglass: "Whatever may be the prejudices of those who may look upon it," he wrote to Prang, "they will be compelled to admit that the Mississippi senator is a man, and one who will easily pass for a man among men. We colored men so often see ourselves described and painted as monkeys, that we think it a great piece of good fortune to find an exception to this general rule."

L. Prang and Company (after a painting by Theodore Kaufmann), 1870, chromolithograph, 14 x 11 ¾ inches. Prints and Photographs Division, Library of Congress.

As described in chapter 12, the crooked behavior of some southern Republican legislators, even if a minority in their own party, proved disastrous after 1870 because it robbed Reconstruction of its moral authority and shifted attention away from its record of economic justice and democratic reform.

Good Government vs. Corrupt Government

Opponents of change in the South ultimately focused national attention on the corruption of the Republican-controlled southern state governments. But sixty years ago, W. E. B. DuBois, a famous African-American civil rights leader and historian, looked at the corruption in a different light. In his pathbreaking history of the period, *Black Reconstruction in America,* DuBois commented that "if there was one thing" that opponents of Reconstruction "feared more than bad Negro government, it was good Negro government." And if the old planter elite feared "good Negro

ODIUM — disgrace

PROFLIGATE — a reckless, wildly extravagant person

Why was corruption so damaging to the Republican coalition?

government," then it must have found the prospect of a poor black and poor white Republican alliance absolutely frightening.

Much to the dismay of the old elites, the economic agenda of Reconstruction extended well beyond investment in transportation and education. Georgia Republicans made clear its pro-labor bias: "We favor laws to foster and elevate labor. We denounce all attempts of capital to control labor by legislation." Repealing the notorious Black Codes, Radical Republicans passed legislation that prompted one planter to complain in 1872 that "under the laws of most southern states, ample protection is afforded tenants and very little to landlords."

The laws that landlords complained about, while legislated in state capitals, were enforced at the level of local government. At the grass-roots level, the concern of planters was not about the corruption of government, but rather the Republican coalition's efficiency in carrying out a radical economic program.

PARISH—a small political unit

MAGISTRATE—a local official with power to settle disputes and enforce laws

"I WONDER HOW *HARPER'S* ARTIST LIKES TO BE OFFENSIVELY CARICATURED HIMSELF?"

Nast gets a taste of his own medicine in this answering cartoon on the cover of the New York *Daily Graphic*. Such consciousness in the press about offensive imagery would not last long. By the 1880s, with the end of a national commitment to black equality, racist stereotypes characterized most published cartoons and illustrations.

Th. Wust, New York *Daily Graphic*, March 11, 1874. American Social History Project.

Radical Reconstruction at the Grass Roots

The organization of mass, local-based political movements of poor blacks and whites by churches, conventions, Union Leagues, Republican Clubs, and militia companies revolutionized southern county and parish politics. For two hundred and fifty years, planters and their allies had monopolized local offices. But beginning in 1867, sheriffs and justices of the peace across the South dispensed a different kind of justice.

Control of village, parish, and county offices by Radical Republicans changed the way southern elites and working people of all races related to one another. When planters and laborers brought contract disputes before locally elected officials, Republican magistrates would often decide in favor of the worker. Almost all of these officials were Republicans, significant numbers of them African Americans and poor whites. For a brief but terribly important period of southern history, Radical Reconstruction had shifted the balance of power in local law enforcement from rich to poor.

A White Man to an African-American Judge: "Well, I'll Be Damned"

As Radical Republicans — many of them African Americans — took control of local and county governments, habits of everyday life, language, and conduct changed. Racial attitudes tolerated or encouraged for two centuries were no longer permissible under the new order. In the following document, ex-slave John R. Lynch, only twenty-two-years-old when appointed justice of the peace in Natchez, Mississippi (and later elected a three-term U.S. congressman), recalls a revealing incident about a white man summoned before his court.

DOCUMENT SIX

[A] case of some significance that came before me was that of a white man that I knew unfavorably and well. He had cursed, abused, and threatened the life of an inoffensive old colored man on account of a misunderstanding over a small business transaction. Upon the complaint of the colored man, a warrant was issued for the arrest of the party against whom the complaint was made. When he was brought before the court and the charges had been read to him and he was asked whether or not he was guilty as charged, he seemed to be somewhat surprised. "Why," he remarked, "do you mean to tell me that it is a crime for a white man to curse a nigger?" "Yes," the court replied. "It is a crime for a white man to curse a Negro as it is for a Negro to curse a white man." "Well," he exclaimed, "that's news to me. You certainly must be mistaken. If there is such a law, I never heard of it." The court then handed him the code and told him where he could find the section bearing upon the point at issue and requested him to read it for himself, which he did.

When he had finished, he exclaimed in a somewhat subdued tone: "Well, I'll be damned." The court then admonished him that if that remark should be repeated, he would be committed to the county jail for contempt of court. He quickly apologized and assured the court that no disrespect was intended. He said that he could not deny having used the language set forth in the affidavit, but he hoped the court would not be severe because he did not know and did not believe that in using that language he was violating any law. Since it was his first offense, he was let off with a fine of five dollars and costs which he promptly paid. It was the first and only time he was brought before me.

—The Autobiography of JOHN ROY LYNCH,
edited by John Hope Franklin, 1970

Examining the document

•John Lynch calls this a "case of some significance." Do you agree? Why, or why not? •Why was the defendant so surprised by the turn of events? •Do you think it was fair for Lynch to fine him? •What does this document tell us about changes in the South during Reconstruction?

Who were the African Americans active in local government? Some had been prominent before the war in free black communities in both the South and North; others had been slaves. Most, but not all, had some schooling, and a few had college educations. With a few notable exceptions, most developed grass-roots ties and built political organizations through activist institutions (e.g., Union Leagues, churches, schools).

Tunis Campbell, an educated free black from New Jersey, and Robert Smalls, an ex-slave from South Carolina, typify the range of backgrounds among elected African-American officials during Reconstruction.

Active in abolitionist circles, Campbell was one of many northern antislavery reformers (black and white) who went South to the Union-occupied Sea Islands during the Civil War. After serving as an officer of the Freedmen's Bureau, Campbell settled on the Georgia coast in McIntosh County. As a state senator and later justice of the peace, he changed how white and black, and rich and poor interacted with one another.

Campbell integrated trial juries and was, as one observer put it, "the champion of [the freedpeople's] rights and the bearer of their burden." When an abusive sea captain refused to pay black sailors, Campbell had him arrested. Planters and foremen, viewing Campbell as a "constant annoyance," came to fear the man they called the "negro magistrate, or majesty." An overseer conceded that he was "powerless" to discipline his field hands because if they complained, "I should only get myself into trouble and have the negro sheriff sent over by Campbell to arrest me."

The story of Robert Smalls—his journey from slave to military hero to South Carolina congressman—is the stuff of legends. On May 19, 1862, early in the Civil War, the slave Robert Smalls, his family, and a few other bondsmen stole aboard a vessel belonging to his master in Charleston (South Carolina) harbor and boldly sailed it, loaded with Confederate arms, several miles downwind to the Union-occupied Sea Islands. Four months later, Smalls was in Washington, D.C., lobbying President Lincoln's cabinet for permission to recruit Sea Island blacks into the Union Army. Empowered "to arm, equip and receive into the service of the United States such volunteers of African descent as [he] may deem expedient," Smalls and several white Union officials recruited the first all-black unit, the First South Carolina Volunteers. By November, this unit was raiding coastal plantations in nearby Georgia, liberating slaves, destroying an enemy salt works, and taking Confederate prisoners.

What difference did the actions of Campbell and Smalls make in everyday life in Georgia and South Carolina?

Six years later, in November 1868, Smalls celebrated his election to the U.S. Congress, representing the Sea Islands and adjoining South Carolina coast. Smalls helped build a Republican political organization that made an immense difference in the lives of working people in his congressional district.

A strike of African-American field laborers against coastal rice plantations in the spring and summer of 1876 was a case in point. The intervention of Smalls and that of his black and white allies was crucial to the success of African-American labor in the work-stoppage.

Planter

While most black Republicans supported the 1876 strike in the South Carolina rice fields, some did not. One African-American legislator, Thomas Hamilton, owned a rice plantation on the Sea Islands. He sternly delivered the following lecture to his workers, who were also his constituents.

DOCUMENT SEVEN

You complain now that you don't get enough for your labor, but would you not have greater cause of complaint if you destroy entirely their [the planters'] ability to pay at all? I am a rice planter and employ a certain number of hands. Now, if my work is not permitted to go on, how can I gather my crops and pay my laborers, and how can my laborers support their families? They [the families] are dependent upon their labor for support; they are not calculated [trained] for anything else; they can't get situations in stores as clerks; they can't all write, nor are they fitted for anything else. There is but one course for you to pursue, and that is to labor industriously and honestly.

— THOMAS HAMILTON,
reported in the Beaufort Tribune, *October 4, 1876*

Examining the document

•Why is Hamilton opposing strikers who are also his political constituents? •What is his advice to them? •Do you think the strikers should have followed his advice?

Protesting wage cuts, plantation workers sometimes used intimidation in the rice fields to enforce strike solidarity. In response, planters questioned the legality of the tactics used by protesters to force nonstrikers to join the walkout. Securing arrest warrants, planters organized posses to seize and detain strikers who used what the planters deemed to be illegal force.

But on several occasions, radical office-holders and law officials intervened. One white Radical Republican judge claimed that he "would *not* do anything to have them arrested and…hoped they would hold out." At the end of the summer, on two separate occasions, Congressman Smalls actually had to rescue planter-organized posses surrounded by hostile strikers. In both instances, exercising his legal authority, Smalls took custody of the strikers for whom the planters had arrest warrants. He then transported the prisoners to Beaufort, the main town on the Sea Islands. There he had the strikers arraigned before a black judge, knowing full well that the magistrate would dismiss the charges and release the men. With this kind of political backing, the strikers were able to win concessions and reverse the wage cuts that had triggered the walkout.

Beaufort had once been the seat of the white South Carolina aristocracy. In 1860, on the eve of the Civil War, Beaufort's planters had led the secessionist movement to form the Confederacy and divide the Union. Barely a generation later, under radical rule, Beaufort had become a very different place. It now had a black mayor, an all-black police force, black judges, and a black representative in the U.S. Congress, Robert Smalls. Edward King, a white newspaperman, commented:

Here [in Beaufort] the revolution penetrated to the quick. One of the most remarkable revolutions ever recorded in history has occurred. A wealthy and highly prosperous community [the aristocracy] has been reduced to beggary; its vassals [servants] have become its lords.

King used the words "remarkable" and "revolution" to describe what happened. *Revolution* means momentous or radical change. In 1865, planters with sizable holdings in land and slaves ruled the Confederacy. Three years later, their human property (slaves), now free citizens, drafted constitutions, elected new state governments, extended political and economic rights to millions of poor blacks and whites, and actively shaped and participated in "one of the most remarkable revolutions" in American history.

> What was the "remarkable" revolution in Beaufort?

Revolutions frequently provoke counter-revolutions. The old planter elites thought that Radical Reconstruction had gone too far. Before long, they launched a violent counterattack that split the Republican party along race, class, and sectional lines (as recounted in chapter 12).

Some radicals, however, thought that Reconstruction did not go far enough. They wanted to confiscate land from the planting class and redistribute it to ex-slaves and poor whites. Predictably, planters and the Democratic party opposed the idea. So did many Republicans. It is a story full of interesting twists and turns that is the subject for chapter 11.

Black Reconstruction in South Carolina— Myth and Reality

Much of what generations of Americans learned about Reconstruction came from popular culture—novels, political cartoons, and two movies that set box-office records. The films— Birth of a Nation *(1915) and* Gone with the Wind *(1939)—probably influenced more Americans' ideas about Reconstruction than all the histories written about the period.*

Birth of a Nation was based on a novel, The Clansman. *Written in 1905 by Thomas Dixon, a southern minister and friend of future president Woodrow Wilson,* The Clansman *celebrates the overthrow of Reconstruction by the Ku Klux Klan. It rewrites the history of Reconstruction and southern race relations from the point of view of the Confederate elite.*

The novel reached tens of thousands of Americans as a book and millions more in its movie version. Birth of a Nation*—arguably the most famous silent movie ever made.*

Compare the portrayal of African Americans in The Clansman *(Document Eight) with the excerpt from Howard Fast's* Freedom Road *in Document Five, and the illustration by Thomas Nast at the beginning of the chapter titled "Colored Rule in the Reconstructed (?) State."*

DOCUMENT EIGHT

The day he [Dr. Cameron] undertook to present his memorial [statement] to the legislature was one he never forgot. The streets were crowded with Negroes who had come to town to hear Lynch, the Lieutenant-Governor, speak in a mass-meeting. Negro policemen swung their clubs in his face as he pressed through the insolent throng up the street to the stately marble Capital. At the door a black greasy trooper stopped him to parley. Every decently dressed white man was regarded a spy.

As he passed inside the doors of the House of Representatives, the rush of foul air staggered him. The reek of vile cigars and stale whiskey, mingled with the odors of perspiring Negroes, was overwhelming. He paused and gasped for breath.

The space behind the seats of members was strewn with corks, broken glass, stale crusts, greasy pieces of paper and picked bones. The hall was packed with Negroes, smoking, chewing, jabbering, perspiring.

A carpetbagger at his elbow was explaining to an old darkey from down east why his forty acres and a mule hadn't come.

On the other side of him a big Negro bawled:

"Dat's all right! De cullud man on top!"

The doctor surveyed the hall in dismay. At first, not a white member was visible. The galleries were packed with Negroes. The speaker presiding was a Negro, the Clerk a Negro, the doorkeepers Negroes, the little pages all coal-black Negroes, the Chaplain a Negro. The Negro party consisted of one hundred and one—ninety-four blacks and seven scalawags, who claimed to be white. The remains of Aryan civilization were represented by twenty-three white men from the Scotch-Irish country.

The doctor had served three terms as the member from Ulster in this hall in the old days, and its appearance was now beyond any conceivable depth of degradation.

The ninety-four Africans, constituting almost its solid membership, were a motley crew. Every Negro type was there, from the genteel butler to the clodhopper from the cotton and rice fields. Some had on second-hand seedy frock coats their old masters had given them before the war, glossy and threadbare. Old stovepipe hats, of every style in vogue since Noah came out of the Ark, were placed conspicuously on the desks or cocked on the backs of heads of the honourable members. Some wore the coarse clothes of the field, stained with red mud.

Old Aleck [known by Dr. Cameron when Aleck was a slave], he noted, had a red woolen comforter wound round his neck in place of a shirt or collar. He had tried to go barefooted, but the Speaker had issued a rule that members should come shod. He was easing his feet by placing the brogans under the desk, wearing only his red socks.

Each member had his name painted in enormous gold letters on his desk, and had placed beside it a sixty-dollar French imported spittoon. Even the Congress of the United States, under the inspiration of Oakes Ames and Speaker [Schuyler] Colfax [corrupt politicians infamous for graft], could only afford one of domestic make, which cost a dollar.

The uproar was deafening.

—*From "The Riot in the Master's Hall," in* The Clansman *by*
THOMAS DIXON, *1905*

Examining the document

•*If a reader did not know anything about Reconstruction, what would he/she conclude after reading this excerpt?*

•*What racial stereotypes does Dixon promote?*

•*Give examples of the language, visual details, and behavior used to create (or reinforce) insulting portrayals of African Americans. How does Dixon's portrayal compare with those presented in Documents Four and Five? Does this affect your thinking about the value of using literature to study history?*

Suggested Activities

LANGUAGE AND IMAGES

Words and images are powerful tools of description. In the Nast illustration at the beginning of the chapter ("Colored Rule in the Reconstructed (?) State") and in Document Eight (the excerpt from *The Clansman*), words and images are used to present a negative view of Reconstruction in South Carolina. Choose either the Nast lithograph or the excerpt from Dixon's novel. Analyze how words and/or images are used to create stereotypes. Then, depending on which you choose, either:

* Rewrite a segment of *The Clansman* excerpt.
* Redraw the Nast illustration.

Your purpose is to use different words and/or images to change a distorted depiction into a more accurate one. Share and discuss your re-creations with classmates in small groups.

> In what general and specific ways are these views similar? Different? How do you know whether these historical novels and the video present an accurate picture? How would you find out? (What questions would you ask? Where would you go to get answers?)

As time permits, the class should obtain and share information that would cast light on these questions.

DISCUSSION

Some historians have sharply highlighted corruption in Reconstruction state legislatures. While corruption is a serious matter, there was vastly greater graft in northern governments, and subsequently in some southern governments after Reconstruction was over. But in the seventy-five years following the Civil War, the media, popular culture, and history books focused much more intensely on corruption in the South during Reconstruction itself. What do you think explains this imbalance in coverage?

IMAGES OF AFRICAN AMERICANS

Frederick Douglass made the following comment about the portrait of Senator Hiram Revels (page 234):

> Whatever may be the prejudices of those who may look upon it, they will be compelled to admit that the Mississippi senator is a man, and one who will easily pass for a man among men. We colored men so often see ourselves described and painted as monkeys, that we think it is a great piece of good fortune to find an exception to the general rule.

With this comment in mind, *closely* examine all of the illustrations and photographs of African Americans in this chapter. Which present African Americans in a positive light? a negative light? both positive and negative? Which do you think present the most honest view of their subjects? Be sure to give examples and explanations as you answer each of these questions.

VIDEO OPTION: *IMAGINING DR. TOER'S AMAZING MAGIC LANTERN SHOW*

Review the conclusions you reached in the prereading exercise (Document One) about why E. Yulee was so upset by Dr. Toer's magic lantern show. Try to imagine what the show was about. Using your imagination, free-write for five minutes on Toer's show and his audience's reaction to it. Then watch *Dr. Toer's Amazing Magic Lantern Show* (one of the ASHP videos that can be used with this text). Compare your imagined version of Toer's show with the video's version. What kind of role do you think activities like the magic lantern show played in educating and organizing African-American voters in the South during Reconstruction?

DISCUSSION/CRITICAL READING AND VIEWING/INQUIRY

The video *Dr. Toer's Amazing Magic Lantern Show* and the excerpts from historical novels by Fast and Dixon are all reenactments of Reconstruction history. All three depict exchanges between African Americans about political issues of the day. All three have a view about the role of African Americans in Reconstruction. In small groups, discuss the following.

- How are these characterizations similar? different? What conclusions do they suggest about African-Americans in Reconstruction politics?

- How do you know whether these historical novels and video present an accurate picture? How would you find out? What questions would you ask? Where would you go to get the answers?

As time permits, the class should gather and share information that could cast light on these matters.

"PLOWING IN SOUTH CAROLINA." An 1866 engraving portrays a freedman as a farmer cultivating his homestead. For most mid-nineteenth century Americans, the image symbolized honesty, responsibility, and independence.

James E. Taylor, *Frank Leslie's Illustrated Newspaper*, October 20, 1866. American Social History Project.

THE PROMISED LAND

ORE READING. *In Document One, ex-slave ley Wyat argues for the freedmen's right to the l "where we are located." In Document Two, s Yulee, an ex-Confederate lawyer and planter Georgia, presents a counterargument.*

Not much is known about the setting of this discussion. Use your imagination in a half-page journal entry to describe the scene. Where are the speakers? Who else is there? What is happening?

n Ex-Slave: "They Have Grown Rich, and My People Are Poor"

DOCUMENT ONE

We has a right to the land where we are located. For why? I tell you. Our wives, our children, our husbands, have been sold over and over again to purchase the lands we now locate upon; for that reason we have a divine right to the land....And then didn't we clear the land and raise the crops of corn, of cotton, of tobacco, of rice, of sugar, of everything? And then didn't...large cities in the North grow up on the cotton and the sugars and the rice that we made!...I say they have grown rich, and my people are poor.

— BAYLEY WYAT, *an ex-slave protesting eviction of blacks from confiscated plantations in Virginia, 1866*

A Southern White Lawyer: "As Well May the Irish Laborer Claim New York City"

DOCUMENT TWO

…as well may the Irish laborer claim New York City, because by his labor all the stores and residences there were constructed. Or claim our railroads because they labored on them with their shovels and wheelbarrows.

— ELIAS YULEE, *a southern white lawyer, in response to Wyat's argument, 1866*

Examining the documents

•*What is Wyat's main point?* •*How does Yulee respond to it?* •*Why did Wyat and Yulee develop such different viewpoints on this matter?* •*Whose argument is strongest— Wyat's or Yulee's? Why?*

"Uncle Sam is Rich Enough to Give You All a Farm"

Of all the whole creation in the East or the West,
The glorious Yankee nation is the greatest
*   and the best.*
Come along! Come along! don't be alarmed,
Uncle Sam is rich enough to give you all a farm.

With this song, Harriet Tubman greeted African- American slaves in South Carolina who were liberated during the Civil War by an all-black Union Army regiment. There was striking symbolism in the fact that Tubman, an ex-slave, accompanied the Second South Carolina Volunteers in an assault against Confederate plantations in the lush rice fields of the Combahee River basin. In the decades before the Civil War, Tubman had led hundreds of slaves to freedom as a "conductor" for the Underground Railroad, a network of guides and safe houses on the route through which escaped slaves were escorted north to freedom.

The last line of Tubman's song echoes a recurring nineteenth-century American theme: that land is the birthright of every American. *Uncle Sam is rich enough to give you all a farm.* America was the land of opportunity, and opportunity meant land. A family with land was independent, no longer subject to landowners or employers for economic survival.

BATTLE OF THE LITTLE BIGHORN. The debate over freedpeople's right to land occurred in the same era as the United States government completed the confiscation of Indian lands. The loss of their homes and their forced removal to reservations provoked many Indians to war. This is part of a series of pictures drawn by the Sioux warrior Red Horse showing the last Indian victory, the 1876 Battle of the Little Bighorn. Red Horse recorded his memories of the battle five years later at the Cheyenne River Agency reservation.

Tenth Annual Report, Bureau of Ethnology, #4700. National Anthropological Archive, Smithsonian Institution.

On the farms envisioned by Tubman and other former slaves, there would be no place for cotton or sugar or tobacco or any other crop associated with slavery, gang labor, and white supervision. Like so many other nineteenth-century Americans, white and black, freedpeople wanted to work the land as self-sufficient farmers. Their "American Dream" was built around forty acres and a mule many expected from the Freedmen's Bureau, a few barnyard animals, and enough seed to plant greens, potatoes, and garden vegetables. What was important was that they owned the land outright; that they were not farm laborers dependent on planters for work and wages, or tenants obligated to landlords; that they were not in debt to mortgage-holding banks, or to local merchants who extended credit for seed and supplies; that with hard work they could feed, house, and clothe their families. A farm might not make emancipated slaves rich, but it certainly would make them free and independent. *Uncle Sam is rich enough to give you all a farm.* Should the United States take the land of the planters who waged war against the Union and give it to the ex-slaves? Was there any precedent for Uncle Sam confiscating land and redistributing it? Who, ultimately, would own this land? Who would work it, and on what terms? The answers to these questions were intricately tied to the politics of the South, its economy, its race relations, and the struggle of African Americans for freedom and equality.

Following the war, there was a decade of conflict in the South as ex-slaves, ex-slaveholders, poor whites, and various interested parties from the North struggled over the issues of land and labor. But questions like these were played out in a much larger historical context, both before and after the Civil War.

The Debate Over U.S. Land Policies

The debate over government land policy was not new. From the end of the American Revolution in the 1780s to the outbreak of the Civil War in the 1860s, the federal government had accumulated millions of acres in land. Its landed wealth came as a result of conquest and swindle. The United States took—some would say grabbed or stole—millions of acres of western lands from Native Americans and Mexicans. As the government amassed vast new territories, southern slaveholders and northerners of many different interests struggled over who should get the land (as recounted in chapters 1 and 2).

"THE SENATORIAL ROUND-HOUSE." The federal government's most generous land program in the late nineteenth century benefitted railroad companies. *Harper's Weekly*'s Thomas Nast commented on railroad lobbyists' control of the U. S. Senate in an 1886 cartoon.

Thomas Nast, *Harper's Weekly*, July 10, 1886. American Social History Project.

"THE POPULAR IDEA OF THE FREEDMAN'S BUREAU— PLENTY TO EAT AND NOTHING TO DO." An 1866 *Frank Leslie's* cartoon comments on popular misunderstanding about the operations of the bureau.

Frank Leslie's Illustrated Newspaper, October 6, 1868. General Research Division, The New York Public Library, Astor, Lenox, and Tilden Foundations.

DOCUMENT THREE

It is greatly to be wished that some competent person would write a full and true history of our dealings with the Indians. Undoubtedly the latter have often suffered terrible injustice at our hands. . . .

[But it] was wholly impossible to avoid conflicts with the weaker race, unless we were willing to see the American continent fall into the hands of some other strong power; and even if we adopted such a ludicrous [ridiculous] policy, the Indians themselves would have made war upon us. It cannot be too often insisted that they did not own the land; or at least their ownership was merely such as that claimed by our own white hunters. If the Indians really owned Kentucky in 1775, then in 1776 it was the property of [frontiersman Daniel] Boone and his associates; and to dispossess one party was as great a wrong as to dispossess the other. To recognize Indian ownership of the limitless prairies and forests of this continent—that is, to consider the dozen squalid [foul, repulsive] savages who hunted at long intervals over a territory of a thousand square miles as owning it outright—necessarily implies a similar recognition of the claims of every white hunter, squatter [illegal settler], horse-thief or wandering cattle-man....

...As a nation, our Indian policy is to be blamed because of the weakness it displayed, because of its shortsightedness, and its occasional leaning to the policy of the sentimental humanitarians; and we have often promised what was impossible to perform; but there has been little wilful wrong-doing.... The tribes were warlike and bloodthirsty, jealous of each other and of the whites; they claimed the land for their hunting grounds, but their claims all conflicted with one another; their knowledge of their boundaries was so indefinite that they were always willing, for inadequate compensation, to sell land to which they had merely the vaguest title....

— THEODORE ROOSEVELT
in The Winning of the West, *vol. 1, 1889*

Roosevelt Claims That "Indians Did Not Own the Land"

The United States has a long history of land confiscation and redistribution. In the following document, Theodore Roosevelt, who later became president of the United States, states his position on the confiscation of Indian lands.

Examining the document

•*How does Theodore Roosevelt justify the removal of Indians from their traditional lands? •What is he driving at when he claims that "If the Indians really owned Kentucky in 1775, then in 1776 it was the property of [frontiersman Daniel] Boone and his associates; and to dispossess one party was as great a wrong as to dispossess the other"? •Why does he make a point of characterizing Indians as "a weaker race"? •Here is an added twist to the question: Roosevelt very much believed that property rights are sacred. How then could he excuse the taking of Indian lands? (Reread the statement carefully because Roosevelt undoubtedly realized that he had to justify a challenge to anyone's property rights.)*

Federal land policies in the West created precedents, both positive and negative, for postwar land policies in the South. In the first half of the nineteenth century, the U.S. government established a pattern of confiscation

What were the precedents for confiscating and redistributing land?

and redistribution. It seized land from the Indian and Mexican nations and then gave much of it away to railroads, land speculators, and small cultivators. By 1860, as a result of public land sales on the open market, speculators owned twenty-five percent of the land in the states of Illinois and Iowa and fifty percent of the land in Minnesota.

In response to popular pressure, Congress made changes in federal land policy. In 1862,

What was the Homestead Act? To whom did it provide land?

it passed the Homestead Act, granting 160 acres of federally owned territory in the West to individuals

or families who paid a modest filing fee and who were willing to improve and live on the land for five years.

The act never created as many homesteads as expected. Most laborers could not afford

Who lost land in the West? Who got land? Who were the biggest winners and losers under the federal government's western land policies?

even the small filing fee, let alone the money for the long trip west and farm equipment. Lumber and mining corporations, land speculators, and cattle companies took

PRECEDENT—an action that sets an example for similar situations in the future

LAND SPECULATOR—one who risks buying land to resell it at great profit

advantage of loopholes in the 1862 act to capture much more land than ever went to homesteaders.

But the biggest beneficiaries were the railroads. Between 1862 and 1890, Congress, state legislatures, and town councils distributed 180 million free acres to railroad companies to encourage construction of new lines. The free acreage was equivalent in size, for example, to the entire land mass of Texas and Oklahoma.

The federal government had confiscated millions of acres of western lands from non-whites, Mexicans, and Indians, and redistributed it to railroads, corporate interests, and selected homesteaders. But, with rare exception, it would not confiscate the land of wealthy white Confederate planters and redistribute it to poor blacks and whites. By the end of the Reconstruction era in 1877, federal land policies had done little to alter the unequal distribution of wealth in the old Confederacy and had done much to redistribute power and wealth to railroads and other large corporations in both the West and the South.

There was nothing inevitable about this outcome. Back in 1865, as the Civil War ended, federal land policy in the South was an open question. As described in chapters 6 and 7, Sherman's Field Order Number Fifteen raised expectations of land ownership among ex-slaves.

Those expectations seemed a step closer to reality in March 1865 when Congress passed the bill creating the Bureau of Refugees, Freedmen, and Abandoned Land, known as the Freedmen's Bureau (see pages 164–165 in chapter 7 and 202–204 in chapter 9). The land provision of that bill stated that the

Bureau would redistribute lands abandoned by Confederate planters by leasing forty-acre tracts to freedmen and "loyal white refugees." After three years the renter could purchase the land. Many ex-slaves saw the Freedmen's bill as a reaffirmation of Sherman's Field Order Number 15. But the bill did not empower the Freedmen's Bureau to conduct large-scale land confiscation. Obviously, it could not lease or sell land it did not have. In 1865, there were potentially one million eligible black and white families in the South but only 800,000 acres under bureau control; that amounts to less than an acre per household.

Rather than distribute land it didn't have, the bureau mainly supervised labor contracts.

What impact did the Freedmen's Bureau have on the issues of land and labor in the South?

In the spring of 1865, military officials and Freedmen's Bureau agents in the occupied South feared that unless black labor was put to work, the economy of the South would collapse. Agents of the Freedmen's Bureau persuaded reluctant freedmen to sign labor contracts with ex-slaveholders. Without land, emancipated slaves had little choice. This put bureau agents in the uncomfortable position of encouraging, and later enforcing, contracts that put emancipated slaves back to work for their former masters.

President Andrew Johnson further dashed the hopes of freedmen for land. Less than two months after the war ended, he issued a sweeping amnesty and began issuing individual pardons granting planters and Confederate leaders full political rights and title to lands abandoned or confiscated during the war.

REAFFIRM — to declare or approve again

Thaddeus Stevens's Plan for Confiscation and Redistribution

Radical Republicans mobilized their party, the Congress, and the country against Johnson's Reconstruction plan. But on the issue of land confiscation and redistribution, the Radicals were hopelessly split.

Yet for a brief historical moment, Thaddeus Stevens, a leader of the Radical Republicans in the House of Representatives, stirred the political pot. He called for the massive confiscation of planter lands and their redistribution to ex-slaves and poor whites in forty-acre tracts. After such redistribution, he claimed, there would still be plenty of confiscated lands left over which the government could then put up for sale. With the receipts, the U.S. Treasury Department could pay off the Union war debt and finance pensions for Union veterans and the families of Union soldiers who died in the Civil War.

Stevens claimed that without land confiscation and redistribution, there was no basis for democracy in the South. Free institutions could not develop if a tiny elite continued to monopolize the land. "No people will ever be republican in spirit and practice," Stevens insisted, "where a few own immense manors [plantations] and the masses are landless." Under such conditions, economic necessity would force poor whites and ex-slaves to work the planters' land on the planters' terms, or starve. How could democracy endure when a few planters controlled the economic survival of the majority of southerners?

REPUBLICAN — one who supports a representative, elected government which owes its power to the people

In 1866 President Johnson sent two generals on a southern inspection tour to gather complaints against the Freedmen's Bureau. The plan backfired: freedpeople repeatedly informed Joseph S. Fullerton (shown here meeting with residents of a North Carolina black settlement) and John Steedman of their support for the bureau. Fullerton was unsympathetic to the former slaves' aspiration for land. When he ran the Louisiana Freedmen's Bureau, he shut down a black orphan asylum and sent the children to work for white masters, ordered the arrest of all New Orleans African Americans who did not have written proof of employment, and returned 62,000 acres of freedpeople's land to planters.

Theodore R. Davis, *Harper's Weekly*, June 9, 1866. American Social History Project.

"THE GREAT LABOR QUESTION FROM A SOUTHERN POINT OF VIEW." An 1865 *Harper's Weekly* cartoon contrasts the idle planter with the industrious former slave. "My boy," the planter says hypocritically, "we've toiled and taken care of you long enough—now you've got to work!"

Harper's Weekly, July 29, 1865. American Social History Project.

DOCUMENT FOUR

We especially insist that the property of the chief rebels should be seized and appropriated to the payment of the national debt, caused by the unjust and wicked war they instigated [started]....There are about 6,000,000 of freedmen in the South. The number of acres of land is 465,000,000. Of this those who own above 200 acres each number about 70,000 persons, holding in the aggregate—together with the states—about 394,000,000 acres. By forfeiting the estates of the leading rebels the government would have 394,000,000 of acres besides their town property, and yet nine-tenths of the people would remain untouched. Divide the land into convenient farms. Give, if you please, forty acres to each adult male freedman. Suppose there are 1,000,000 of them. That would require 40,000,000 acres, which deducted from 394,000,000 leaves 354,000,000 acres for sale. Divide it into suitable farms, and sell it to the highest bidders. I think it, including town property, would average at least $10 per acre. That would produce $3,540,000.

The whole fabric of southern society *must* be changed and never can it be done if this opportunity is lost. Without this, this government can never be, as it has never been, a true republic....How can republican institutions, free schools, free churches, free social intercourse exist in a mingled community of nabobs [men of wealth and high position] and serfs [tillers of the land]? If the South is ever made a safe republic let her lands be cultivated by the toil of...free labor....

Nothing is so likely to make a man a good citizen as to make him a freeholder [landholder]. Nothing will so multiply the production of the South as to divide it into small farms. Nothing will make men so industrious and moral as to let them feel that they are above want and are the owners of the soil which they till....No people will ever be republican in spirit and practice where a few own immense manors and the masses are landless. Small and independent land-holders are the support and guardians of republican liberty.

— *Excerpts from speeches by Radical Republican Congressman*
THADDEUS STEVENS, *1865,*
as published in the Congressional Record

"No People Will Ever Be Republican in Spirit and Practice Where a Few Own Immense Manors and the Masses are Landless"

In the following excerpts from the Congressional Record, *Thaddeus Stevens makes the case for confiscation and redistribution of land in the South.*

Examining the document

- *What is Stevens's plan?*
- *To what groups of people do you think the plan might appeal?*
- *What is the basis for his argument that the breakup of large plantations and their redistribution as smaller farms will enhance democracy, promote good citizenship, and multiply production? Do you agree?*

Stevens's bill never got out of committee and onto the floor of the House of Representatives for a vote. It died despite Stevens's considerable power, prestige, and persuasive skills, and despite the appeal of confiscation to several large groups —freedmen, poor whites, Union veterans, and families of deceased soldiers. It died because Stevens's Radical allies, while supporting political and civil equality for African Americans, generally drew the line at property seizure and land redistribution.

What was Thaddeus Stevens's plan? What arguments did he make in favor of the plan? Why did it fail to pass Congress?

The whole notion of property confiscation touched a raw nerve. Northern journals, including leading Republican publications like the *New York Times* and the *Nation,* worried that the confiscation of property from the rich and its redistribution to the poor in the South might set a precedent for doing the same in the North. Might it not encourage industrial workers to seize the property of large northern corporations? The *Nation* warned that the "division of rich man's lands among the landless...would give a shock to our whole social and political system from which it could hardly recover without the loss of liberty."

Why did property confiscation touch a raw nerve? Why did the Nation *and the* New York Times *oppose confiscation and redistribution of Confederate plantations?*

The Republicans who controlled the Reconstruction governments in the South were just as divided over issues of land confiscation and distribution as were Republicans in the U.S. Congress.

After 1867, there was some talk of land confiscation and redistribution at the conventions that drafted new constitutions for the states seeking readmission to the Union under the Radical Republicans' plan of Reconstruction. But both supporters and opponents of land seizure knew that Congress, after killing the Stevens bill, would not readmit states with constitutions that provided for confiscation and redistribution of planter property. As a result, none of the new state constitutions addressed the issue of land confiscation.

The South Carolina legislature hoped that by taxing planter land at its true value, it could force much of it onto the market for sale. It created a Land Commission that purchased and then resold property by providing relatively easy terms for long-term payment. Other reconstructed states, however, did woefully little to provide land for ex-slaves and poor whites. Generally taking their cues from northern party members, southern Republicans—particularly white elected officeholders and even some free blacks— were unyielding in their opposition to any form of land confiscation and redistribution.

Among ex-slaves, however, the sentiment was widespread that government should give them access to land. But with the exception of South Carolina, ex-slaves could not mobilize enough votes among divided southern Republican legislators, let alone Democrats, to pass meaningful land legislation. Most freedpeople remained landless.

"It Concerns Massachusetts as Much as Mississippi"

DOCUMENT FIVE

[Land confiscation] is a question not of humanity, not of loyalty, but of fundamental relation of industry to capital; and sooner or later, if begun at the South, it will find its way into the cities of the North.... An attempt to justify the confiscation of Southern land under the pretense of doing justice to the freedmen, strikes at the root of property rights in both sections. It concerns Massachusetts as much as Mississippi.

— NEW YORK TIMES, *July 9, 1867*

Examining the document

•*What arguments does* the New York Times *make against confiscation and redistribution of Confederate lands?*
•*To whom would these arguments appeal?*
•*Are property rights in a market (capitalist) economy consistent with policies of confiscation and redistribution?*

"Then I Can Take Care of Myself"

DOCUMENT SIX

FREEDMAN: Sir, I want you to help me in a personal matter.
GENERAL: Where is your family?
FREEDMAN: On the Red River.
GENERAL: Have you not everything you want?
FREEDMAN: No sir.
GENERAL: You are free!
FREEDMAN: Yes sir, you set me free, but you left me there.
GENERAL: What do you want?
FREEDMAN: I want some land; I am helpless; you do nothing for me but give me freedom.
GENERAL: Is not that enough?
FREEDMAN: It is enough for the present; but I cannot help myself unless I get some land; then I can take care of myself and my family; otherwise I cannot do it.

—*Reported by the* JOINT CONGRESSIONAL COMMITTEE ON RECONSTRUCTION, *1867*

The widespread demand for land among ex-slaves is reflected in this conversation between a freedman and a general at Fort Smith, Arkansas, shortly after the end of the Civil War.

Sharecropping

Most freedmen remained landless. Still, in a postwar economy where the demand for agricultural wage labor far outstripped the supply, freedmen had considerable bargaining power. Some struck, others slowed down cotton and rice production, and significant numbers refused to sign labor contracts. Planters and freedmen found themselves in a standoff. Neither side got what it wanted. Most ex-slaves didn't get forty acres, let alone a mule. And most ex-slaveholders could not recruit and keep a cheap labor force of black contract labor because freedmen generally refused to work in gangs under white supervision on cotton, rice, and sugar plantations.

In the end the two sides compromised. The result was sharecropping. The system got its name because both the tiller of the soil and the owner of the land received a share of the harvest. In return for seed, materials, and the right to work the land, the farmer shared his harvest with the landlord. Freedmen considered sharecropping preferable to wage contracts. It allowed them to work individually at their own pace and to avoid white-supervised gang labor. For the planter, sharecropping was often the only way he could get freedpeople to produce cotton, sugar, rice, or tobacco.

An Alabama newspaper that reflected the views of local planters, the *Selma Argus*, recognized that sharecropping was "an unwilling concession to the freedman's desire to become a proprietor...." In an editorial, the *Argus* commented that if African-American farm labor was permitted to rent and sharecrop, "the power to control him is gone."

Yet sharecropping was very different from land ownership. Sharecropping gave farmers an important measure of control over their work, yet still left them dependent on a landlord for land, and often seed, equipment, and credit.

Even so, during Radical Reconstruction, the system of sharecropping frequently worked to the advantage of the cropper and to the disadvantage of the landlord. That's because local magistrates and justices of the peace who settled disputes between tenants and landlords tended to be Republicans. In fact, in many instances the local officials were African Americans. But with the end of Reconstruction, the Democratic party regained control of local governments and appointed magistrates and justices sympathetic to the old planting class. Public officials now allowed landlord-merchants to manipulate the payment of shares for seed and materials in ways that reduced croppers to a permanent state of debt, poverty, and dependence.

How was sharecropping a compromise? Who were the parties that compromised? What did each side get? What did each side have to give up or concede?

GANGS — work groups

PROPRIETOR — owner

Did the failure to redistribute land undermine the freedom of emancipated slaves? There are a lot of "what if" questions to ponder. What if Congress had passed Thaddeus Stevens's land confiscation and redistribution bill? What if confiscation and redistribution had broken the economic and political hold of planters over the lives of ex-slaves and poor whites? What if Congress had distributed forty acres and a mule to every ex-slave and poor white farmer in the South? Would poor whites have served as such a fertile recruiting ground for the Ku Klux Klan if they had obtained land and an economic and political stake in Reconstruction? Would the history of democracy and race relations in the United States have turned out differently if the Union had confiscated the land of planters and redistributed it to poor blacks and whites?

"You Turned Us Loose to the Sky"

DOCUMENT SEVEN

You say that you have emancipated us. You have and I thank you for it. But what is your emancipation?

When the Israelites were emancipated they were told to go and borrow of their neighbors—borrow their coin, borrow their jewels, load themselves down with the means of subsistence; after they should go free in the land which the Lord God gave them. When the Russian serfs had their chains broken and were given their liberty, the government of Russia—aye the despotic government of Russia—gave to these poor emancipated serfs a few acres of land on which they could earn their bread.

But when you turned us loose, you gave us no acres. You turned us loose to the sky, to the storm, to the whirlwind, and worst of all, you turned us loose to the wrath of our infuriated masters.

— FREDERICK DOUGLASS,
summing up the failure of Reconstruction

Examining the document

•*What does Douglass mean when he argues that the emancipators "turned us loose to the wrath of our infuriated masters"?*
•*Is Douglass against emancipation?*
•*What does he see as the main failure of Reconstruction?*

Suggested Activities

CONGRESSIONAL HEARING/ROLE PLAY

It is 1865. The war is over and a committee in the House of Representatives is about to hold a hearing on a confiscation and redistribution bill proposed by Thaddeus Stevens (see Document Four). The list of the witnesses who will testify on the merits or drawbacks of the bill include all or some of the following:

- Congressman Thaddeus Stevens
- Bayley Wyat
- Elias Yulee
- the editor of the *New York Times*
- Cornelius Vanderbilt, president of the New York Central, one of the largest railroad corporations in the United States
- the owner of a New England textile factory that imports cotton from the South
- Frederick Douglass
- a southern planter
- a disabled Union veteran
- a poor white southern farmer who does not own the land he works
- the widow of a Union soldier

And from the ASHP's video *Dr. Toer's Amazing Magic Show:*

- Dr. J. W. Toer
- Marly Green
- Mr. Jones

Those not testifying will serve as members of the hearing committee, or may, as advisers, help classmates prepare arguments for each role. Elect a chairman to run the hearing. Presenters should make a three- or four-minute opening statement, explaining why they support or oppose Stevens's bill. Then have committee members cross-examine the witnesses. After the hearing, the committee will discuss the testimony and whether or not to approve the bill.

WHAT IF

What if the Stevens plan of confiscation and redistribution had been passed by Congress and signed into law by the president? Would the history of Reconstruction, American democracy, and race, class, and sectional relations in the United States have been different? Write two pages explaining your thinking on this question. Share and discuss what you wrote.

LETTER WRITING

Pretend you are Frederick Douglass. (See Document Seven. Also use the index to locate other references to or quotations from Douglass in this book.) As Douglass, write a letter to Theodore Roosevelt responding to his statement about land confiscation from the Indians in Document Three. Your teacher will arrange for the class to share and discuss the letters.

"THE GREAT LABOR QUESTION FROM A SOUTHERN POINT OF VIEW"

Write a one-page analysis of the illustration which appears by this title in the chapter. What is the point of the lithograph? How does it make that point? Does it make it effectively? How might a planter react to such an illustration? Is the illustration favorable to the "southern point of view" it claims to depict?

IN-DEPTH RESEARCH

Look up the word *reparations*. Go to the library and research the issue of government reparations (granted by the U.S. Congress in 1988) to the families of Japanese Americans and Japanese immigrants who were removed from their homes and confined to tightly guarded camps in the western United States during World War II. Report your findings to the class. Then, as a class, discuss and debate the following:

Can the same reasoning that was used to justify reparations to Japanese-Americans be applied in the cases of ex-slaves and Indian tribes? Are the situations similar? After the Civil War, should the U.S. government have paid reparations to slaves? Should it have given reparations to Indian tribes whose land was confiscated?

REDRAWING AN ILLUSTRATION

Study the illustration titled "The Popular Idea of the Freedmen's Bureau—Plenty to Eat and Nothing to Do." Reread pages 250–251 in this chapter which discuss the role of the Freedmen's Bureau. Look in the index for other references to the Freedmen's Bureau. Now redraw the illustration from the point of view an ex-slave working for his ex-master under a contract supervised by the Freedmen's Bureau. You do not have to be an accomplished artist to do this activity. What's important is the concept behind the picture, not the skill with which you draw it.

Discuss and share drawings with classmates.

"HE WANTS A CHANGE, TOO." A cartoon by Thomas Nast in *Harper's Weekly*, 1876.

Thomas Nast, *Harper's Weekly*, October 28, 1876, American Social History Project.

CHAPTER TWELVE

RETREAT

BEFORE READING. *The Ku Klux Klan was an organization committed to white supremacy and the use of any means possible to defeat the multiracial Reconstruction coalition in the South. It launched violent attacks against carefully selected targets.*

Read Documents One and Two. Then write a paragraph answering, as best you can, the following questions:

1. What kinds of people were targets of the Klan?
2. Why do you think the Klan chose them as targets?

To the Governor: "They Say That I Shall Not Teach School"

DOCUMENT ONE

DEAR SIR: Please allow me to say that I am yet here and it is about all that I can say. Since the election it has been so that I cannot stay at home in peace. On Friday night, there came a crowd of men to my house and after calling, knocking, climbing and shoving at the door they said that I was President of the [Union] League and at the head of the militia organization and if I did not stop then I would have to abide by the consequences. They said they intended to give me another call and they did, but I was not at home. I lay in swamps and woods.

…It is a plot to drive me out of the country because I am a school teacher. They say that I shall not teach school any longer in this country. Please your honor, send some protection up here.

—*Letter from* THOMAS H. JONES
to South Carolina's Republican governor, January 14, 1871

KKK Tells Teacher: "We Gave You Orders to Stop"

DOCUMENT TWO

They [the Klansmen] said that I had committed a great wrong; I had kept a Sunday-school which I was forbidden to do. They told me that this thing of teaching…was something they did not allow; that the church they belonged to never sanctioned [allowed] any such thing; that it was not sanctioned by the neighborhood or the country and it must not be done, and finally they told me it should not be done and when I proceeded on with the Sunday-school, they said to me, "We gave you orders to stop and you have continued against our orders; now you have got to stop."

— SAMUEL ALLEN, *a church Sunday-schoolteacher, in testimony before the U.S. Senate Select Committee, 1871*

In the late 1860s, southern states—some much more than others—began to make halting progress toward a new society, one in which African Americans could live as free and equal citizens. As African Americans built schools and churches, cultivated land, and participated in the political life of the South, they and their allies could see the outlines of a new world taking shape. But the gains they made drew an increasingly ugly and violent response. Led by ex-Confederate leaders and carried out by vigilante groups like the Ku Klux Klan, the growing violence—ranging from voter intimidation to beatings, house burnings, and lynchings—soon threatened to split the Republican coalition and halt the progress of Reconstruction.

Why did the opponents of Reconstruction resort to terror tactics?

Initially, northern Republicans used the powers of the federal government to intervene and protect their southern allies. As assaults continued, however, northern resolve weakened. Northern society faced difficult changes of its own, and the national Republican party was in the process of abandoning some of its earlier commitments. By the mid-1870s, African Americans and their allies in the southern Republican party were increasingly left to face the violence on their own.

RESOLVE—will and determination

KKK and Vigilante Violence

From the outset of Radical Reconstruction, planters and former Confederate leaders, working through the Democratic party, tried to undermine the Republican coalition wherever it took government power. When normal means of political persuasion and even economic intimidation failed to discourage significant numbers of African Americans and poor whites from voting Republican, the Democratic party turned increasingly to more violent means. Using the KKK, other white vigilante organizations, and its own militia, the Democratic party launched a war against Reconstruction.

The Ku Klux Klan, founded in Tennessee in 1866, spread terror across the South in the late 1860s and early 1870s. By 1870, scores of white vigilante organizations similar to the Klan took root in the South. In addition, the Democratic party armed and drilled its own paramilitary organizations in every state. These militias and the Klan, which actively recruited poor whites, were led by the self-styled "best men" of the South—planters, generals, lawyers, and doctors. In fact, the founder of the Klan, Nathan Bedford Forrest, was the notorious Confederate general responsible for the murder of black Union soldiers taken prisoner at Fort Pillow, Tennessee, during the Civil War.

The Klan targeted the symbols of freedom most important to Radical Reconstruction. It threatened, assaulted, and murdered

VIGILANTE — someone who operates beyond the law to punish those he considers offenders

MILITIA — troops that can be rallied into service when needed

PARAMILITARY — unofficial army or police

locally prominent Republicans, black and white. It assailed and intimidated the white allies of freedpeople. It molested black and white Republican voters. It attacked the Union Leagues. It destroyed farms owned by African-American landholders. It burned churches and schools to the ground. These were not random acts of violence but carefully calculated assaults on the people and institutions identified with Radical Reconstruction.

What was the KKK? Where was it started? Who led it? What was its purpose?

"A PROSPECTIVE SCENE IN THE 'CITY OF OAKS,' 4TH OF MARCH, 1869." A September 1868 edition of the Tuscaloosa, Alabama, *Independent Monitor* proposes the treatment its Republican opponents should receive if they lose the upcoming presidential election. The editor of the Democratic newspaper was the Grand Cyclops of the Ku Klux Klan in Tuscaloosa.

Tuscaloosa *Independent Monitor*, September 1, 1868. Alabama Department of Archives and History, Montgomery, Alabama.

Congress Responds to KKK Violence

At first, the barbarity and savagery of the Klan's attacks moved northern public opinion to demand action. Newspapers, politicians, and ordinary citizens expressed outrage over the Klan's murderous campaign. In response, the U.S. Senate and House of Representatives took two actions.

First, in 1869, it approved the Fifteenth Amendment to the U.S. Constitution prohibiting the federal and state governments from denying anyone the right to vote "on account of race, color, or previous condition of servitude." A year later, as required by the Constitution, three-fourths of the states ratified the amendment and it became law.

Second, the Senate and House established a joint congressional committee to investigate the violence and to draft legislation against it. In 1868–69, and again in 1871, this committee and its various subcommittees held hearings on Klan violence in Washington and throughout the South. (Many of the documents in this chapter are from testimony gathered by Congress during these hearings.)

KLANSMAN. A captured member of the Ku Klux Klan poses for a Holly Springs, Mississippi, photographer after turning state's evidence in the 1871 prosecution of Klan members.

Herb Peck Jr. Collection.

How did northern public opinion and Congress respond to Klan violence at first? in the long-term?

What was the short-term response of the Grant administration to Klan violence? What was the long-term response?

Fearing the possible destruction of the GOP in the South, congressional Republicans on the joint committee drafted far-reaching legislation that would protect voters from intimidation and punish those who committed acts of political terrorism. The Enforcement and Ku Klux Klan Acts passed by Congress in 1870 and 1871 established broad principles for legal and military intervention to protect the rights and lives of African Americans and their allies in the South.

President Grant, elected in 1868, initially enforced the legislation. In 1871, he dispatched federal troops to the South, declared martial law in parts of South Carolina, and vigorously prosecuted Klan terrorists under provisions of the Enforcement Acts. The federal government arrested, tried, and convicted hundreds of Klan members in North and South Carolina and Mississippi.

But four years later, in response to the growing impatience of the northern Republicans with the South and its problems, the Grant administration back-pedalled. In 1875, when the Republican governor of Mississippi pleaded with the president to send troops to guarantee free elections, Grant refused. His curt answer told the story of changing federal commitment to Reconstruction and the enforcement of civil rights. He "had tired" of the issue.

STRAWMAN. An unrepentant southern rebel discovers the true nature of the federal government's commitment to defend African-American rights. "Come on, boys!" he shouts in this 1874 cartoon, "Old Grant's bluster about our killing Republicans is only a military scarecrow, after all."

Harper's Weekly, September 26, 1874. American Social History Project.

"DEDICATED TO THE MEN OF THE SOUTH WHO SUFFERED EXILE, IMPRISONMENT AND DEATH FOR THE DARING SERVICE THEY RENDERED OUR COUNTRY AS CITIZENS OF THE INVISIBLE EMPIRE."

By the turn of the century, popular novels like Thomas Dixon Jr.'s *The Traitor* transformed the bloody record of the Ku Klux Klan (now softened by the euphemism "Invisible Empire") into tales of gallantry, sacrifice, and latter-day knighthood.

(L. D. Williams) Thomas Dixon Jr., *The Traitor: A Story of the Fall of the Invisible Empire* (1907). American Social History Project.

The Retreat on Land Reform

President Grant grew "tired" of Reconstruction over a number of years. From 1867 to 1877, there was a slow but uneven erosion of support for Reconstruction by Grant, the Republican party, and the northern electorate. When the federal government intervened in 1871 to stop KKK violence, its commitment to Reconstruction was already feeble. Neither dramatic nor sudden, the withdrawal from Reconstruction by its northern backers took place in fits and spurts. Occasionally, public officials in Washington and the national GOP would step forward to defend Reconstruction, only to take two steps back. The retreat occurred over a number of issues: land reform, civil rights, partisan party politics, the national economy, corruption, and the organized campaign of vigilante violence in the South.

The first retreat was on the issue of land reform. As seen in chapter 11, Republicans drew the line at land confiscation and redistribution. Northern businesses did not want Republicans setting a radical example for redistributing property from the wealthy to the poor. Even more telling, textile manufacturers, bankers, import-export houses, and northern merchants had a big stake in the continued cultivation of cotton on southern plantations. Fearing that a break-up of big southern estates would disrupt cotton production, hurt their profits, and undercut the national economy, these northern industrialists, financiers, and traders were unyielding in their opposition to any kind of Reconstruction land reform.

Why was there so much opposition in the Republican party to land reform in the South?

The Retreat on Civil Rights

The second retreat was on civil rights. Radicals in Congress pushed the Fourteenth and Fifteenth Amendments, but northern public opinion did not necessarily march to their drumbeat. Because of the reluctance of some northern states to ratify, the votes of reconstructed southern states became crucial to the passage of both amendments. Under the provisions of the March 1867 Reconstruction Act, southern states *had* to ratify the Fourteenth Amendment to be readmitted to the Union. The irony of this condition is that without the votes of southern states, the Fourteenth Amendment might not have received the three-fourths approval required for ratification.

In northern states, there was an uneasy mix of support for and opposition to African-American civil rights. In 1867, a constitutional convention in New York state refused to grant the vote to African Americans.

What kind of support did the Fourteenth and Fifteenth Amendments have in the North?

Commenting on setbacks to his party, Republican editor Horace Greeley observed that "the negro question lies at the bottom of our reverses. Thousands have turned against us because we propose to enfranchise the Blacks." When African Americans were granted the right to vote in the South before they were in several northern states, radicals realized that their civil rights agenda was in trouble.

RATIFY—to approve and make valid

ENFRANCHISE—to give the right to vote

The Retreat of the Republican Party

The third retreat was the changing commitment of the Republican party. Between 1868 and 1870, the principles and idealism of Radical Republicanism that had briefly guided the party gave way to crude political careerism.

The power and influence of the Radicals decreased for a number of reasons. Thaddeus Stevens, congressional leader of Radicals in the House, died in 1868; Radicals suffered defeats at the polls in 1868 and again in 1870; and Charles Sumner, the leader of Radical Republicans in the Senate, became more and more isolated.

Moderates, known as the "Stalwarts," hastened the decline of the Radicals, capturing control of the Republican party. These men had little interest in political principles, let alone the democratic ideals of Radical Reconstruction. Rather they focused single-mindedly on the spoils of political office. Their main goal was to get political power and keep it. Political careerism replaced radical idealism as the order of the day in the Grand Old Party.

The Stalwarts pushed the nomination of General Ulysses S. Grant for president. A popular war hero, Grant ran successfully in 1868 and was reelected in 1872. Grant was neither an enemy nor an enthusiastic supporter of Reconstruction. Rather, politics—particularly the Stalwart politics of winning and holding office—influenced his stand on Reconstruction. With electoral support

Who were the Stalwarts? What was their position on Reconstruction?

for Reconstruction waning in the North, Grant decided during his first term to withdraw large numbers of federal troops from the South. The absence of federal troops made it easier for the Democratic party, the KKK, and other vigilante organizations to wage a campaign of terror in the South against African Americans and their poor white allies.

After 1870, and particularly during Grant's second term (1873–77), the Republicans increasingly became a party of big business. Many northern Republican businessmen

What was Grant's position on Reconstruction?

Why did the business wing of the Republican party become increasingly wary of Reconstruction?

"CLASP HANDS OVER THE BLOODY CHASM." Thomas Nast denounces the Liberal Republican platform during the presidential election campaign of 1872. The Liberal Republicans, led by presidential candidate, New York newspaper editor Horace Greeley, split off from the Republican party. Among other policies, the Liberal Republicans promoted reconciliation with white southern politicians. In the view of the ardently Republican cartoonist, the call for national unity would be accomplished at the cost of freedpeople's rights.

Thomas Nast, *Harper's Weekly*, August 24, 1872. American Social History Project.

and their political allies saw the South as a rewarding field for investment. As such, they became suspicious of southern Radical Reconstruction governments that intervened to protect the rights of poor black and white labor over those of landed property holders.

Retreat and Corruption

The fourth area of retreat was around the issue of corruption. Graft in the South was only one aspect of widespread corruption throughout the Union. Corruption (in the tens of millions of dollars involving the skimming of government funds by corporations and politicians) in the Grant administration and northern statehouses and city halls dwarfed that in southern Reconstruction governments. Yet the sensational charges of southern corruption did real damage. Radical Reconstruction had taken the high moral ground. To many northerners, the appeal of Reconstruction was its idealism and its identification with the democratic principles of freedom and equality. Even the appearance of corruption (and there was certainly substance that went beyond appearances) could undermine the integrity of Reconstruction and weaken its fragile support. And that's what happened when a number of northern Republicans began to have second thoughts about their endorsement of Reconstruction.

If there was so much corruption in the North, why did Republican graft in the South become an even bigger issue?

GRAFT — illegal gain of money or influence

CAREERISM — seeking advancement by all possible means

Retreat and Depression of 1873

When the nation sank into depression in 1873, many businessmen withdrew their support for Reconstruction. One corporate observer commented that "there is a general impression [among businessmen] in the country that the financial crisis of 1873 was owing in great part to the paralysis of the South." "What the South now needs is capital to develop her resources," wrote

Why did the 1873 depression prompt many to rethink their support for Reconstruction?

another. "But this cannot obtain [happen] until confidence in her state governments can be restored, and this will never be done by federal bayonets." The writer called for the complete withdrawal of northern troops. "We have tried this long enough. Now let the South alone."

"A TRAMP'S MORNING ABLUTIONS." Uprooted by depression, thousands of men wandered the country in search of work. As this 1877 engraving of a summer morning scene in New York's Madison Square shows, city parks all over the United States served as homes for many of the country's unemployed. The "tramp menace," many argued, required a repressive response.
Frank Leslie's Illustrated Newspaper, July 21, 1877. American Social History Project.

"GATHERING THE DEAD AND WOUNDED." A *Harper's Weekly* engraving shows some of the grim results of a terrorist attack on the African-American citizens of the rural town of Colfax, Louisiana, in April 1873.
Harper's Weekly, May 10, 1873. American Social History Project.

The Mississippi Plan

Leaving the South alone only encouraged the southern enemies of Reconstruction. After the arrest and prosecution of Klan members in 1871, the Democratic party leadership did not abandon the use of violence and terror. It found other ways and organizations to accomplish the same brutal ends. In Mississippi, it created, armed, and trained paramilitary units as part of a plan to overthrow that state's

What was the Mississippi Plan?

Reconstruction government. "The Mississippi Plan," as it came to be called, served as a model of successful Democratic terror in the South.

The Democratic party carried out its Mississippi Plan in two steps. First, it moved to divide white Republicans from black Republicans. To drive whites from the ranks of the southern GOP, the Democrats launched a campaign that ran the gamut from race baiting to economic pressure to physical violence. Unable to resist, one white Republican revealed that the Democrats simply made it "too damned hot for [us] to stay out" of their party and activities. "No white man," he explained, "can live in the South in the future and act with any other than the Democratic Party unless he is willing to live a life of social isolation and remain in political oblivion."

The second step, like the first, involved economic intimidation and physical coercion. Only it was directed at blacks, not whites. Democratic landlords warned black farm workers, tenants, and sharecroppers that they would lose their livelihoods if they voted Republican. When defiant black voters continued to organize for Republican candidates, Democratic "rifle clubs" escalated the violence. In December 1874, open war broke out in Vicksburg, Mississippi. By the time the gun smoke cleared, Democratic party vigilantes had killed thirty-five black citizens.

By refusing to intervene, the Grant administration in effect encouraged Democrats all over the South to reproduce the Mississippi Plan in their states. Terror and brute force carried the day for the Democrats in Mississippi and several other southern states where Republicans still held power. By 1876, the Radical Republican coalition was in tatters, and the Democrats were poised to dominate southern politics for the next hundred years.

GAMUT — complete range or series

OBLIVION — the condition of being completely forgotten

INTIMIDATION — threat

"RIFLE CLUBS" — title commonly used in nineteenth-century America for armed paramilitary groups linked to political organizations

The Mississippi Democratic Party: Stealing the Vote

Voting in this era was not done by secret ballot. That in part explains why opponents of Reconstruction in Mississippi were able, for example, to intimidate Sam Scott, a black sharecropper, into voting Democratic.

DOCUMENT THREE

Dick Sprauls said that I would get a bullet through me if I voted the Republican ticket; or I would be driven home without anything to eat and be liable to be bushwacked [ambushed]. I voted the Democratic ticket only to save the lives of myself and my family. My having voted the Democratic ticket against my feelings and sense of right, so worried me last night that I could not sleep.

— SAM SCOTT, *in testimony before the congressional subcommittee on Klan intimidation on a Mississippi plantation*

South Carolina: A Campaign of Chilling Violence

In 1876, using the Mississippi Plan as their model, the Democratic party in South Carolina organized a chilling campaign of violence to steal the election for governor. Their strategy succeeded with the election of Wade Hampton. Below are excerpts from their plan. Note, in particular, item sixteen.

Examining the documents

•*Why did Sam Scott vote (Document Three) for the Democratic ticket? Why did he worry about his decision?*
•*What were the main elements of the 1876 election plan of the South Carolina Democratic party (Document Four)?* •*How did the plan propose "to control the vote" of African Americans?* •*Why did the plan call for the organization of "Negro" Democratic clubs?*

DOCUMENT FOUR

3. [It is decreed] That the Democratic Military Clubs are to be armed with rifles and pistols and such other arms as they may command. They are to be divided into two companies, one of the old men, the other of the young; an experienced captain or commander to be placed over each of them. That each company is to have a first and second Lieutenant. That the number of ten privates is to be the unit of organization. That each captain is to see that his men are well armed and provided with at least thirty rounds of ammunition. That the Captain of the young men is to provide a Baggage wagon in which three days rations for the horses and three days rations for the men are to be stored on the day before the election in order that they may be prepared at a moment's notice to move to any point in the County when ordered by the Chairman of the Executive Committee....

11. Every Democrat must feel honor bound to control the vote of at least one Negro, by intimidation, purchase, keeping him away or as each individual may determine, how he may best accomplish it....

16. Never threaten a man individually. If he deserves to be threatened, the necessities of the times require that he should die. A dead Radical is very harmless—a threatened Radical or one driven off by threats from the scene of his operations is often very troublesome, sometimes dangerous, always vindictive [vengeful]....

21. In the month of September, we ought to begin to organize Negro [Democratic] clubs, or pretend that we have organized them.... Those who join are to be taken on probation and are not to be taken into full fellowship until they have proven their sincerity by voting our ticket.

—Excerpts from the original draft of the South Carolina 1876 Democratic party campaign plan formulated by ex-Confederate general
MARTIN W. GARY

1877: A Decisive Year

In February 1877, Democrats and Republicans made a deal over the disputed 1876 presidential election that nailed the coffin shut on Reconstruction. Contested returns from three southern states had left the winner of the 1876 presidential election in doubt. For a price, the Democrats agreed to recognize as victor the Republican candidate for president, Rutherford B. Hayes of Ohio. The price—or more accurately, the prize—was the South. Republicans conceded control of the southern states to the Democrats and agreed to abandon Reconstruction. When Hayes took office in March 1877, he promised to prohibit federal troops in the South from taking part in political affairs and to provide federal assistance for railroad development to the new Democratic-controlled state governments.

In 1867, the Republican party had taken dramatic action to defend the interests of recently emancipated African Americans. Now, a decade later, it deserted southern freedpeople and took dramatic action to defend the inter-

How did the deal over the 1876 presidential election seal the fate of Reconstruction?

ests of huge railroad corporations. Using troops recently withdrawn from the South, the Hayes administration decisively intervened on behalf of railroad owners and against railroad workers in suppressing the great nationwide railroad strike of 1877.

Starting as a spontaneous walkout to protest severe wage cuts and layoffs in railroad yards in Martinsburg, West Virginia, the strike spread along rail lines across the

"THE MODERN ST. GEORGE."
Republican president Rutherford B. Hayes is portrayed freeing the South from the "mis-rule" of Reconstruction government in this lithograph cartoon from the satirical weekly *Puck*.

Joseph Keppler, *Puck,* May 2, 1877.
Collection of The New-York Historical Society.

nation, sparking labor uprisings of industrial workers in cities like Pittsburgh, Chicago, St. Louis, and San Francisco. Most Republican party officials supported the use of military force by federal troops, state militias, and local police, whose intervention subdued the strikers and created a temporary and uneasy peace.

How did the Republican party change between 1867 and 1877?

The movement of the Grand Old Party from Radical Republicanism to corporate Republicanism reflected larger, more fundamental changes in the United States. For more than fifty years, from 1820 to 1877, conflicts pitting free labor against slave labor,

North against South, and white against black had defined the course of American history. That historical era came to an end in 1877. The nation had resolved some of these conflicts, others it had not. The North defeated the South. The courage and actions of millions of black and white Americans, together with the Thirteenth Amendment, had put an end to the system of slavery. Yet the issues of race and free labor remained unresolved.

How was 1877 a turning point in American history?

Racial divisions and bigotry continued to plague American democracy for the remainder of the nineteenth and twentieth centuries. Still, the struggle for equality continued. African Americans and their allies of other races mobilized by the millions to extend the unfinished revolution of the Civil War and Reconstruction into the twentieth century, most notably during the civil rights movement of the 1950s, 1960s, and 1970s. But as we approach the twenty-first century, the unresolved issue of racial inequality still eats away at the very core of American democracy.

The Civil War marked the triumph of a system of free labor over slave labor. But the railroad strikes of 1877 signaled the beginning of another conflict that divided Americans and raised new questions about the future of American democracy. Big business and industrial workers disagreed over the meaning of free labor. Conflict between them escalated.

The dramatic events of 1877—the end of Reconstruction and the outbreak of the great railroad strike—raised vital questions about the future of race and labor relations in American democracy. More than 125 years later, American democracy is a work in progress, and those same questions are still on the agenda.

"WAITING FOR THE REDUCTION OF THE ARMY." As this 1878 cartoon from the New York *Daily Graphic* indicates, in the aftermath of the nationwide railroad strikes of 1877, Indians, trade unionists, immigrants, and tramps were increasingly grouped together in the press as symbols of disorder and opposition to the nation's progress.

Ph. G. Cusachs, New York *Daily Graphic*, June 14, 1878. American Social History Project.

A Union League Defends Itself Against the KKK

In 1867, as seen in chapter 10, Union Leagues sprouted across the South. Established initially as grass-roots political clubs, the leagues functioned as the organizing arm of the radical wing of the Republican party. While they educated members on political issues, the leagues also served economic, social, and paramilitary functions. They mobilized members to help in the construction of schools and churches; negotiated contracts for sharecroppers (on occasion even initiating strikes and boycotts); and created paramilitary groups to defend the gains of Radical Reconstruction.

In Sumter County, Alabama, the Union League was particularly militant, having succeeded in winning major demands for sharecroppers. Then in the spring of 1868, the Klan made the Sumter Union League a target for harassment. A scalawag (a white, southern, Radical Republican), Daniel Price, explains what happened in a letter to the U.S. military commander for the eastern district of Alabama.

DOCUMENT FIVE

In order to keep you posted on affairs in Sumter and to get a little advice, I write this. You know the designs of the Ku Klux's and also that they are extending all over the land. Well they have made their appearance in this city, and the conservatives have been telling the colored men for a week or two, that they (the K.K.s) would be here and that they were going to break up the League. They have reported marvelous tales of these night-walkers and to some degree frightened a great many colored men, and last week it was currently reported that they were coming on last meeting night (Friday) and certainly would destroy the League and run myself out of the county, that the Negroes should not hold their meetings any longer in this place, and that the K.K.s would kill every man [who did not stop going to league meetings].

Considering all of these things a good many of the colored men, of their own accord, brought their muskets, rifles, shot-guns, etc. to the meeting and during the meeting the K.K.s made their appearance (on the street) sure enough in considerable numbers but on finding out from some of their class who had been on the watch that there were some 3 to 400 colored men in the…chamber and that 2/3 of that number were prepared for them, they fell back….

— DANIEL PRICE *in a letter to C. W. Pierce,*
U.S. Military Commander for Eastern Alabama, April 1868

The KKK Assassinates an African-American Leader

Six months later, Klan harassment escalated into the assassination of Ben Brown, a league official, sharecropper, former Union soldier, and African-American leader in Sumterville, Alabama. Brown, just elected president of the Sumter County Union League, met his death at the hands of thirty white vigilantes. They shot him because he refused to disband the league and leave the county. Daniel Price, in a letter to Governor William Smith, told of Brown's violent end and called for assistance. The governor refused to answer the letter or dispatch help.

DOCUMENT SIX

I am under the impression the reason the Democrats act in such a lawless manner, they wish to provoke the colored man into lawlessness so as to make political capital in the North....I am afraid to leave town and am in constant dread of being murdered....This state of things cannot long continue. Either we must have protection or leave....We have fallen upon evil times when an American citizen can not express his honest opinions without being in great danger of being murdered.

— DANIEL PRICE, *in a letter to Alabama governor William Smith,*
October 7, 1868

Violence in a Mississippi Courtroom

After the murder of Ben Brown, several black and white leaders of the Sumter County Union League, including Daniel Price, fled to Meridian, Mississippi. There, they confronted Klan violence once again. In March 1871, three African-American leaders were charged with delivering "incendiary [fiery] speeches" at a public meeting. At the trial, a gunfight erupted. White Klan members killed the judge and defendants. A riot ensued. One witness to the events, a local Democratic party leader, said, "It was not known how many Negroes were killed by the enraged whites, but the number has been estimated at twenty-five to thirty." As the following testimony indicates, the Klan moved to intimidate those who practiced constitutional free speech in Meridian.

DOCUMENT SEVEN

QUESTION: You say that a man may make a Republican [party] speech there, provided he said it in pretty mild form?

SMITH: Yes, sir; he has to be a little mild and cautious and guarded.

QUESTION: You said something about incendiary speeches; I want you to get precisely at what is understood there as an incendiary speech. What is offensive to the Democratic ear in that sense?

SMITH: They are pretty generally disposed to regard — when Negroes propose to assert all their rights, and to defend themselves against violence in the exercise and enjoyment of their rights, and to do it at all hazards, they would call that incendiary.

— *Testimony of* J. R. SMITH, *Postmaster, Meridian, Mississippi*

Examining the documents

•How did Union League members in Sumter County, Alabama, resist the Klan (Document Five)? •Why did league leaders flee to Meridian, Mississippi (Document Seven)? What awaited them there? •What was considered an "incendiary" speech in Meridian? •Would you consider such a speech incendiary?

Suggested Activities

NEWSPAPER ARTICLE

You are an investigative reporter for a northern newspaper, writing a story on the KKK and paramilitary activity in the South. You have attended the various hearings reflected by the documents above, examined relevant letters, and even attended Dr. Toer's Amazing Magic Show. Drawing from this material, write your story. Your piece should be analytical, selective in its coverage, lively, and illustrated by short quotations from those on both sides who were on the scene when violence was threatened and actually occurred. Choose carefully the events you cover and the words you quote. It is the selection of your material that will make your story interesting and believable to readers.

Consider some of the following questions:

* Why did the planter class and their allies in the Democratic party turn to violence? What was the goal of the violence?
* What form did the violence take? Was it planned?
* Who were the targets of the violence? Were these targets random or carefully selected?
* How did the targets of violence respond?
* Did the violence achieve its intended goals? Why, or why not?

"HE WANTS A CHANGE, TOO"

Take ten minutes to study closely all the images and words in the frontpiece illustration for this chapter on page 260. Then write a one-page story or poem based on what you see. Share and discuss your writing with classmates.

LINKING WORDS AND VISUAL IMAGES

First, in a single sentence, write down what you consider to be the most important point made in this chapter. Second, select a picture from this chapter that best reflects that most important point. Third, in a paragraph or two explain your choices of that most important point and the picture that best captures it. Share and discuss your choices with classmates.

THE UNFINISHED REVOLUTION

"THE FREED SLAVE." During the 1876 Centennial Exposition celebrating 100 years of national independence, this statue (by an Austrian sculptor) commemorating Emancipation attracted the interest of African-American visitors to the Philadelphia fairgrounds.

Fernando Miranda. *Frank Leslie's Illustrated Newspaper*, August 5, 1876. American Social History Project.

TIMELINE

"THE UNFINISHED REVOLUTION"

This timeline highlights events, trends, and themes—and the links between them—discussed in the epilogue.

1865	The Thirteenth Amendment to the Constitution abolishes slavery.
1865–1875	Freedpeople build churches, schools, and colleges that become the central unifying institutions of free African-American communities in the South.
1866	The Civil Rights Act grants freedpeople citizenship, provides them "full and equal benefits of all laws," and empowers federal courts to defend these rights from interference by the states.
1868	The Fourteenth Amendment affirms citizenship and "equal protection under the law" for ex-slaves and prohibits states from depriving "any person of life, liberty, or property, without due process of law."
1870	The Fifteenth Amendment affirms citizens' right to vote regardless of "race, color, or previous condition of servitude."
1870–71	Congress passes three acts making force or fraud a federal crime when used to prevent citizens from voting. The third, the Ku Klux Klan Act, outlaws organizations that employ disguise and violence to deny others their civil rights.
1875–90	More than 10,000 freedpeople leave the South and migrate to Kansas and other midwestern states.
1890–1910	Southern states establish most of their "Jim Crow" laws segregating schools, transportation, and other public facilities.
1896	In the case *Plessy v. Ferguson,* the Supreme Court makes segregation the law of the land by declaring that "separate but equal" facilities do not violate the equal protection clause of the Fourteenth Amendment.
1909	African American and white reformers organize the National Association for the Advancement of Colored People (NAACP). W. E. B. DuBois becomes the editor of the NAACP's newspaper, *The Crisis,* which emerges as a leading and militant voice for civil rights.
1914–70	Several million African Americans leave the rural South and resettle in the urban North in the largest internal population migration in U.S. history.
1917–35	African-American writers, artists, and intellectuals centered in New York, rejecting white values and stereotypes, produce a creative stream of poetry, novels, dance, painting, sculpture, and photography during the period that comes to be called the Harlem Renaissance.
1954	The Supreme Court in the *Brown v. Board of Education* case, outlaws school segregation. The issue had been brought before the court by the National Association for the Advancement of Colored People (NAACP), which argues that the Fourteenth Amendment and the Reconstruction era civil rights laws make segregation unconstitutional.

1957	African-American clergy, led by Dr. Martin Luther King Jr., form the Southern Christian Leadership Conference (SCLC). Most of the clergy are drawn from churches that originated during Reconstruction. In the 1950s and 1960s, the clergy and churches play key roles in civil rights struggles across the South and confront organized and violent opposition from southern segregationists.
1960	Students from historic African-American colleges, whose origins go back to Reconstruction, form the Student Nonviolent Coordinating Committee (SNCC). Using nonviolent methods, SNCC activists face police and vigilante violence as they organize sit-ins to integrate segregated lunch counters and develop voter-registration drives in southern states where African Americans have been denied the ballot.
1964	The Civil Rights Act of 1964 is passed to enforce the Fourteenth Amendment ratified nearly a century earlier.
1965	The Voting Rights Act of 1965 is passed to enforce the Fifteenth Amendment ratified nearly a century earlier.

Where in the larger context of American history do we locate Reconstruction? This is not a question about timelines, but rather one about the connections between Reconstruction and:

- the events that preceded it, most notably slavery and the Civil War.
- the events that followed it, most significantly the African-American liberation and civil rights movements of the twentieth century.

The Civil War and Reconstruction marked, in the words of historian Eric Foner, "an unfinished revolution" in American democracy and race relations. This unfinished revolution began the work of reversing the ugly legacy of slavery, continued into the civil rights era, 1955–75, and no doubt will endure into the next century.

Historians have referred to Reconstruction as "the first civil rights movement" and to the civil rights movement as the "second Reconstruction." There are complicated links between the two periods which reflect both the positive and negative heritages of Reconstruction. After 1877, Reconstruction gave way to a century of racial segregation, lynching, and undemocratic rule by one party (ironically calling itself the Democratic party) that threatened the rights and lives of black men and women in the South. The civil rights struggles of the 1950s, 1960s, and early 1970s were a democratic, grass-roots response to the conditions of institutionalized violence and segregation that followed the defeat of Reconstruction.

Reconstruction did not and could not stop the racist tide of the Ku Klux Klan, the Democratic party, and their white supremacist allies. But as "the first civil rights movement," Reconstruction established the legal building blocks for the movements of the 1950s and 1960s: the Thirteenth, Fourteenth, and Fifteenth Amendments, and the Civil Rights Acts of 1866 and 1870–71 (the Ku Klux Klan and Enforcement Acts). In turn, when ex-slaves built the schools, colleges, and independent churches so central to the development of a free African-American community after the Civil War, they laid a social foundation that would support a "second Reconstruction" one hundred years later.

The modern civil rights movement—with nearly all of its leadership drawn from black churches and colleges that trace their history back to Reconstruction—would use civil rights legislation and amendments drafted after the Civil War in the nineteenth century to win important victories that desegregated schools and extended voting rights in the twentieth century.

The political, social, and economic links between Reconstruction, the civil rights movement, and the present tell us volumes about the history of race, democracy, labor, and migration in the United States over the last hundred years. Some of that history is grim, some of it inspiring, and all of it important to the future of America.

How did Reconstruction establish the legal and social foundation for the civil rights movement of the 1950s and 1960s?

"THE NORTH CAROLINA RACE WAR." Numerous attacks on African-American communities occurred during the late nineteenth century. As this illustration of the 1898 "race riot" in Wilmington, North Carolina, shows, many national periodicals expressed little sympathy toward the black victims of violence. In a fashion reminiscent of arguments at the close of Reconstruction, commentators claimed that the "misrule" of corrupt black Wilmington officials had brought violence upon themselves. The illustration of gun-toting terrorists appearing on the cover of *Collier's Weekly* only bolstered popular misconceptions about black aggression.

H. Ditzler, *Collier's Weekly*, November 26, 1898. Prints and Photographs Division, Library of Congress.

Race

By 1877, slavery was dead, but racism was alive and thriving.

Until the Civil War, the history of racism and slavery ran parallel to one another. While slavery existed long before the first Africans in chains came to the Western Hemisphere, it took a very different form in the Americas. Europeans had enslaved other Europeans, and Africans had enslaved other Africans. But with the beginning of the transatlantic slave trade in the fifteenth century, for the first time members of one race (whites) enslaved huge numbers of another race (Africans). Unlike most earlier systems of bondage, the status of slave passed from black parent to black child. Slavery and race became inseparable.

Throughout the 250-year history of slavery in North America, a system of laws, attitudes, ideas, and behavior promoted white superiority and black inferiority. There was no basis in nature or science for the superi-ority of one race or the inferiority of another. To the contrary, these racial attitudes and laws were the product of the unequal human and power relationships between slaveholders and slaves. While it was the slaveholders who developed this whole racist structure, it had a profound influence on the ideas and actions of many nonslaveholding whites as well.

When the Thirteenth Amendment abolished slavery, racist attitudes and behavior, reinforced by more than two centuries of history, did not disappear. Nevertheless, for a fleeting but terribly important moment in American history, Reconstruction held out the possibility for the creation of new democratic structures by a coalition of ex-slaves, poor whites, and northern Republicans. The defeat of that Reconstruction coalition had alarming repercussions for American equality, freedom, and race relations.

New forms of racism— different from, yet historically linked to, the old system of slavery—developed in the South after Reconstruction. Between 1890 and 1900, the broad outlines of post-Reconstruction racism took shape. Denied land,

ANTILYNCHING CRUSADER. Memphis, Tennessee, newspaper editor Ida B. Wells was in the forefront of the campaign to stop violence against African Americans. In 1892, she revealed the role of local white businessmen in the lynching of three black competitors. She is shown here with Betsy Moss and her two children, the widow and orphans of one of the murdered black businessmen, Memphis grocer Tom Moss. A white mob destroyed Wells's office and she was forced to flee north, where her public lectures and writing brought lynchings to national attention.

W. F. Griffin. Special Collections, University of Chicago Library.

African Americans became econo-mically dependent, politically disenfranchised, socially segregated, and routinely targeted for acts of chilling and often officially approved violence. From 1890 to 1900, an average of 175 African Americans were lynched each year, many burned or dismembered beyond identification. Public officials in the South did not condemn lynching and did not punish those responsible. By their silence and inaction, but more often by highly visible and vocal encouragement, southern politicians and government leaders endorsed racial violence.

What new forms of racism were developed in the South after Reconstruction?

DISENFRANCHISE — to take away the right to vote

Were slavery and racism always linked? What was different about the slavery established by Europeans as part of the transatlantic trade in the fifteenth century?

Labor, Land, and Economic Dependence

Legally free, black agricultural workers (and many poor whites) nonetheless became a dependent work force of sharecroppers and tenants laboring under a mountain of debt owed to landlords and local merchants.

Initially, as pointed out in chapter 11, sharecropping was not a defeat for ex-slaves but a compromise. During Reconstruction, ex-slaves wanted land, independence, and freedom from cotton or anything else that suggested the old system of slavery. On the other hand, ex-masters had every incentive to keep freedmen landless, dependent, and working in the cotton fields. For the old planting classes, the key to the profitable cultivation of cotton (or rice or tobacco or sugar) for world markets was cheap labor. During Reconstruction, African Americans

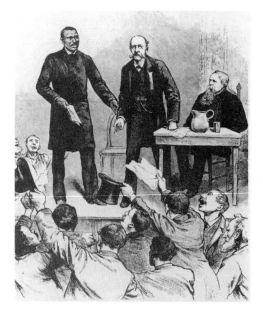

"AN INJURY TO ONE IS AN INJURY TO ALL."
Most late-nineteenth-century trade unions barred African Americans from membership, but the strongest labor organization of the era espoused racial equality. While its southern locals were segregated by race, the national Knights of Labor included many black members and occasionally challenged racial injustice. During the Knights' 1886 convention in Richmond, Virginia, the refusal of the integrated New York delegation to accept segregated accommodations and the prominent role played by African Americans in the proceedings made national headlines. Here, New York delegate Frank J. Ferrell is shown introducing Knights leader Terence V. Powderly to the convention.

Joseph Becker, *Frank Leslie's Illustrated Newspaper,* October 16, 1886. American Social History Project.

successfully resisted planter schemes to make them work the old plantations as gang labor under white supervision. Nevertheless, most freedpeople remained landless.

The compromise was sharecropping. Ex-slaves did not own the land, but they were granted the right to work farms as individual families. They received a share of the crop, as did the landlord. Yet even if ex-planters could not restart a system of gang labor similar to slavery, they did get something they wanted: cotton to sell on world markets.

Later, as cotton prices plummeted and Democrats replaced Republicans in power throughout the South, the sharecroppers lost many of their rights and became caught in an ever-deepening cycle of debt and dependency. With low cotton prices, croppers received less and less money for their shares. Their landlords offered them credit, but only on the condition that they grow more cotton. More cotton meant overstocked markets, lower prices, and even more debt.

Why did sharecropping work to the disadvantage of freedpeople after Reconstruction?

Democracy

Democratic rights spelled out by the Fourteenth and Fifteenth Amendments and the civil rights legislation of the 1860s and 1870s came under intense attack after Reconstruction.

In the 1890s, when indebted white and black sharecroppers and tenants began joining a new radical farmer's party, the Populist party, to redress their common economic grievances, the ruling Democratic party successfully divided them along racial lines by establishing Jim Crow laws.

"Jim Crow" was a character from white theater companies, called minstrel shows, that ridiculed African-American behavior. The new laws that denied African Americans their civil rights, taking away the vote and establishing a formal system of segregation in public places (schools, trains, bathrooms, etc), bore the name of this racist caricature.

The segregation of southern public facilities that resulted from these new laws was much more developed in urban than rural areas. Segregation in the cities served to divide a small but rapidly growing southern industrial labor force by granting white workers small privileges denied their black counterparts.

The use of Jim Crow laws to disenfranchise African Americans was a tricky business because the Fifteenth Amendment of the U.S. Constitution guarantees that the "right of citizens to vote shall not be denied... on account of race, color, or previous condition of servitude." Southern states made a mockery of the Constitution

_____

Who was Jim Crow? What were Jim Crow laws?

_____

by requiring poll taxes and literacy tests as conditions for voting, and then claiming that these requirements were color-blind. In fact, color counted heavily as southern states used these techniques to disqualify the vast majority of African-American voters. Poll taxes and literacy tests were used much more selectively and infrequently to disenfranchise poor whites. For seventy-five years, the federal government refused to intervene to protect the constitutional rights of African-American and other disenfranchised voters.

EMANCIPATION DAY 1888. African Americans continued to celebrate their freedom through the late nineteenth century. Crepe-paper bunting, American flags, and Lincoln's portrait grace the exterior of a general store as the black citizens of Richmond, Virginia, commemorate the twenty-fifth anniversary of the signing of the Emancipation Proclamation.

#1388, Cook Collection. Valentine Museum, Richmond, Virginia.

JUSTICE OF THE PEACE. After the collapse of Reconstruction, some African Americans continued to hold local elective positions in the South, particularly sheriffs and judges. This 1889 engraving shows a black justice of the peace presiding over a Jacksonville, Florida, police court.

Matthew Somerville Morgan, *Frank Leslie's Illustrated Newspaper,* February 23, 1889. General Research Division, The New York Public Library, Astor, Lenox, and Tilden Foundations.

CARICATURE — a distorted representation

POLL TAXES — taxes to vote

EXODUSTERS. Beginning in the mid-1870s, thousands of African Americans chose to leave the South in the hope of finding equality on the western frontier. This engraving shows the arrival of "exodusters" (their name derived from the Bible) in St. Louis, Missouri, en route to Kansas in 1879.

Frank Leslie's Illustrated Newspaper, April 19, 1879. General Research Division, The New York Public Library, Astor, Lenox, and Tilden Foundations.

From 1890 to 1965, U.S. presidents, senators, and congressmen bowed down before a powerful bloc of southern Democratic legislators in the U.S. Congress. These legislators were products of one party—the party of white supremacy rule in what came to be known as "the solid South." Elected unopposed term after term, they created a political bloc that wielded tremendous power. While they never had anything approaching a majority in either house of Congress, they nonetheless chaired key committees and controlled enough votes to promote their agenda of segregation, political disenfranchisement, and white supremacy.

What was "the solid South"? Why were white southern Democrats able to wield so much power in the U.S. Congress?

BLOC—a group with a common interest or aim

Migration

As Reconstruction came to an end, Henry Adams, a freedman and Union Army veteran from Louisiana, commented: "This is a horrible part of the country. It is impossible for us to live with these slaveholders of the South and enjoy the right as they enjoy it." Adams, who tried to organize freedpeople to migrate to Africa, declared that he had recruited 60,000 African Americans who were ready to leave the post-Reconstruction South.

Scarcely any freedmen and women made it to Africa. But tens of thousands, comparing themselves to Moses and the Jews fleeing slavery in Egypt, did leave the South. In Alabama, once the Democratic party seized control of the Reconstruction government in 1874, freedmen meeting in convention in Montgomery talked about "repeating the history of the Israelites" in the Bible and "seeking new homes…beyond the reign and rule of pharaoh." Taking their cues from the Book of Exodus in the Old Testament and calling themselves "exodusters," thousands of African Americans fled to a new Israel—the state of Kansas. Few of these migrants prospered in Kansas. But whatever their economic hardships in the Midwest, even fewer returned south.

In the nineteenth century, however, the vast majority of African Americans did not flee the South. For some, poverty and debt tied them to the region. Many more stayed because of family, religious, and emotional ties to the African-American community. Some, probably the majority, remained because they were a farming people who intimately knew the region's soil, woods, and rivers, and clung to the hope that they could still obtain land and a measure of independence. Frederick Douglass, for one, counseled freedmen and women to dig even deeper roots in the South and continue the struggle for freedom and equality.

Who were the exodusters?

In response to attacks on their democratic rights, economic livelihoods, and social mobility, African Americans in the South developed a variety of responses ranging from accommodation to defiance.

In an 1895 address in Atlanta, Georgia, educator Booker T. Washington advised the southern African-American community to "cast down your bucket where you are." He preached the virtues of self-help, thrift, and hard work. If African Americans were to survive in a segregated society, he argued, they must develop manual skills to work as farmers, domestics, mechanics, or in jobs servicing the black community. In the process, they would accumulate the skills and resources

All Colored People
THAT WANT TO
GO TO KANSAS,
On September 5th, 1877,
Can do so for $5.00

IMMIGRATION.

WHEREAS, We, the colored people of Lexington, Ky., knowing that there is an abundance of choice lands now belonging to the Government, have assembled ourselves together for the purpose of locating on said lands. Therefore,

BE IT RESOLVED, That we do now organize ourselves into a Colony, as follows:—Any person wishing to become a member of this Colony can do so by paying the sum of one dollar ($1.00), and this money is to be paid by the first of September, 1877, in installments of twenty-five cents at a time, or otherwise as may be desired.

RESOLVED, That this Colony has agreed to consolidate itself with the Nicodemus Towns, Solomon Valley, Graham County, Kansas, and can only do so by entering the vacant lands now in their midst, which costs $5.00.

RESOLVED, That this Colony shall consist of seven officers—President, Vice-President, Secretary, Treasurer, and three Trustees. President—M. M. Bell; Vice-President—Isaac Talbott; Secretary—W. J. Niles; Treasurer—Daniel Clarke; Trustees—Jerry Lee, William Jones, and Abner Webster.

RESOLVED, That this Colony shall have from one to two hundred militia, more or less, as the case may require, to keep peace and order, and any member failing to pay in his dues, as aforesaid, or failing to comply with the above rules in any particular, will not be recognized or protected by the Colony.

IMMIGRATION. An 1877 handbill urges African Americans to leave Kentucky and join a new settlement in Kansas.

Kansas State Historical Society.

necessary to make the black community economically independent and prosperous.

In the twentieth century, black nationalist movements, particularly in the North, also advanced the values of economic self-reliance and independence. But there was a big difference: Not only were these movements much more militant (particularly on the issue of political rights), but they promoted segregation on terms defined by blacks, not whites. Washington, on the other hand, counseled caution, even passivity. "The wisest among my race, " he said, "understand that agitation of questions

Why did so many African Americans stay in the segregated South?

PHARAOH—the king of Egypt

ACCOMMODATION—compromise, adjustment, adaptation

NATIONALISM—belief that a people should act independently of other peoples, races, or nations

of social equality is the extremest folly."

In the 1890s, W. E. B. DuBois, a young professor at Atlanta University, challenged Washington's views. Rather than accommodate the reality of the segregated post Reconstruction South, he wanted to change it. Unlike Washington, he demanded decent schools, unrestricted and equal use of all public accommodations, and the right to vote. DuBois asserted that "we will not be satisfied to take one jot or tittle less than our full manhood rights.... We claim the right of freemen to walk, talk, and be with them that wish to be with us."

In response to racism and segregation in the South, how did the strategies of Washington and DuBois differ?

In response to segregation and racial oppression, Washington and DuBois presented sharply contrasting strategies and gave voice to an important debate that continued into the twentieth century. But the truth of the matter is that in the half century after Reconstruction, large masses of black southerners did not march to the drumbeat of either Washington or DuBois.

There was one organized movement, however, that did enlist tens of thousands of black southerners at the grass roots—the Great Migration. First slowly, then with a rush during and after World War I (1914–18), the Great Migration moved the center of gravity of the African-American community from south to north, from rural to urban, and from agricultural to industrial labor. In what came to be the greatest internal migration in U.S. history, millions made the journey north, to the new "Land of Hope."

The differences between the "exodusters" of the 1870s and the Great Migration of the early twentieth century involved much more than numbers. Exodusters abandoned the South for Kansas, but not the dream of land ownership they thought was key to

SILENT PARADE. Thousands of Harlem residents march on July 28, 1917, in a demonstration organized by the NAACP to protest race riots in St. Louis, Missouri.

Schomburg Center for Research in Black Culture, The New York Public Library, Astor, Lenox, and Tilden Foundations.

independence. Half a century later, the millions who joined the Great Migration forsook not only the South but also the hope of tilling the soil. They journeyed north in search of industrial jobs and decent wages denied them in the South. Many traveled in mass by rail in train cars inscribed with chalk slogans that told the story of their dreams: "Farewell—We're Good and Gone," "Bound for the Promised Land," and "Bound for the Land of Hope."

How and where did the center of gravity of the African-American community shift?

What was the difference between the exodusters in the nineteenth century and African Americans who migrated north in the twentieth century?

The Great Migration north after World War I was an organized, active response to southern racism. It was a grass-roots movement that had to overcome white resistance. Desperate to keep, control, and exploit cheap black farm labor, southern white landlords resorted to violence and intimidation to prevent people from leaving. But African Americans formed migration clubs that created networks that stretched from the rural South to the industrial North, helping thousands to migrate.

In sharp contrast to the South, the new northern "Promised Land" provided freedom to vote and freedom from the daily humiliations of segregated life. But even with greater economic opportunity, there were disturbing racist undercurrents.

Northern industrialists often divided the work force along racial lines, giving unskilled jobs to black labor and more skilled work to white labor. These "divide and conquer" tactics depressed the pay of industrial labor

MIGRANT. A documentary photographer working for the federal government recorded this young woman preparing to leave Belcross, North Carolina, for a job in Onley, Virginia, in July 1940.

Jack Delano, 1940, Farm Service Administration.
Prints and Photographs Division, Library of Congress.

of all races, but African Americans in general received even lower wages—usually much lower—than whites.

As African Americans from the South flooded northern urban labor and housing markets, they competed with native-born and immigrant workers for jobs, living space, and ultimately political power. On a few occasions, these tensions exploded into race riots and even an occasional lynching, with African Americans once again the victims of monstrous violence.

The migrants were not passive when racism showed its northern face. They created com-

What forms did racism take in the industrial North? Was there more economic opportunity for African Americans in the North as compared to the South?

munities, built political organizations in the cities, and joined groups like the National Association for the Advancement of Colored People (founded in 1909) to defend and expand their rights. By 1919, the NAACP had 91,000 members.

The NAACP sought to mobilize both African Americans and whites around civil rights issues. On the other hand, in the 1920s, the Universal Negro Improvement Association (UNIA), led by Marcus Garvey, appealed to African-American racial pride. The UNIA organized a large grass-roots base, mostly in urban northern centers, and linked two powerful themes—back to Africa and economic empowerment. In the mid and late twentieth century, African-American leaders and movements would return to these themes time and time again.

In the 1920s, during the period that came to be known as the Harlem Renaissance, New York-based artists, poets, writers, and playwrights consciously moved away from white values and created works that had a unique African-American voice and identity.

What was the Harlem Renaissance? More popular forms of African-American culture found a still wider audience: the singing of Florence Mills and Ethel Waters, the dancing of Bill "Bojangles" Robinson, and the unique sounds of New York, Chicago, and Kansas City jazz.

In the 1930s, African-American workers joined new industrial unions by the tens of thousands. In 1941, when African-American union leader A. Philip Randolph prepared to mobilize black working people for a huge march on Washington, President Franklin Delano Roosevelt issued an executive order to end job discrimination in federal government agencies.

Randolph called off the march. But his threat to organize African Americans from every corner of the nation to converge on Washington underscored an important reality: racism was not a simply a southern problem, but a national one. However, the form and focus of racism—and African-American resistance to it—tended to differ from region to region.

In the South, the inescapable daily realities of Jim Crow laws stood between every African-American man, woman, and child and their aspirations for freedom and justice. The completion of the "unfinished revolution" of Reconstruction was utterly impossible without first destroying the system of Jim Crow. Thus, in the twentieth-century South, the struggle for freedom and against racism was first and foremost one for civil rights.

In the urban centers of the North and West, the issue of civil rights, while hugely important, did not carry the same emotional weight it had in the South. African Americans could generally vote and move about in public places without "whites only" signs constantly assaulting their dignity. Other powerful realities influenced

How was racism— and the resistance to it— similar and different in the South and North during the second half of the twentieth century?

racism and the response of the African-American community. There were no formal Jim Crow laws in the North, but, nonetheless, there was growing inequality between races. In this context, the issue of African-American identity in a white-dominated society assumed more and more importance. Discrimination in industrial employment, housing, and government services would focus black communities in the North much more on issues of economic, political, and cultural empowerment.

The second American Revolution—an unfinished revolution for freedom and equality—began in the era of the Civil War and

Reconstruction. That revolution continues today in both the South and North. The conditions and terms of the struggle have differed over time and regions, but the historical lines connecting the twentieth century to the Civil War and Reconstruction are unmistakable.

During the Civil War and Reconstruction, African-American men and women had begun to define what their freedom would mean to them and all Americans in the post-slavery era. Harriet Tubman defined it on June 3, 1863, when she marched with Colonel James Montgomery at the head of an army of black deliverance to liberate 727 slave men, women, and children from their South Carolina masters. Field hands on Edward Philbrick's Coffin Point plantation defined it when they rebelled against "King Cotton" and refused to work as gang labor for twenty-five cents an hour. Twenty Savannah ministers defined it on January 12, 1865, when they told General William Tecumseh Sherman and Secretary of War Edwin Stanton "the way we can best take care of ourselves is to have land, and turn it and till it by our own labor." In February 1865, African-American soldiers defined it when they marched as part of the liberating Union Army into Charleston, South Carolina, singing "Glory, Glory, Hallelujah." Eight months later, the South Carolina Black Convention defined it when delegates spoke out against the Black Codes and for "equity and justice." Squatters on the Delta Plantation defined it in 1867 when they drove off Union soldiers and defended their right to the land. Union Leagues defined it by building multiracial coalitions and facing down KKK violence. Elected African-American legislators, judges, and congressmen defined it every time they stood up for the rights of common men and women in the South, black and white. Black men and women constantly defined and redefined that freedom by governing their own churches, by reconstituting their families, by building schools, by voting and holding office, and by laboring independent of white supervision.

Millions over the decades continued to define and redefine freedom when they migrated, marched, petitioned, boycotted, and mobilized to fight for civil rights, for more power over their own lives, and for the most fundamental principles of American democracy.

Freedom was not something abstract to these men and women. Every victory and every setback gave it new meaning. 1876 was a defeat. But even under the most adverse conditions, ex-slaves and the generations that followed continued to stretch the boundaries of their freedom—and the freedom of all Americans.

In 1938, Langston Hughes, one of the leading figures of the Harlem Renaissance, wrote about the unfulfilled vision and future possibility of American freedom. His poem, "Let America Be America Again," concluded with these lines:

> O, Let America be America again—
> The land that has never been yet—
> And yet must be—the land where *every* man is free.
> The land that's mine—the poor man's, Indian's,
> Negro's, ME—
> Who made America,
> Whose sweat and blood, whose faith and pain,
> Whose hand at the foundry, whose plow in the rain,
> Must bring back our mighty dream again.
>
> > O, yes,
> > I say it plain,
> > America never was America to me,
> > And yet I swear by this oath—
> > America will be!

Recommended Reading

SLAVERY

GENERAL HISTORIES AND SURVEYS
John Blassingame, *The Slave Community* (1979).

Eugene Genovese, *Roll Jordan Roll: The World the Slaves Made* (1974).

Nathan Huggins, *Black Odyssey: The Afro-American Ordeal in Slavery* (1977).

Peter Kolchin, *American Slavery, 1619–1877* (1993).

Peter J. Parish, *Slavery: History and the Historians* (1989).

Kenneth Stampp, *The Peculiar Institution* (1956).

CULTURE AND SOCIAL RELATIONS
Edward D. C. Campbell Jr. with Kim S. Rice, eds., *Before Freedom Came: African-American Life in the Antebellum South* (1991).

Elizabeth Fox-Genovese, *Within the Plantation Household* (1988).

Herbert Gutman, *The Black Family in Slavery and Freedom, 1750–1925* (1976).

Lawrence Levine, *Black Culture and Black Consciousness: Afro-American Folk Thought from Slavery to Freedom* (1977).

Albert Raboteau, *Slave Religion: "The Invisible Institution," in the Antebellum South* (1978).

Sterling Stuckey, *Slave Culture: Nationalist Theory and the Foundation of Black America* (1987).

SLAVE RESISTANCE
Herbert Aptheker, *American Negro Slave Revolts: Nat Turner, Denmark Vesey, Gabriel, and Others* (1943).

Eugene Genovese, *From Rebellion to Revolution: Afro-American Slave Revolts in the Making of the Modern World* (1979).

Vincent Harding, *There Is a River: The Black Struggle for Freedom in America* (1981).

THE ANTISLAVERY MOVEMENT
Nathan Huggins, *Slave and Citizen: The Life of Frederick Douglass* (1980).

Aileen S. Kraditor, *Means and Ends in American Abolitionism: Garrison and His Critics on Strategy and Tactics, 1834–1850* (1967).

James Brewer Stewart, *Holy Warriors: The Abolitionists and American Slavery* (1976).

Harriet Beecher Stowe, *Uncle Tom's Cabin* (1852).

FREE BLACKS
Ira Berlin, *Slaves Without Masters: The Free Negro in the Ante-Bellum South* (1976).

DOCUMENTS
John Blassingame, ed., *Slave Testimony: Two Centuries of Letters, Speeches, Interviews, and Autobiographies* (1977).

Henry Louis Gates Jr., ed., *The Classic Slave Narratives* (1987).

James Mellon, ed., *Bullwhip Days: The Slaves Remember — An Oral History* (1988).

Willie Lee Rose, ed., *A Documentary History of Slavery in North America* (1976).

Recommended Reading

THE ROAD TO WAR

GENERAL HISTORIES

Bruce Levine, *Half Slave and Half Free: The Roots of the Civil War* (1992).

David Potter, *The Impending Crisis, 1848–1861* (1976).

Kenneth Stampp, *America in 1857: A Nation on the Brink* (1990).

Kenneth Stampp, ed., *The Causes of the Civil War* (1974).

POLITICAL PARTIES AND LEADERS

David Donald, *Lincoln Reconsidered* (1961).

Eric Foner, *Free Soil, Free Labor, Free Men: The Ideology of the Republican Party Before the Civil War* (1970).

Michael F. Holt, *The Political Crisis of the 1850s* (1978).

JOHN BROWN AND DRED SCOTT

Donald Fehrenbacher, *Slavery Law and Politics: The Dred Scott Case in Historical Perspective* (1981).

W. E. B. DuBois, *John Brown* (1919).

Stephen Oates, *To Purge This Land With Blood: A Biography of John Brown* (1970).

SLAVERY AND WESTWARD EXPANSION

Eugene Berwanger, *The Frontier Against Slavery: Western Anti-Negro Prejudice and the Slavery Extension Controversy* (1967).

James Rawley, *Race and Politics: Bleeding Kansas and the Coming of the Civil War* (1969).

THE SECESSION CRISIS

Steven N. Channing, *Crisis in Fear: Secession in South Carolina* (1970).

Daniel W. Crofts, *Reluctant Confederates: Upper South Unionists in the Secession Crisis* (1989).

David Potter, *Lincoln and His Party in the Secession Crisis* (1962).

Kenneth Stampp, *And the War Came: The North and the Secession Crisis, 1860–1861* (1950).

LITERATURE

Harriet Beecher Stowe, *Uncle Tom's Cabin* (1852).

Walt Whitman, *Leaves of Grass* (1855).

Recommended Reading

THE CIVIL WAR

OVERVIEWS

David Donald, *Liberty and Union* (1978).

Eric Foner, *Politics and Ideology in the Age of Civil War* (1980).

James McPherson, *Battle Cry of Freedom: The Civil War Era* (1988).

Peter J. Parrish, *The American Civil War* (1985).

THE MILITARY: STRATEGY AND SOLDIERS

Richard E. Berringer, Herman Hattaway, Archer Jones, and William N. Still Jr., *Why the South Lost the Civil War* (1986).

Gerard F. Linderman, *Embattled Courage: The Experience of Combat in the American Civil War* (1987).

Bell Wiley, *The Life of Billy Yank* (1952).

Bell Wiley, *The Life of Johnny Reb* (1943).

AFRICAN AMERICANS IN THE WAR

Ira Berlin, Barbara J. Fields, Steven F. Miller, Joseph P. Reidy, and Leslie S. Rowland, eds., *Free at Last: A Documentary History of Slavery, Freedom and the Civil War* (1992).

Dudley Taylor Cornish, *The Sable Arm: Negro Troops in the Union Army* (1966).

Joseph T. Glaathaar, *Forged in Battle: The Civil War Alliance of Black Soldiers and White Officers* (1991).

Thomas Wentworth Higginson, *Army Life in a Black Regiment* (1869).

James McPherson, *The Negro's Civil War: How American Negroes Felt and Acted During the War for the Union* (1965).

Benjamin Quarles: *The Negro During the Civil War* (1953).

Edwin S. Redkey, ed., *A Grand Army of Black Men* (1992).

LINCOLN AS A WAR LEADER

Stephen B. Oates, *With Malice Towards None: The Life of Abraham Lincoln* (1977).

John L. Thomas, ed., *Abraham Lincoln and the American Political Tradition* (1986).

THE DRAFT RIOTS

Iver Bernstein, *The New York City Draft Riots: Their Significance for American Society and Politics in the Age of Civil War* (1990).

Adrian Cook, *Armies of the Streets: The New York City Draft Riots of 1863* (1979).

WOMEN IN THE WAR

Mary Boykin Chesnut, *Mary Chesnut's Civil War* (1981).

Mary E. Massey, *Bonnet Brigades* (1966).

THE VISUAL IMAGES OF WAR

Mark E. Neely, Harold Holzer, and Gabor Boritt, *The Confederate Image: Prints of the Lost Cause* (1987).

Nina Silber, *The Romance of Reunion: Northerners and the South, 1865–1900* (1993)

Philip Van Doren Stern, *There They Were: The Civil War in Action as Seen by its Combat Artists* (1959).

W. Fletcher Thompson, Jr., *The Images of War: The Pictorial Reporting of the American Civil War* (1959).

LITERATURE

Stephen Crane, *Red Badge of Courage* (1895).

Recommended Reading

RECONSTRUCTION

OVERVIEWS

W. E. B. DuBois, *Black Reconstruction in America* (1935).

Eric Foner, *Reconstruction: America's Unfinished Revolution, 1863–77* (1988).

Eric Foner and Olivia Mahoney, *America's Reconstruction: People and Politics After the Civil War* (1995).

John Hope Franklin, *Reconstruction After the Civil War* (1961).

Kenneth Stampp, *The Era of Reconstruction* (1965).

LAND AND LABOR

Eric Foner, *Nothing But Freedom: Emancipation and Its Legacy* (1983).

Stephen Hahn, *The Roots of Southern Populism* (1983).

Edward Magdol, *A Right to the Land: Essays on the Freedmen's Community* (1977).

Roger Ransom and Richard Sutch, *One Kind of Freedom: The Economic Consequences of Emancipation* (1977).

RECONSTRUCTION POLICIES DURING THE CIVIL WAR

Louis S. Gerteis, *From Contraband to Freedman: Federal Policy Toward Southern Blacks, 1861–1865* (1973).

Willie Lee Rose, *Rehearsal for Reconstruction: The Port Royal Experiment* (1965).

THE FREEDMEN'S BUREAU

Peter Kolchin, *First Freedom* (1972).

William McFeely, *Yankee Stepfather: General O. O. Howard and the Freedmen* (1968).

Claude F. Oubre, *Forty Acres and a Mule: The Freedmen's Bureau and Black Land Ownership* (1978).

TRANSITION FROM SLAVERY TO FREEDOM: CHURCH, SCHOOL, AND FAMILY

Stephen W. Angell, *Bishop Henry McNeal Turner and African-American Religion in the South* (1992).

Jacqueline Jones, *Labor of Love, Labor of Sorrow: Black Women, Work and the Family from Slavery to the Present* (1985).

Leon Litwack, *Been in the Storm So Long: The Aftermath of Slavery* (1979).

Robert C. Morris, *Reading, 'Riting, and Reconstruction: The Education of Freedmen in the South, 1861–1870* (1981).

Clarence Walker, *A Rock in a Weary Land: The African-American Episcopal Church During the Civil War and Reconstruction* (1982).

NATIONAL RECONSTRUCTION POLITICS

LaWanda and John Cox, *Politics, Principle and Prejudice, 1865–1866* (1963).

Eric L. McKitrick, *Andrew Johnson and Reconstruction* (1960).

Brooks D. Simpson, *Let Us Have Peace: Ulysses S. Grant and the Politics of War and Reconstruction* (1992).

Hans L. Trefousse, *Andrew Johnson* (1989).

REFORM MOVEMENTS AND CIVIL RIGHTS DURING THE RECONSTRUCTION ERA

Ellen DuBois, *Feminism and Suffrage: The Emergence of an Independent Women's Movement in America, 1848–1869* (1979).

Robert Kaczorowski, *The Politics of Judicial Interpretation: The Federal Courts, Department of Justice, and Civil Rights, 1866–1876* (1985).

Recommended Reading

AFRICAN AMERICANS AND RECONSTRUCTION COALITIONS

Michael Fitzgerald, *The Union League Movement in the Deep South: Politics and Agricultural Change During Reconstruction* (1989).

Thomas Holt, *Black Over White: Negro Political Leadership in South Carolina During Reconstruction* (1977).

Dorothy Sterling, ed., *The Trouble They Seen* (1976).

KU KLUX KLAN

Allen W. Trelease, *White Terror: The Ku Klux Klan Conspiracy and Southern Reconstruction* (1971).

LAND AND INDIAN POLICIES

Patricia Nelson Limerick, *The Legacy of Conquest* (1987).

NOVELS

Howard Fast, *Freedom Road* (1944).

Thomas Dixon Jr., *The Clansman* (1905).

Albion Tourgée, *A Fool's Errand* (1879).

EPILOGUE

MIGRATION

Malaika Adero, ed., *Up South: Stories, Studies and Letters of this Century's Black Migrations* (1993).

James L. Grossman, *Land of Hope: Chicago, Black Southerners and the Great Migration* (1989).

Nell Irvin Painter, *Exodusters: Black Migration to Kansas After Reconstruction* (1971).

BOOKER T. WASHINGTON AND W. E. B. DUBOIS

August Meier, *Negro Thought in America, 1880–1915: Racial Ideologies in the Age of Booker T. Washington* (1963).

SEGREGATION

Howard M. Rabinowitz, *Race Relations in the Urban South, 1865–1890* (1978).

C. Vann Woodward, *The Strange Career of Jim Crow* (1974).

John Cell, *The Highest Stage of White Supremacy: The Origins of Segregation in South Africa and the American South* (1982).

THE MODERN CIVIL RIGHTS MOVEMENT

Clayborne Carson, David Garrow, Gerald Gill, Vincent Harding, Darlene Clark Hine, eds., *The Eyes on the Prize Civil Rights Reader* (1991).

Recommended Reading

ASHP VIDEOS & CD-ROMS

FOUR AMERICAN SOCIAL HISTORY
PROJECT VIDEOS SUPPLEMENT MATERIAL
IN THIS TEXT. THEY ARE:

Doing as They Can (Slavery)
Dr. Toer's Amazing Magic Lantern Show
   (Reconstruction)
1877: The Grand Army of Starvation (The 1877
   Railroad Strike)
Up South (The Great Migration)
Who Built America: Working People & The Nation's
   Economy, Politics, Culture, and Society,
   Volume 2 (1992).
Who Built America, the CD-ROM: From the Centennial
   Celebration of 1876 to the Great War of 1914
   (Voyageur, 1994).

FOR DISTRIBUTION INFORMATION
CONTACT:

The American Social History Project
99 Hudson Street, Third Floor
New York, NY 10013
TEL (212) 966-4248, EXT. 201
FAX (212) 966-4589

A

abolitionists, 12, 14, 18, 28-33, 42, 46-48, 50-52, 61-63, 64, 65, 77, 79, 82

African-American
  churches, 20, 28, 145, 181-83, 184-89, 201, 220-21, 237
  colleges, 177
  communities, 28, 151-69, 175-89, 201, 220-21, 278, 279-80, 285, 287-89
  culture, 19-20, 24-27, 175-89, 288
  family, 174-76
  northern residents, 28, 30-31, 88, 90-94, 286-88
  soldiers, 57, 58, 64, 65, 66, 72, 76, 78, 107-25, 133, 135, 165, 166, 174, 176, 237
Alabama, 176, 256, 273-74, 284-85
Allen, Samuel, 262
Alston, J. T., 67
American Antislavery Society (AAS), 11, 32
amnesty, 199-200, 201, 251
Andrews, Sydney, 178
Anthony, Susan B., 205, 206, 207, 209
Appomattox surrender, 58
Arkansas, 59, 135
Atkins, Smith D., 77

B

Baldwin, James, 188
Baskind, Bruce, ix-x
Beaufort, SC, 239
Beauregard, P.G.T., 57, 108
Beecher, William, 168

Berlin, Ira, 80-81
Black Codes, 145, 200-201, 202, 203, 204, 220, 235, 289
Black conventions. See colored conventions
Bloody Kansas, 12, 46-47
blues, 185
Boston, John, 72
Boyd, W. T., 67
Bradford, Sarah, 45
bread riots, 57, 89, 98-105
Brer Rabbit, 24-27
Brown, John, 12, 14, 50-53, 133, 134
Brown, Simon, 185
Brown v. Topeka Board of Education (1954), 206, 212, 213-14, 278
Bull Run, battle of, 57, 70
business, 15, 18, 37-39, 60, 86-88, 135, 151-53, 157, 232-34, 250, 265, 267, 268, 271, 272
Butler, Benjamin, 57, 68-69, 73, 74, 79, 105, 117

C

California, 39-40, 41
Campbell, Tunis, 237
carpetbagger, 229, 230-32
Charleston Mercury, 56
Chesnut, Mary Boykin, 85, 89
Cinque, Joseph, 19
civil rights, 178, 181, 189, 212-14, 266, 278-89
civil rights acts, 145, 203-4, 214, 278, 279
Civil War
  advantages of North, 131-33
  advantages of South, 130

Johnson, William H., 113
Joint Congressional Committee on
   Reconstruction, 201-2, 255
Jones, Thomas H., 261
Jordan, Josie, 16

K

Kansas, 12, 46-47, 48, 285
Kansas-Nebraska Act, 12, 14, 46-47
Kentucky, 61, 81, 119
Ku Klux Klan, 58, 122, 257, 261-65, 267,
   268, 273-75, 279
Ku Klux Klan Act, 264, 278, 279

L

labor, 86-88, 134-35, 150, 235, 244-59,
   271, 272, 288
labor, gang, 156, 157
labor, wage, 91-93, 151-52, 156-57,
   162-63, 165, 197, 231, 233, 237-39, 256
labor contracts, 251, 256
land, 245-59, 281-82
land and independence. *See* self
   sufficient farming
Land Commission (South Carolina), 254
land confiscation, 211, 230, 239, 245-55,
   257. *See also* land redistribution
land redistribution, 58, 127-29, 132, 136,
   140-41, 141, 145, 164-69, 211, 230, 239,
   245-55, 257, 265
Lee, Robert E., 58, 130, 131, 133
"Let America Be America Again"
   (Hughes), 289
Levine, Lawrence, 184
Liberator, the, 18, 19, 30

Lincoln, Abraham, 12, 15, 47, 53, 57-62,
   64-65, 68-69, 73, 78-82, 132, 135, 145,
   160, 195-97
Louisiana, 79, 211, 213, 234
Lynch, John Roy, 236
lynching, *87*, 88, 91, 281

M

McClellan, George B., 76
McPherson, James M., 80-81, 88
"Malitis," 16
Manigault, Charles, 172
Maryland, 61, 72, 81, 119
Massachusetts, 30
Mexican-American War, 11, 40
Mexico and Mexicans, 11, 39-41,
   248, 250
migration, 284-88
militia, 220-21, 237
Militia Act, 76
Miller, G. P., 66
Milliken's Bend, battle of, 119
Missick, Victoria, ix-x
Mississippi, 268-70, 275, 283
Mississippi Plan, 268-69
Missouri, 61, 81, 119
Missouri Compromise, 11, 14, 40
Montgomery Advertiser, 73
Mundy, Marcellus, 78

rifle clubs, 269-70
Roosevelt, Franklin, 228, 288
Roosevelt, Theodore, 249

S